INTERNATIONAL TRADE FINANCE

International Trade Finance
A Pragmatic Approach

TARSEM SINGH BHOGAL

ARUN KUMAR TRIVEDI

palgrave
macmillan

© Tarsem Singh Bhogal and Arun Kumar Trivedi 2008

All rights reserved. No reproduction, copy or transmission of this publication may be made without written permission.

No paragraph of this publication may be reproduced, copied or transmitted saved without written permission or in accordance with the provisions of the Copyright, Designs and Patents Act 1988, or under the terms of any licence permitting limited copying issued by the Copyright Licensing Agency, 90 Tottenham Court Road, London W1T 4LP.

Any person who does any unauthorised act in relation to this publication may be liable to criminal prosecution and civil claims for damages.

The authors have asserted their rights to be identified as the authors of this work in accordance with the Copyright, Designs and Patents Act 1988.

First published in 2008 by
PALGRAVE MACMILLAN
Houndmills, Basingstoke, Hampshire RG21 6XS and
175 Fifth Avenue, New York, N.Y. 10010
Companies and representatives throughout the world.

PALGRAVE MACMILLAN is the global academic imprint of the Palgrave Macmillan division of St. Martin's Press, LLC and of Palgrave Macmillan Ltd. Macmillan® is a registered trademark in the United States, United Kingdom and other countries. Palgrave is a registered trademark in the European Union and other countries.

ISBN-13: 978–0–230–55378–1 hardback
ISBN-10: 0–230–55378–8 hardback

This book is printed on paper suitable for recycling and made from fully managed and sustained forest sources. Logging, pulping and manufacturing processes are expected to conform to the environmental regulations of the country of origin.

A catalogue record for this book is available from the British Library.

A catalog record for this book is available from the Library of Congress.

10 9 8 7 6 5 4 3 2 1
17 16 15 14 13 12 11 10 09 08

Printed and bound in Great Britain by
CPI Antony Rowe, Chippenham and Eastbourne

HG3753 .B56 2008
0134111580442
Bhogal, Tarsem Singh.

International trade
   finance : a pragmatic
      2008.

2009 01 27

Contents

List of Tables	*xii*
List of Figures	*xiii*
Preface	*xv*
About the Authors	*xvii*
Acknowledgements	*xviii*
Glossary	*xix*

1 *International Trade and Inherent Risks*   *1*
   Background of International Trade   1
   Exporters' Risks   2
   Importers' Risks   2

2 *Services Offered by Commercial Banks*   *4*
   Finance for Exports   6

3 *Methods of Trade*   *7*
   Cash on Delivery   7
   Advance Payment   7
   Open Account   8
   Collections   8
   Letters of Credit   8
   Methods of Payment/Settlement of Account   9

4 Foreign Exchange Rates — 11
Introduction — 11
Foreign Currency Transactions — 11
Bank's Accounting System — 11
Foreign Exchange Market — 12
Exchange Rates Quotation — 12
Spot Exchange Rates — 13
Forward Exchange Rates — 13
Fixed Forward Exchange Rates — 13
Option Forward Exchange Rates — 14
How Exchange Rates are Determined — 14
Factors Influencing Exchange Rate — 14
Forward Exchange Rates — 15
Foreign Exchange Spot Transaction – Mechanism — 15
Forward Exchange Contract — 17
How the Forward Exchange Rate is Calculated — 18

5 Bills of Exchange, Collections, Purchasing and Discounting — 20
Definition of a Bill of Exchange — 20
Clauses on Bills of Exchange — 24
Types of Acceptances — 26
Endorsement of Bills of Exchange — 27
Collection of Bills — 32
Mechanism – Sight Bill for Collection — 34
Mechanism – Documentary Usance Bills for Collection — 35
Bills Purchased — 37
Bills Discounted — 37
Mechanism – Bills Discounted — 38
Bills Processing Cost (Indicatives) — 38

6 Documentary Letters of Credit — 40
Who Does What? — 43
Advantages and Disadvantages of Letters of Credit — 45
Letter of Credit – Mechanism — 47
Letter of Credit Contracts and Regulations — 48
Sale Contract — 50

7 Letters of Credit – Types — 52
Clean Letter of Credit — 53
Documentary Letter of Credit — 53
Circular or Traveller Letter of Credit — 53
Revocable Letter of Credit — 53
Irrevocable Letter of Credit — 54

Irrevocable Confirmed Letter of Credit	56
Revolving Letter of Credit	57
Revolving Letter of Credit – Mechanism	58
Red Clause Letter of Credit	59
Red Clause Letter of Credit – Mechanism	60
Transferable Letter of Credit	62
Transferable Letter of Credit – Mechanism	62
Transferable Credit – Limitations	63
Procedure for Effecting Transfer of a Letter of Credit	66
Back-to-Back Letter of Credit	66
Back-to-Back Letter of Credit – Mechanism	69
Status of Issuing Bank of the Prime Letter of Credit	71
Credit Check on Letter of Credit Applicant	71
Third Country or Transit Letter of Credit	77
Deferred Payment Letter of Credit – Mechanics	79
Standby Letter of Credit	81
Standby Letter of Credit – Mechanism	82
Skeleton Letter of Credit	86
Omnibus Letter of Credit	86
Straight Letter of Credit	86

8 *Methods of Payment Settlement* **87**

Payment L/C	87
Channels of Payment Settlement	87
Payment L/C – Bill on Issuing Bank	88
Mechanism of Settlement – Acceptance L/C	89
Method of Settlement – Usance Bill on Issuing Bank	90
Method of Settlement – Negotiation	92
Negotiation Under 3 months Usance L/C Bill on Issuing Bank	94
Negotiation of Documents Under Reserve	95
Negotiation of Documents Under Reserve	96
Advising/Confirming Bank – Procedural Aspect	97

9 *Financial Load Variations – Eight Types of Letters of Credit* **98**

Payment Letter of Credit – Bill Drawn on Issuing Bank	98
Payment Letter of Credit – Bill Drawn on Confirming Bank	100
Deferred Payment Letter of Credit	101
Acceptance Letter of Credit – Bill Drawn on Issuing Bank	102
Acceptance Letter of Credit – Bill Drawn on Confirming Bank	103
Sight Negotiation Letter of Credit – Bill Drawn on Issuing Bank	104
Usance Negotiation Letter of Credit – Bill Drawn on Issuing Bank Paid at Maturity	105

Usance Negotiation Letter of Credit – Bill
Drawn on Issuing Bank Reimbursement on Sight Basis   107

10   *Incoterms*   *109*

Background   109
Ex Works (......Named Place. "EXW")   111
Free Carrier (......Named Place. "FCA")   111
Free Alongside ship (...Named Port of Shipment. "FAS")   112
Free on Board (...Named Port of Shipment. "FOB")   112
Cost and Freight (..Named Port of Destination. "CFR")   112
Cost, Insurance and Freight (..Named Port of Destination. "CIF")   113
Carriage Paid to (...Named Place of Destination. "CPT")   113
Carriage and Insurance Paid to (..Named Place
of Destination. "CIP")   114
Delivered at Frontier (...Named Place. "DAF")   114
Delivered Ex Ship (...Named Port of Destination. "DES")   114
Delivered Ex Quay (Duty Paid) (…Named Port
of Destination. "DEQ")   114
Delivered Duty Unpaid (Named Place of Destination "DDU")   115
Delivered Duty Paid (...Named Place of Destination. "DDP")   115
Cost Sharing between Sellers and Buyers – Incoterms   116

11   *Documents in Foreign Trade – Significance*   *117*

Genesis   117
Bill of Exchange   118
Invoice   119
Pro-forma Invoice   120
Bill of Lading   120
Types of Bills of Lading   122
Air Waybill   123
Certificate of Origin   124
Certificate of Inspection   124
Packing List   125
Post Parcel/Courier Receipt   125
Forwarding Agent's Receipt   125
Rail, Road Consignment Notes/Truck and Carrier Receipt   125
Consular Invoice   125
Veterinary Certificate/Health Certificate   126
Non-negotiable Sea Waybill (UCP Article 21)   126
Multimodal Transport Document (UCP Article 19)   126
Combined Transport Document   127
FIATA Bill of Lading   127
Other Documents   127

12	**Negotiation of Documents**	**128**
	Meanings of Negotiation	128
	Role of Advising and Confirming Banks	129
	Role of Issuing Bank	129
	Negotiation of Documents Under Reserve	130
	Letter of Credit – Processing Cost (Indicatives)	131
13	**Factoring and Forfaiting**	**132**
	Factoring: Genesis	132
	Factoring and Cash Flow	132
	Factoring and Legal Implications	133
	Factoring Mechanism	133
	Advantages of Factoring	134
	Disadvantages of Factoring	134
	Invoice Discounting	135
	Advantages to Exporter	135
	Export Factoring	136
	Forfaiting: Genesis	137
	Fixed Rate Export Finance	137
	Forfaiting – Capital Goods Sale	137
	Forfaiting – Secondary Markets	138
	Risks in Export Finance	138
	Advantages to the Exporter	139
	Disadvantages to the Exporter	139
	Requirements of a Forfaiter	139
	Documents Required by the Forfaiter	140
	Forfaiting Procedures in Practice	141
	Mechanism of a Forfaiting Transaction	141
14	**Electronic Documents (eUCP)**	**143**
15	**Scrutiny of Documents – Procedures**	**149**
	Buyer's Responsibilities	150
	Seller's Responsibilities	150
	Responsibilities of Other Parties (Banks)	150
	The Issuing Bank	151
16	**Common Irregularities in Documents**	**160**
	Compliance of Terms	160
17	**Guarantees and International Bonds**	**164**
	Guarantees as Security	164
	Distinction between Guarantees and Indemnities	166

Advantages of Guarantees as Security	167
Disadvantages of a Guarantee as Security for a Credit Facility	168
Procedures for Taking as Security	168
International Bonds/Bank Guarantees	171
Parties	171
Bank's Role	171
Format of Bank Guarantees/Bonds	172
Categories of Bank Guarantees/Bonds	173
Types of Bank Guarantees/International Bonds	173
Retention or Maintenance Bonds	179
Banking Facility	179
Other Types of Bonds	179
Precautions	180
International Bonds/Guarantees – Precautions	180
Time for Payment	181
Arbitration Clause	181
Issuing Bank Guarantees – Action Steps	182
International Bonds and Bank Guarantees – Specimens	184

18 *SWIFT and Letters of Credit* *192*
Introduction	192
SWIFT Code Words	201
Specimens of Formats for Swift Messages Used by Banks	204

19 *ICC DOCDEX RULES ICC Rules for Documentary Instruments Dispute Resolution Expertise* *222*
Article 1: Dispute Resolution Service	222
Article 2: Request	223
Article 3: Answer	224
Article 4: Supplements	225
Article 5: Acknowledgements and Rejections	225
Article 6: Appointment of Experts	226
Article 7: Appointed Experts' Procedure	227
Article 8: DOCDEX Decision	227
Article 9: Deposit and Publication of the DOCDEX Decision	228
Article 10: Costs of DOCDEX	228
Article 11: General	229
Appendix to the ICC Rules for Documentary	229

20 *Export Risks Insurance and ECGD* *233*
Genesis	233
Background	233
Operation on Break-Even Basis	234

ECGD's Safeguard Finance 234
Specific Guarantee 236
Types of ECGD Guarantees 237
Buyer Credit (BC) Facility 239
Insurance for Cash Payments 240
Overseas Investment Insurance 241
Financing Facilities for Exporters 241
Project Financing Facility 242
Subsidiaries Guarantee 243
Supplementary Stocks Guarantee 244
Comprehensive Bill Guarantee 245
Comprehensive Open Account Guarantee 245
Specific Bank Guarantee 245
Buyer Credit Guarantees 245
Money Laundering and Terrorist Activities 246

21 Marine Insurance 248
Introduction 248
Importance of Marine Insurance 248
Definition 249
Classification of Marine Insurance Cover 249
Marine Insurance Associations 250
Types of Insurance Instruments 250
Contents of a Marine Insurance Policy 252
Insurance Certificate 253

Annexes 255
Specimen of Application for L/C 255
General Guidance for Completion of L/C Application Form 261
Negotiation of Documents Under Reserve 265

Index 269

List of Tables

4.1	Example of exchange rates spot/forward against GBP	13
5.1	Bill of exchange indicative processing cost	38
7.1	Comparison of commercial and standby letter of credit	83
18.1	SWIFT statistics. SWIFTNet FIN traffic (in number of messages) January 2007 YTD (Posted 28 February 2007)	192

List of Figures

4.1	Action flow diagram customer sells GBP against USD	16
4.2	Action flow diagram customer sells USD against GBP	17
4.3	Fixed forward contract	18
4.4	Forward contract with option over third month	18
4.5	Exchange margins – premium and discount in forward contract	19
5.1	Bill of exchange – specimen	21
5.2	Types of bills of exchange	23
5.3	Example of a blank endorsement of a bill of exchange	28
5.4	Example of a special endorsement of a bill of exchange	29
5.5	Example of a restrictive endorsement of a bill of exchange	29
5.6	Example of a conditional endorsement of a bill of exchange	30
5.7	A specimen of customer's instructions for collections of bills of exchange	33
5.8	Mechanics of a sight bill for collection	34
5.9	Mechanics of a documentary usance bill for collection	36
5.10	Mechanics of a bill discounting	38
6.1	Letter of credit – mechanism	47
6.2	Letter of credit – contracts and regulations	49
7.1	Types of letters of credit	52
7.2	Revolving letter of credit – mechanism	58
7.3	Red clause letter of credit – mechanism	60
7.4	Transferable letter of credit – mechanism	62
7.5	Back to back letter of credit – mechanism	69
7.6	Third country/transit letter of credit – mechanism	78
7.7	Deferred payment letter of credit – mechanism	80
7.8	Standby letter of credit – mechanism	82
8.1	Channels of payment settlement	88
8.2	Payment letter of credit – bill on issuing bank	89
8.3	Acceptance letter of credit – mechanism of settlement	90

8.4	Usance bill on issuing bank – mechanism of settlement	91
8.5	Negotiation sight letter of credit – bill drawn on issuing bank	93
8.6	Negotiation – 3 months usance L/C bill on issuing bank	95
9.1	8 types of letters of credit – financial load variations	98
9.2	Payment L/C – bill of issuing bank	99
9.3	Payment L/C – bill on confirming bank	100
9.4	Deferred payment L/C	101
9.5	Acceptance L/C – bill on issuing bank	102
9.6	Acceptance L/C – bill on confirming bank	104
9.7	Sight negotiation letter of credit – bill drawn on issuing bank	105
9.8	Usance negotiation L/C – bill drawn on issuing bank paid at maturity	106
9.9	Usance negotiation L/C – bill on issuing bank re-imb. on sight basis	107
10.1	Incoterms – cost sharing between buyers and sellers	116
11.1	Specimen of bill of exchange	118
12.1	Letter of credit – inactive processing cost	131
13.1	Factoring – mechanism	133
13.2	Forfaiting transaction – mechanism	142
17.1	Guarantee as security – mechanism	165
17.2	Distinction between guarantee and indemnity	166
17.2a	Distinction between guarantee and indemnity	166
17.3	Bid bond – mechanism	175

Preface

The global trading system is undergoing a period of transition. Shifting economic circumstances, major advances in technology and the emergence of new players on the global scene, all underscore that we are on the cusp of big changes. Persistent imbalances, driven largely by macro-economic factors continue to be a cause of concern in some major economies. Even in such a climate of uncertainty, one thing is certain that there is a great need to strengthen the global trading system by working it more equitable and relevant for those who trade in the twenty-first century with Uniform Customs and Practice.

Looking in the retrospect we find that in 2005, the value of world merchandise exports rose by 13 per cent to $10.1 trillions and the value of world commercial services export by 11 per cent to $2.4 trillions. The volume and value of international trade is a testimony to make us believe that the world order has changed quite swiftly over the past ten years at a much faster pace than that of the previous 20 years. It is difficult to contemplate what the world trade/economies will look like in 2010. One thing is certain, however, change is inevitable. Bankers and trading communities operating in such a climate will have to face the challenges that are immense.

Technology has indeed opened up new markets with geographic boundaries becoming non-existent to the web-enabled community. What we see today is the beginning of the reaction to this expansion as an outcome of globalisation and internationalisation, adding to multi-complexities to the players in the international trade.

In this spectrum, industry practitioners will solicit solace resorting to basics and learning the lesson of the laser. How to focus rather than find a solution from the ponderance? So we did, encouraged by these international inter-active developments.

Based on our learning experience and working as practitioners facilitating international trade, in our capacity as bankers, we have worked on a treatise in your hands 'International Trade Finance' 'A Pragmatic Approach'. In fact, we have been motivated to write this book in view of the urge from the beginners as well as industry practitioners to understand and grasp the type and nature of various documents in use in international trade and mechanism of settlement of payments thereof.

The book is organised into 21 chapters endeavouring to address key topics relating to the gamut of international trade, letter of credit mechanism, collection of bills, trade customs and practice and so on. We do not pretend that all technical concerns are answered but we are confident that we have gone much further than any other published material on the subject. Dealing with complicated implementation issues in a forthright and comprehensive fashion and design. We have given lucid account of provisions vis-à-vis trade customs and practice protecting the interest of the parties involved in international trade. We have striven to present and explain transaction flow through diagrams easing the job of a learner enabling to understand and grasp the hard-core subject matter.

We sincerely believe that this book will be regarded as an essential tool for both the beginners and practitioners in international trade. We are sanguine that the readers will position this book within easy reach for navigating solutions to assorted trade related issues and/or a constant travel companion when in business across the world.

T. S. Bhogal and A. K. Trivedi

About the Authors

Tarsem Singh Bhogal

Tarsem S. Bhogal, has been Principal of the Staff Training Centre, Association of Indian Banks in the UK from 1990 to August 2006. Earlier, he had been a senior faculty of an International Bank's Regional Staff Training and Development Centre in London. Bhogal set up a Regional Staff Training Centre of a public sector bank in northern India. He has been a practical banker who managed banking operations in Kenya, India and the United Kingdom starting banking career with The Standard Bank Limited. Bhogal is a Fellow of The Institute of Financial Accountants, Member of Chartered Management Institute and ordinary member of the Chartered Institute of Banker (now Institute of Financial Services) London, U.K.

Dr Arun Kumar Trivedi

Arun K. Trivedi is the Vice President and Chief Representative of IndusInd Bank, London. He has been Head, Global Banking, IndusInd Bank. He is a former faculty of International Banking, Foreign exchange and Foreign Trade at the National Institute of Bank Management, Pune. Professional international banking experience includes Head Forex Treasury, Vysya Bank (now INGVysya and Chief (Treasury), State Bank of Patiala. He is Fellow of Securities Investment Institute, London (UK), Fellow of the Indian Institute of Bankers and Life Member, Indian Society for Training and Development, New Delhi. Dr. Trivedi is also author and co-author of various books on the subjects viz International Banking, Treasury operations, Risk Management.

Acknowledgements

We are grateful to the following authorities for their permission to publish information in this book relating to their products and services. As the systems and procedures of international trade change with improvements of information technology and other developments, we would like to request the readers to visit their websites to obtain the latest information.

1. Export Credit Guarantee Department – www.ecgd.gov.uk

2. International Chamber of Commerce (ICC) Paris – www.iccwbo.org

3. Society for Worldwide International Financial Telecommunication. – www.swift.com

Disclaimer
The authors have made reasonable efforts to ensure the accuracy of the information given in this book at the time but assume no liability for any inadvertent error or omission that may appear. The information may change from time to time and practical procedures may also differ from one bank to another, authors do not accept any liability for the consequences of error or omission.

T. S. BHOGAL and DR A. K. TRIVEDI

Glossary

ACCEPTANCE: A word sometimes used to denote an accepted bill of exchange, but strictly the writing across the face of a bill by which the drawee assents to the order of the drawer.

ACCOMMODATION BILL: A bill to which a person adds his name to oblige or accommodate another person, without receiving any consideration for so doing (in other words to lend the person money).

ACH (Automated Clearing House): An electronic clearing system in which payment orders are exchanged among financial institutions, primarily via magnetic media or telecommunication networks and handled by a data processing centre.

ACH RETURN: An item not accepted by the receiving bank and returned to the originator.

AD VALOREM: According to the value, generally in connection with taxes or duties.

AIRWAY BILL: A document issued in the case of transport by airfreight.

ALL MONIES DEBENTURE: A deed of debenture expressed to cover all monies owing by a company at any time on any account.

AML: Anti-money laundering.

ANSI (American National Standards Institute): ANSI is a private non-profit organisation that administers and coordinates the US voluntary standardization and conformity assessment system. It is the official US representative on the International Organization for Standardization (ISO). It has approximately 1,000 company, organisation, government agency, institutional and international members.

GLOSSARY

APACS (Association for Payment Clearing Services): APACS is the umbrella body for the UK payments industry. Three autonomous clearing companies operate under the umbrella of APACS – Voca, CHAPS Clearing Company and the Cheque and Credit Clearing Company.

APPRECIATION: Describes a currency strengthening in response to market demand rather than by official action such as revaluation.

APS (Assured Payment System): An arrangement in an exchange-for-value system under which completion of timely settlement of a payment instruction is supported by an irrevocable and unconditional commitment from a third party (typically a bank, syndicate of banks or clearing house).

ARBITRAGE: Buying a currency in one centre and selling it in another to take advantage of temporary rate discrepancies. Preferably the two transactions should take place simultaneously, but this is not essential. Arbitrage transactions can take place over many centres and through many currencies before being brought (hopefully) to a satisfactory conclusion.

ASSIGNMENT: A transfer or making over of a right to another person, as in the assignment of the proceeds of a life policy as security to a lending banker.

AUTHENTICATION: The methods used to verify the origin of a message or to verify the identity of a participant connected to a system and to confirm that a message has not been modified or replaced in transit.

AUTHORISED DEPOSITORY: A person authorised by an order of the Treasury to keep bearer securities in safe custody. The term arose under the Exchange Control Act, 1947, and included banks, members of the Stock Exchange, solicitors practising in the United Kingdom, and certain other financial institutions.

BACK OFFICE: The part of a firm that is responsible for post-trade activities. Depending upon the organisational structure of the firm, the back office can be a single department or multiple units (including documentation, risk management, accounting or settlements etc). Some firms have combined a portion of these responsibilities usually found in the back office, particularly those related to risk management, into what they term a middle office function.

BACS: Bankers Automated Clearing Services

BACSTEL-IP: The delivery channel, which provides vocal customers with a secure, and direct online telecommunications access to the payment network.

BANK BILL: A bill of exchange drawn on a bank or bearing the endorsement of a bank.

GLOSSARY

BANK DRAFT: This is an instrument drawn by the buyer's bank, normally on a correspondent bank in the exporter's country. The buyer sends the draft to the exporter, who then obtains payment via his own bank. It is possible for the buyer's bank to draw a draft on itself, which is less convenient to an exporter in the United Kingdom if he wants payment in GB Pounds, and, in any case, will not finally be paid until it is presented to the bank on which it is drawn.

BANK RATE: Formerly the advertised minimum rate at which the Bank of England would discount approved bills of exchange, or lend against certain securities. Bank Rate was discontinued in October 1972 and replaced by the minimum lending rate.

BARGE B/L: A Bill of Lading issued for transportation of goods by barge i.e. small boat.

BARRATRY: It is a wrongful act willfully committed by the master or crew of the ship.

BEAR: A speculator on the Stock Exchange who anticipates a fall in the value of a certain security and therefore sells stocks which he does not possess in the hope of buying them back more cheaply at a later date, thus making a profit.

BENEFICIARY: One entitled to receive the benefit such as cash or goods. In case of a letter of credit the beneficiary is the seller or exporter of goods.

BERTH B/L: The term used to distinguish a B/L issued by a liner, or a vessel trading under liner conditions, from a B/L issued by a vessel carrying cargo under a charter party.

BIC (Bank Identifier Code): A unique address that identifies precisely the financial institutions involved in international financial transactions. A BIC consists of eight or eleven characters comprising the first three or four of the following components: Bank Code, Country Code, Location and Branch Code. BIC are allocated by SWIFT.

BID: Normally the rate at which the market in general, or market-maker in particular, is willing to buy a currency. "Bid", "pay" "take" and "buy" all mean that the quoting or contracting party is interested in buying a currency. Beware, however, when the quotation is a cross-rate for two foreign currencies; then the currency, which is of interest should always be specified.

BILATERAL NET SETTLEMENT SYSTEM: A settlement system in which participants' bilateral net settlement positions are settled between every bilateral combination of participants.

BILATERAL NETTING: An arrangement between two parties to net their obligations. The obligations covered by the arrangement may arise from financial contracts, transfers or both.

BILL OF EXCHANGE: An unconditional order in writing, addressed by one person to another, signed by the person giving it, requesting the person to whom it is addressed to pay, on demand or at a fixed or determinable future time, a sum certain in money to, or to the order of, a specified person, or to the bearer.

BILL OF LADING: A receipt for goods upon shipment, signed by a person authorised to sign on behalf of the owner of the ship. The bill of lading is also a document of title to the goods. It is capable of ownership being transferred by endorsement and delivery.

BILL BROKER: A merchant engaged in buying and selling bills of exchange.

BIMETALLISM: A currency system having a double standard, under which gold and silver coins are in circulation, containing the full weight of metal represented by their face value.

BIOMETRIC: This term refers to a method of identifying the holder of a device by measuring a unique physical characteristic of the holder, for example, by fingerprint matching, voice recognition or retinal scan.

BIS (Bank of International Settlements): The BIS is an international organisation which fosters co-operation among central banks and other agencies in pursuit of monetary and financial stability, its banking services are provided exclusively to central banks and international organisations.

BLUE CHIP: A term used to describe the ordinary shares of first-class industrial companies.

BOLERO: Bolero is a secure platform, which enables paperless trading between buyers, sellers and their logistics service and bank partners.

BOTH TO BLAME COLLISION CLAUSE: When damage may be caused by collision of goods into one and another.

BOTTOMRY BOND: Borrowing of money to complete the voyage by ship owners by offering the ship as security. The lenders lose the money if the ship is lost.

BREAKING BULK: To open hatches and commence discharge.

BROKER: Intermediary who negotiates foreign exchange deals between banks. In most money centres brokers do not act as intermediaries between banks and commercial users of the market.

BROKERAGE: Commission charged by a broker for his services. In some countries, this fee is referred to as "commission". Brokerage charges can vary depending on currency amount and maturity of the foreign exchange contract.

BULL: A speculator on the Stock Exchange who anticipates a rise in the value of a certain security and therefore buys such stocks, not intending to pay for the purchase, but hoping to sell them later, at a profit.

BULLION: Gold or silver in bars or in species. The term is also used to describe quantities of gold, silver, or copper coins when measured by weight.

BUSINESS DAY: Also Banking Day, Clear day, Market day and open day. A day on which foreign exchange contracts can be settled, e.g. a foreign exchange contract covering the sale of US dollars against GB Pound can be finalised only on a day when both New York and London are open for normal banking business (of course, other cities in the US and UK are suitable for payment, but only if they are acceptable to both parties to a transaction).

BUYER'S OPTION: A beneficial holder of a buyer's option can take delivery at any time between first day and last day of the option, e.g. between a spot and a forward date or even between two forward dates, without incurring further costs or for that matter gaining extra profits.

BUYING RATE: The rate (see Bid) at which the market in general, or a market-maker in particular, is willing to buy a foreign currency.

CAPITAL: Money contributed/used to run a business, often raised by an issue of shares; sums of invested money; the amount of money used or available to carry on a concern.

CARRIER'S AGENT: An agent of the shipping company.

CASH: Deposits with the central bank, banknotes and coin.

CARRIER'S LIEN: The shipping company has a "Lien" on the goods for any unpaid freight.

CASPIANA CLAUSE: Where the ship owners are permitted to discharge the cargo at a port other than the destined port stated in the B/L.

CHAIN OF TITLE: The proof of title to land, the sequence of deeds and documents from the good root of title to the holding deed.

CHAPS (Clearing House Automated Payment System): The UK electronic transfer system for sending same-day value payments from bank to bank. It operates with the Bank of England in providing the payment and settlement service.

CHARTER PARTY B/L: A Bill of Lading issued by a charter party i.e. the party to whom the owner has leased the vessel for a certain period or a certain voyage.

CHEQUE: A bill of exchange payable on demand drawn on a banker. The buyer could draw a cheque payable at his own domestic bank, and forward it to the exporter. It may take some weeks for such a cheque to be cleared through the banking system, though it is sometimes possible for the exporter to obtain funds against the cheque by having it purchased by his own bank.

CHIPS: Clearing House Inter-bank Payment System is a computerized funds transfer system for international dollar payments linking over 140 depository institutions with offices or subsidiaries in New York. Funds transfers through CHIPS, operated by the New York Clearing House Association, account for over 90% of all international payments relating to international trade. Final settlement occurs through adjustments in special account balances at the Federal Reserve Bank of New York.

CLAUSED B/L: See Unclean B/L below

CLEAN FLOAT: When an exchange rate reflects only normal supply and demand pressures, with little or no official intervention.

CLEAN BILL: A bill of exchange having no documents attached.

CLEAN B/L: When the goods received on board are in good order and no adverse remark, such as "boxes broken" etc., are marked on the Bill of Lading.

CLEARING BANK: A bank, which is a member of the London Banker's Clearing House.

CLEARING HOUSE: A central location or central processing mechanism through which financial institutions agree to exchange payment instructions or other financial obligations, for example securities, etc. The institutions settle for items exchanged at a designated time based on the rules and procedures of the Clearing House. In some cases, the Clearing House may assume significant counterparty, financial or risk management responsibilities for the clearing system.

COMBINED TRANSPORT DOCUMENT: A Bill of Lading issued by a transporting authority covering more than one mode of transport of goods.

COMBINED TRANSPORT OPERATOR: A transporter who provides for the cargo to be transported through more than one mode of transport.

COMMERCIAL DEALS OR TRANSACTIONS: Foreign exchange deals between a bank and a non-banking party.

COMMISSION: Charges made by a bank to execute a foreign exchange contract with a commercial organisation. (In some countries, this charge is made in the exchange rate).

CONFERENCE LINER B/L: A Bill of Lading issued by a shipping company running cargo vessels on regular line or regular schedule basis.

CONFIRMATION: After transacting a foreign exchange deal over the telephone or telex, the parties to the deal send to each other written confirmation giving full details of the transaction.

CONSIDERATION: The price paid. The term has been defined as "some right, interest, profit or benefit, accruing to one party, or some forbearance, detriment, loss, or responsibility given, suffered or undertaken by the other".

CONSIGNEE: One who is to receive the consignment.

CONSIGNOR: One who sends or forwards the consignment.

CONSOLIDATION: A person or company (Freight Forwarder) undertaking Consolidation of Consignments.

CONSUMER SPENDING: The current expenditure of individuals, including purchases of so-called "consumer durable" articles, such as television, radios, washing machines and machinery for use in the home.

CONTAINERISED CARGO: When the goods are transported duly packed in special large sized containers (20x8x8 feet) for handling cargo more efficiently.

CONTRACT OF AFFREIGHTMENT: An undertaking to carry the goods to the agreed port of destination. Bill of Lading is a contract of affreightment.

CONVERTIBLE CURRENCY: A currency, which can be freely exchanged for other currencies or gold without special authorisation from the appropriate central bank.

COPY BILL OF LADING: An unsigned additional copy of a B/L, which is of no value but may serve the purpose of evidence of shipment of goods.

CORRESPONDENT BANKING: An arrangement under which one bank holds deposits owned by other banks and provides payment and other services to those respondent banks. Such arrangements may also be known as agency relationships in some domestic contexts. In international banking, balances held for a foreign correspondent bank may be used to settle foreign exchange transactions. Reciprocal correspondent banking relationships may involve the use of so-called Nostro and Vostro accounts to settle foreign exchange transactions.

COVER: Foreign exchange deal which protects the value of an import or export transaction against exchange rate fluctuations.

CROSS-BORDER SETTLEMENT: A settlement that takes place in a country other than the country in which one trade counterparty or both are located.

CROSS-RATE: An exchange rate between two foreign currencies, in particular, other currencies against dollars outside the United States. For example, when a dealer in London buys (or sells) Euros against US Dollars, he uses a cross-rate.

CURRENCY: The recognised means of making payments, which circulate from hand to hand, or pass current, in a country.

CURRENCY BAND: The margin within which a currency is allowed to fluctuate by the monetary authorities.

D/P BILL: A bill with documents attached, presented for payment by the acceptor or drawee, the documents to be surrendered against such payment.

D/A BILL: A bill with documents attached, presented for acceptance by the drawee. The documents must be surrendered against such acceptance.

DATED STOCK: Gilt-edged stock issued by the government having a date by which it will be repaid.

DEALER (TRADER): A specialist in a bank or commercial company authorised to effect foreign exchange transactions and allowed to take speculative positions.

DEBENTURE: An acknowledgement of indebtedness, usually given under seal incorporating a charge on the assets of an incorporated company.

DEED: A written document executed under seal, evidencing a legal transaction.

DEMAND: An authoritative claim or request. A demand draft is one payable on presentation. Current account balances are repayable on demand.

DEMURRAGES: Extra charge to be paid if a vessel is not loaded or unloaded within a time allowed.

DEPOSIT BANK: A bank taking money from customers on current deposit or other accounts on the terms that the money is to be repaid on demand or at the end of an agreed term: usually confined to banks which take any sum on deposit, and do not specify any minimum amount.

DEPOSIT RATE: The rate of interest paid by a bank on a deposit account.

DEPRECIATION: A currency, which loses in value against one or more other currencies, especially if this happens in response to natural supply rather than by an official devaluation.

DEPRECIATION: Loss in value of assets by wear and tear, obsolescence, etc.; or normal deterioration in value which takes place during the life of an asset.

DEPRECIATION OF A CURRENCY: a diminution or lessening of the power of the monetary unit over the market, the diminution being shown by a rise in prices.

DETAILS: All information required for a foreign exchange transaction – name, rate, date(s) and where payment is to be effected.

DEVALUATION: The reduction of the official par value of the legal unit of currency, in terms of the currencies of other countries. Deliberate downward adjustment of a currency in relation to gold or other currencies.

DEVIATION CLAUSE: The shipping company may change the route to reach the agreed destination.

DIRECT DEBIT: It is a pre-authorised payment system used in collecting recurring bills by electronic means. Generally, the borrower signs a pre-authorisation agreement giving his bank the right to debit an account for the amount due on a designated day.

DIRECT QUOTATION: A foreign exchange rate, which values a foreign currency in terms of the national currency, for example, dollars quoted in Frankfurt in Euros terms.

DIRTY FLOAT: When the value of a floating currency is influenced by the intervention of the central bank.

DISCOUNT: Usually refers to the value of a currency in the forward market. When a currency is at a discount compared to the spot rate, it is worth less, or in other words, is cheaper to buy in the forward market than for spot settlement.

DOCUMENTARY BILL: A bill of exchange which is accompanied by various documents, such as a bill of lading, invoice and insurance policy.

DOMESTIC BANKING: The normal course of business between a banker and his customer (as opposed to "wholesale" banking), or the banking business in this country (as opposed to international foreign banking).

DOMICILE: A place of permanent residence; the place at which a bill of exchange is made payable.

DRAWEE: The person or company on whom a bill of exchange or cheque is drawn. When the person has accepted a bill he is known as the acceptor.

DRAWER: The person who writes out and signs a cheque or bill of exchange.

EBA: European Banking Association: A discussion forum for payments practitioners, the Euro Banking Association plays a major role in the financial industry as a developer of European payment infrastructures. The initiation and coordination of a cost effective and efficient euro clearing system are core activities of the association and have lead to the creation of Europe's leading private large-value clearing system EURO 1, the low-value payment system and STEP 1, and the first pan-European automated clearing house, STEP 2.

EBPP (Electronic Bill Presentment and Payment): The process by which companies bill customers and receive payments electronically over the internet. There are two types of presentments model: the direct model, in which a biller delivers the bill to customers via its own website or via a third-party's site; and the consolidator model, in which bills multiple billers are delivered to a single website, to be presented in aggregate to the consumer for viewing and payment.

ECB (European Central Bank): The ECB is the central bank for Europe's single currency, the Euro. The ECB's main task is to maintain the Euro's purchasing power and thus price stability in the Euro area. The ECB was established as the core of the Euro-system and ESCB (European System of Central Banks). The ECB and the national central banks together perform the task they have been entrusted with. The ECB has legal personality under public international law.

EDI (Electronic Date Interchange): The electronic exchange between commercial entities (in some cases also between public administrations), in a standard format, of data relating to a number of message categories, such as orders, invoices, customs documents, remittance advices and payments. EDI messages are sent through public data transmission networks or banking system channels. Any movement of funds initiated by EDI is reflected in payment instructions flowing through the banking system. EDIFACT, a United Nations body, has established standards for electronic data interchange.

EDIFACT (Electronic Data Interchange for Administration Commerce and Transport): Along with ANSI X12, EDIFACT was one of the first information standards created for e-business transactions.

EFT (Electronic Fund Transfer): A service which routes payments to the appropriate bank or building society.

EFTPOS (Electronic Fund Transfer at Point of Sale): The term refers to the use of payment cards at a retail location. The payment information is captured either by paper vouchers or by electronic terminals, which in some cases are designed also to transmit the information. Where this is so, the arrangement may be referred to as "electronic fund transfer at the point of sale".

ELIGIBLE LIABILITIES: The GB Pound deposits of the banking system as a whole, excluding deposits having an original maturity or more than two years, and any GB Pound resources gained by switching foreign currencies into GB Pound. Inter-bank transactions and GB Pound certificates of deposit (both held and issued) are taken into the calculation of individual banks' liabilities on a net basis, irrespective of the term.

ENDORSEMENT IN BLANK: An endorsement in blank consists of the name only of the payee or endorsee of a bill of exchange, written on the back of the bill. Such an endorsement specifies no endorsee, and the bill becomes payable to bearer.

EURO-CURRENCY: Currency held by non-residents and placed on deposit with banks outside the country of the currency. Major Euro-markets exist in Germany, Switzerland, France and the United Kingdom, and, from time to time, there are active dealings in Netherlands and Belgium and even Japan. The Euro element is of less importance now that deposit markets have been established in the Far East (the Asian currency market) and in the Western hemisphere.

EURO-DOLLARS: Dollars belonging to non-residents of the US, which are invested in the money markets in Europe, particularly in London. Side by side with the Euro-dollar market, there exist the Asian and the Western hemisphere markets. Euro-dollar settlements are made over the banking accounts in the United States and form an integral part of the US money supply.

EXCHANGE CONTRACT: Verbal or written agreement between two parties to deliver one currency in exchange for another for a specific value date, or sometimes a specific period, as in the case of an option contract.

EXOTIC CURRENCIES: Currencies in which there is no active exchange market. Most of the currencies of the underdeveloped world would fall within this category.

FATF (Financial Action Task Force): It is an inter-governmental body whose purpose is the development and promotion of policies, both at national and international levels, to combat money laundering and terrorist financing. It is a "policy-making body" which works to generate the necessary political will to bring about national legislative and regulatory reforms in these areas.

FED WIRE: Federal Wire is a high-speed electronic communication network linking the Federal Reserve Board of Governors, the 12 Federal Reserve Banks and 24 branches, the US Treasury Department and other federal agencies.

FINANCE BILL: A bill drawn by a firm or company for the purpose of arranging a short-term loan. The bill is drawn by arrangement on another firm or on a bank or accepting house. No sale of goods is involved. When the bill is accepted, it is discounted.

FIRM QUOTE (QUOTATION): When a foreign exchange dealer gives a firm buying or selling rate, or both, for immediate response or with a definite time limit.

FIXED EXCHANGE RATE: Official rate set by monetary authorities for one or more currencies. In most instances, even fixed exchange rates are allowed to fluctuate between definite upper and lower intervention points.

FLEXIBLE EXCHANGE RATES: Exchange rates with a fixed parity against one or more currencies but with frequent up or down valuations.

FLOATING EXCHANGE RATE: When the value of a currency is decided by supply and demand only.

FLOATING POUND: The GB Pound left to find its own level on the Foreign Exchange through the operation of the laws of supply and demand.

FLUCTUATIONS: Up and down movements of an exchange rate in response to supply and demand.

FOREIGN EXCHANGE MARKET: Worldwide network which connects the various national exchange markets by telephone and telex, either direct or via the brokers, to transact foreign exchange business.

FOREIGN EXCHANGE: Conversion of one currency into another.

FOREIGN BILL: A bill of exchange drawn abroad and payable in this country; or drawn in this country and payable abroad.

FORWARD RATES: Discounts or premiums between the spot rate and the forward rates for a currency.

FORWARD BOOK: Various net exposures for forward maturities which a bank has incurred by deliberate policies or as a result of dealing activities.

FORWARD EXCHANGE: Buying or selling currencies for delivery later than spot. Also called "future".

FORWARD/FORWARD: Simultaneously buying and selling the same currency for different maturity dates in the forward market. This also describes a dealer's forward book when he has long and short positions for different maturities, for example, long of Euro three months and short of Euro in the six months maturity.

FORWARD MARGINS: Discounts or premiums between the spot rate and the forward rates for a currency.

FORWARD MATURITIES: Business days for which deals can be transacted later than the spot date.

FORWARD PURCHASE: Engagement to buy a currency in exchange for another at a future date.

FORWARD SALE: Agreement to deliver a currency in exchange for another on a future date.

FORWARD RATE: The rate at which foreign currency can be bought or sold for delivery at a future time.

FORWARD CONTRACT: Exchange agreement between two parties to deliver one currency in exchange for another at a forward or future date.

FORWARDING AGENT'S B/L: A certificate of shipment issued by a shipping company's agent stating that the named consignment has been forwarded.

FREEHOLD: An estate in land, which is properly described as an estate in free simple absolute possession, signifying the highest type of land ownership, which anyone can possess.

FREIGHT PREPAYABLE/TO BE PREPAID: Freight to be paid before shipment of the cargo.

FREIGHT PAID/PREPAID: It is a clause when the freight is paid to the carrier prior to the transportation of the consignment.

GILT-EDGED: Securities of the highest class (e.g. government stocks) which are readily realizable.

GOOD ROOT OF TITLE: A document, which deals with the whole legal and equitable interest in land, describes the property in detail and shows no adverse factor influencing the title. It is the starting point of the chain of title when proving title to land.

GREEN CLAUSE: This clause is written on a letter of credit and is distinct to Red Clause, primarily covers the degree to which each one ties up the applicant's funds and exposes him to a foreign exchange risk. The merchandise is taken as collateral security against the advance of funds allowed by this clause. The advance funds may be given against warehouse receipts. Such clauses are not common these days and are of academic interest.

GROUND RENT: The rent paid to a freeholder who has granted a lease on his land and/or buildings.

HEDGE AGAINST INFLATION: An investment in land or shares, which are expected to appreciate in value in times of inflation, thus protecting the investor against loss due to the fall in the value of money.

HEDGING: Act of buying or selling the currency equivalent of a foreign asset or liability in order to protect its value against depreciation (appreciation) or devaluation (revaluation).

HOLDING DEED: The deed, which transferred the ownership of land to the person who is now holding it.

HOUSE AIR WAYBILL: A document issued by a consolidator for instruction to the break bulk agent.

HOUSE BILL OF LADING: A Certificate of Shipment of a specified consignment usually issued by a Freight Forwarder in association with a group age or consolidated international consignment.

HULL LOADING: It is where the vessel is loaded away from the port or a small ship goes into the other big ship.

INCONVERTIBLE CURRENCY: Currency, which cannot be exchanged for other currencies, either because this is forbidden by the foreign exchange regulations or because there are no buyers who wish to acquire the currency.

INDICATION (INDICATION RATE): When a dealer states "for indication" or "indication rate", this means that he does not want to transact business at the given rate or rates. The use of this expression can lead to confusion and it is preferable to substitute the less ambiguous term "for information only".

INDIRECT QUOTATION: Foreign exchange rate, which values the local or national currency in terms of the foreign currency. For example, in London foreign exchange rates show the value of £1 in other currency terms.

INFLATION: The result of the excessive issue of paper money, so that too much money is chasing too few goods, with the result that the value of the money in terms of goods steadily falls (i.e. prices rise).

INHERENT VICE: Deterioration of perishable goods by the passage of time or period.

INLAND BILL: A bill of exchange both drawn and payable within a country.

INTEREST ARBITRAGE: Switching into another currency by buying spot and selling forward, and investing the proceeds in order to obtain a higher interest yield. Interest arbitrage can be inward, i.e. from foreign currency into the local one, or outward, i.e. from the local currency to the foreign one. Sometimes better results can be obtained by not selling the forward interest amount, but in that case, if the exchange rate moved against the arbitrageur, the profit on the transaction might be less and even turn into a loss.

INTERVENTION: When central banks operate in the exchange markets to stabilize the rates and sometimes to influence the external value of a currency.

INTEREST PARITY: One currency is in interest parity with another when the difference in the interest rates is equalized by the forward exchange margins. For instance, if the operative interest rate in the United States is 5% and in the United Kingdom 6%, a forward premium of 1% for US Dollars against GB Pounds would bring about interest parity.

INTRINSIC VALUE: Genuine or real value. When used of a coin it means that the metal in the coin is worth the face value of the coin.

INVESTMENT: Using money to buy something which, it is hoped, will bring in some return and will not lose its value.

JETTISION: Means the throwing overboard of cargo or ship's gear to save the ship.

JOBBER: A dealer on the Stock Exchange who carries on business with the public and with other jobbers through the medium of stockbrokers.

L.A.S.H. B/L (Lighter Abroad Ship): A smaller ship that goes into mother ship.

LEADS AND LAGS: Process of accelerating or delaying foreign exchange cover when a currency adjustment seems imminent.

LEASEHOLD: Granting of the use of land by the freeholder to a lesser for a term of years.

LEGAL TENDER: The authorised notes and coin which may be lawfully offered in payment of a debt in a country.

LIEN: Lien is a legal right to obtain goods belonging to someone else until the charges on them have been paid, or until some pecuniary claim against the owner has been satisfied.

LIMITED LIABILITY: The limitation of the shareholders of a company of their liability for the debts of the company to the nominal amount of the shares they hold or to the amount they have guaranteed.

LINER B/L: A Bill of Lading issued by a shipping company operating passenger ships.

LONG POSITION (or just LONG): Incurred when a dealer purchases a currency in excess of his immediate requirements. Obviously a long position in one currency is compensated by a short position in another, even if the other currency is the national one.

LONG BILL: A long bill is a bill of exchange having a usance of three months or more.

MAIL TRANSFER (MT): In this case, the buyer's bank sends instructions by airmail to a correspondent bank, asking it to credit the exporter or his bank with GB Pound or foreign currency. Bank charges for remitting funds by MT are to be met by either the buyer or exporter and depend on what the parties have agreed. This method is slower than other methods of transfer of funds between banks in two different countries.

MANAGED FLOAT: When the monetary authorities intervene regularly in the market to stabilize the rates or to aim the exchange rate in a required direction.

MARGIN (SPREAD): Difference between the buying and selling rates, but also used to indicate the discounts or premiums between spot and forward.

MARITIME LIEN: Shipping company's lien over the cargo for freight not paid and the captain and the crew also have lien over the cargo for not being paid their salary by the shipping company.

MARKET-MAKER: The bank which makes buying and selling quotations in one or more currencies, either for spot and/or forward, to most comers.

MASTER OF THE VESSEL: Captain of a merchant vessel.

MASTER AIR WAYBILL: An air waybill covering a consolidated shipment showing the consolidator as the shipper.

MATE RECEIPT: Is an acknowledgement of the goods issued by the wharfinger or master of the ship when the goods are delivered on the wharf before the arrival of the ship named to carry the goods.

MATURITY DATE: Due date of an exchange contract, that is, the day that settlement between the contracting parties will have to be effected.

MORTGAGE: The conveyance of a legal or equitable interest in real or personal property as security for a debt or for the discharge of an obligation.

NEAR MONEY: A term sometimes applied to bills, cheques, promissory notes, postal and money orders.

NEGOTIABLE BILL OF LADING: Original copy of B/L duly signed by the ship owner or his authorised agent which gives the transferee a good title to goods.

NEW JASON CLAUSE: Means the ship owners will not be responsible for any accidental damage to the goods, before or after the shipment but in their custody.

OCEAN B/L: When the buyer names a particular ocean going vessel to transport the consignment.

OFFER FOR SALE: An invitation to the public to buy shares of a new issue from an Issuing House, which has bought the issue from the company concerned.

OFFSHORE FUNDS: A name given to mutual investment funds registered abroad in countries which offer tax advantages.

ON-BOARD B/L: A Bill of Lading indicating that the goods named therein have been received on board of the ship.

ON-DECK SHIPMENT: Received on the deck for shipment. It is similar to "On Board B/L".

OPEN DAY: Also known as Banking day, Business day, Clear day and Market day. A day on which foreign exchange contracts can be settled; e.g. a foreign exchange contract covering the sale of US dollars against GB Pounds can be finalised only on a day when both New York and London are open for normal banking business (of course, other cities in the US and UK are suitable for payment, but only if they are acceptable to both parties to a transaction).

OPEN MARKET OPERATIONS: The purchase or sale of securities in the Stock Exchange or Money Market by the central bank for the purpose of expanding or contracting the volume of credit.

OPTION FORWARD RATE: The rate at which foreign currency can be bought or sold for delivery between two future dates at the option of the buyer or seller. The option is as to the precise day of completion.

OVER-VALUATION: Describes the exchange rate of a currency, which is in excess of its purchasing power parity. This means that the country's goods will be uncompetitive in the export markets.

OVERNIGHT LIMIT: Net long or short position in one or more currencies that a dealer can carry over into the next dealing day.

PACKAGE DEAL: When a number of exchange and/or deposit orders have to be fulfilled simultaneously.

PALLETISED CARGO: Cargo of heavy weight placed on wooden frame etc. to facilitate lifting.

PAPER MONEY: Documents representing money, such as banknotes, promissory notes, bills of exchange or postal orders. (The last three of these are sometimes referred to as "quasi-money").

PAR: The nominal value of securities, or the exact amount, which has been paid for them.

PARAMOUNT CLAUSE: Bills of Lading issued in the United Kingdom bear the "Paramount Clause" which means that the carriage of goods is subject to the terms and conditions of the "Carriage of Goods Act of 1924".

PARTIAL SHIPMENT: Shipment of the cargo in part of the entire or complete consignment for shipment.

PIP: The fifth place after the decimal point, for example $/£1.72105. The last digit represents five pips.

PLEDGE: A delivery of goods or the documents of title to goods, by a debtor to his creditors as security for a debt, or for any other obligation. It is understood that the subject of the pledge will be returned to the pledgor when the debt has been paid or the obligation fulfilled.

POINT: The fourth place after the decimal point is called a "point", for example $/Euro1.4012. The last digit (2) represents two points.

PORT CONGESTION SURCHARGE: Extra charges for causing congestion at the port by over staying in the port.

PORT BILL OF LADING: It is a Bill of Lading, which is signed by an authorised person after the receipt of goods/shipment by the person at the port of shipment.

PREMIUM: A currency is at a premium, especially in the forward market, when fewer units can be bought for a forward maturity than on the spot.

PRIME BANK BILL: A bill of exchange drawn on and accepted by a first-class bank.

QUALITATIVE CONTROL: Directives from the Bank of England to the lending banks and financial institutions as to classes of customers who may be allowed to borrow.

QUANTITATIVE CONTROL: Directives from the Bank of England to the lending banks and financial institutions as to the total amount of money which they may lend.

QUARANTINE: Isolation imposed on a passenger while travelling.

QUASI NEGOTIABLE B/L: It is a Bill of Lading that if the transferor has a defective title the transferee does not get good title to the B/L.

RAILWAY RECEIPT: A Railway Receipt is document issued by Railway authorities for transportation of goods by railway.

RED CLAUSE: It is a clause added to a letter of credit, which authorises the advising/confirming bank to advance a certain specified percentage of the credit amount to the beneficiary before the beneficiary is in a position to present documents.

RECEIVED FOR SHIPMENT B/L: A document issued by a shipping company acknowledging the receipt of goods for shipment.

RESERVE ASSETS: These assets, to be held by banks and other financial institutions, are those which the Bank of England is ready to convert into cash, either directly or through the discount market. They comprise Treasury Bills, (Repos), cash held with Bank of England, investments in Gilt Edged Securities etc.

RESPONDENTIA BOND: An instrument by which the owner of the ship hypothecates the cargo as security for repayment of money borrowed at a foreign port.

RESTRAINT OF PRINCES: Action by a Government or King for arresting the ship or the cargo etc.

RESTRICTIVE ENDORSEMENT: One which prohibits the further negotiation of a bill or cheque.

RETAIL BANKING: The traditional course of business between a banker and his domestic customers, as opposed to "wholesale" banking.

REVALUATION: When the official value of a currency is updated by a deliberate decision of the monetary authorities.

RIGHTS ISSUE: The offer by a company of new shares direct to its existing members. The price is usually set below the market price of the existing shares in order to make the offer attractive. The rights to subscribe, therefore, have themselves a market value, and can be sold.

ROLLOVER: Prolongation of a maturing contract by swapping it onto a forward date.

SAILING VESSEL B/L: Bill issued by the owner of the "sailing vessel" (S.V.)

SCRIP: The document or provisional certificate which is given to a person who has agreed to take up bonds in connection with a government loan and has paid the first instalment. Scrip is principally associated with the issue of bonds or debentures.

SCRIP ISSUE: A capitalization of reserves by issuing fully paid-up shares free to present shareholders in proportion to their current holding.

SELLER'S OPTION: Forward contract, which allows the seller to deliver the foreign currency on any date within the option period.

SELLING RATE: Rate at which a market maker will sell a foreign currency for a suitable maturity date.

SHIPPER: Name of the exporter/consignor.

SHORT BILL: A short bill is one which has only a few days to run to maturity, irrespective of the original tenor of the bill or a bill of exchange payable as soon as sighted or seen by the drawee.

SHORT POSITION: It is position of a foreign exchange dealer when a dealer is short outright of a foreign currency.

SHORT FORWARD DATE AND RATE: The term "short forward" can refer to periods of up to two months, although it tends to be used more and more for maturities of less than one month. Dealers may use the term "Shorts" as well.

SLING LOSS: Damage to goods by use of slings (Hooks).

SOUS-PALAN CLAUSE: The carrier reserves the right to unload the cargo to lighten the ships cargo. This situation may arise out of port congestion.

SPECIAL DEPOSIT: An instrument of monetary policy, designed to restrict credit. The Bank of England may call upon all banks and financial institutions to deposit a percentage, usually 1 per cent, of their total deposits with the Bank of England. This restricts the ability of the lending institutions to extend credit.

SPECULATION: The purchase or sale of shares on an estimate of whether the share value will rise or fall, with the intention of making a quick profit, or avoiding a loss.

SPECULATOR and SPECULATION: Individual, an act of buying and selling a currency before the currency has to be paid for or delivered in the hope that a favourable exchange rate adjustment will take place.

SPOT RATE: The normal rate of exchange quoted in the foreign exchange markets, i.e. the rate for transactions in which the funds are to be paid over in each centre two working days later.

SPOT RATE (EXCHANGE RATE): The spot rate is also the exchange rate of a currency and is the one against which appreciations and depreciations (devaluations and revaluations) will be calculated.

SPOT: Generally the spot date falls two business days after the transaction date, though in some markets spot transactions may be executed for value next day.

SPOT DEAL (TRANSACTION): Foreign currency purchase or sale effected for spot value.

SPREAD: Difference between the buying and selling rates, but also used to indicate the discounts or premiums between spot and forward.

SQUARE: Purchases and sales are in balance and thus the dealer has no position.

STAG: A Stock Exchange expression for a person who applies for shares in any new company with the sole object of selling as soon as a premium is obtainable and never intending to hold or even fully subscribe for the shares.

STALE B/L: Where a B/L is dated after the bill of exchange or received in the importer's country after the goods have arrived.

STEAM SHIP B/L: A Bill of Lading issued by Steam Ship owner (S.S.) for the cargo.

STEAMER ARRIVAL: Date of the arrival of the steam ship.

STOCKBROKER: One who purchases or sells stocks or shares for his clients on the Stock Exchange.

STOP-LOSS ORDER: Order given to ensure that, should a currency weaken by a certain percentage, a short position will be covered even though this involves taking a loss. "Realize Profit Orders" are less common.

STRAIGHT B/L: It is an American term for a bill of lading in which it is stated that the goods are consigned to a specified person.

SWAP: Transaction involving the simultaneous buying and selling of a currency for different maturities.

SWAP MARGIN: Discounts or premiums between the spot rate and the forward rates for a currency.

TELEGRAPHIC/SWIFT TRANSFER: This is identical to Mail Transfer except that the instructions are conveyed by telex or cable or electronically. Transfers can also be made via the S.W.I.F.T. (Society for Worldwide Interbank Financial Telecommunications) network.

TENANT RIGHT: A right of the tenant of property, whether expressly stated or implied, such as a right to remove fixtures at the end of the tenancy, or to receive an allowance for seeds or fertilizer put on the land.

TENOR: The term or meaning applied to a bill of exchange or financial instrument when it is payable on sight or a given number of days/months after the date of the instrument.

TERM BILL: A bill of exchange which is payable at the end of a period, as opposed to a bill payable at sight or on demand.

THIN MARKET: When there is little activity in the market and even small orders will affect the rate structure.

THIRD PARTY B/L: A B/L issued not by the ship owner but some other shipping company.

THROUGH BILL OF LADING: It is a bill of lading, which provides (or ought to provide) for continuous responsibility of several railway and shipping undertakings from one place to another.

TOKEN MONEY: Coins where the value of the metal in them is less than the value attached to them by law, such as the cupro-nickel and bronze coins of the UK.

TRADE BILL: A bill of exchange drawn and accepted by commercial firms.

TRAMP SHIPPING: Freight or cargo vessel running on irregular line.

TRANSACTION LOSS (OR PROFIT): Real or opportunity loss or profit on a foreign exchange transaction covering the movement of goods or services or even to undo another foreign exchange transaction.

TRANSACTION DATE: Day on which a foreign exchange transaction is entered into.

TRANS-SHIPMENT: Transfer of cargo from one ship to another prior to reaching the destination.

TRANSLATION LOSS (OR PROFIT): Estimated loss or profit resulting from the revaluation of foreign assets and liabilities for balance sheet purposes.

TREASURY BILL: Bills issued by the treasury in return for sums of money lent to the government by bankers, brokers, etc. They form part of the floating debt of the country.

TRUCK WAY BILL: A document issued by a Road Transporter for transportation of goods by a truck.

TWO-WAY QUOTATION: When a dealer quotes both buying and selling rates for foreign exchange transactions.

UNCLEAN B/L: When the Bill of Lading indicates the packing of goods is defective or broken.

UNDATED STOCK: Gilt-edged security issued by the government on a perpetual basis and does not have a date by which it will be redeemed.

UNDER-VALUATION: An exchange rate is under-valued when it is below its purchasing power parity. The consequence of under-valuation is that goods produced in the under-valued country will be too cheap in the export markets.

UNITISED CARGO: Items such as motor vehicles, tractors and other machinery, which are delivered and accepted by the shipping company as units.

USANCE BILL OF EXCHANGE: It is a period of time between the date a bill of exchange is presented and the date it is paid. In the strict sense, the term means the time allowed by customs for the period of a bill of exchange in trade between two different countries. A bill of exchange drawn in one country and payable in another at a term which is governed by the custom or usage of such transactions.

VALUE TODAY: Transactions executed for same-day settlement; sometimes also referred to as "cash transactions".

VALUE DATE: Maturity date of a spot or forward contract.

WHARFAGE: Charges for storing goods at the wharf.

WHOLESALE BANKING: Borrowing or lending, usually in large sums, by big banks amongst themselves through the medium of the inter-bank market; dealing with other financial institutions, as opposed to retail banking which consists of the traditional course of business between a bank and its customer.

YANKEE BONDS: Dollar denominated bonds issued in the United States by foreign banks and corporations. These bonds pay semi-annual interest, unlike Eurobonds, which pay annual interest, and are registered with Securities and Exchange Commission.

YIELD CURVE: Comparison of the market return, or yield, of a security and its maturity. This usually is plotted on a graph showing the comparative yields of similar investments, such as bonds.

Z-BOND: Long-term, deferred interest Collaterised Mortgage Obligation (CMO) bond that pays no interest until all prior bonds in a CMO bond offering have been retired. Z-Bond is similar to Zero Coupon bond.

CHAPTER 1

International Trade and Inherent Risks

BACKGROUND OF INTERNATIONAL TRADE

Ever since World War II there has been a considerable increase in world trade between independent sovereign states. In international trade, importers and exporters are quite often confronted with problems arising from the movements of goods from one country to another and are simultaneously subject to the different legislation, customs and practices of these countries. Importers and exporters have certain concerns such as:

Exporters want to be certain that they are paid when their goods have been shipped or dispatched because the goods will be out of their control.

Importers want to be certain that they receive goods that conform to what has been ordered.

Commercial banks play an important role in international trade. Commercial banks act as intermediaries between importers and exporters. They have insight and wide practical experience in foreign trade coupled with legal knowledge of provision in different countries. Banks have correspondents in most countries, through whom they deal with the counter parties. Some banks may have their own branches in other countries.

As banks are major financial institutions they are trustworthy and can be relied upon by their customers. They provide advisory services on various subjects to their importing and exporting customers. They collect payment from overseas countries from importers in foreign countries and also remit funds to the exporters abroad on behalf of their customers.

Banks offer various types of services to local and international business communities. These services include financial facilities to exporters and importers by way of loans and overdrafts, discounting and purchasing of bill of exchange. There are many more inherent risks in buying and selling goods overseas than locally. Some of the risks in foreign trade are explained in brief hereunder.

EXPORTERS' RISKS

Arrangements for selling goods abroad are often more complex than those connected with home market sales due to following reasons:

Geographical Factors: The exported goods are sold to buyers who, for geographical reasons, are likely to be less known to the seller's own country.

Legal System: The buyer will often be subject to a different legal system and trade customs from those in the exporter's country.

Language: The languages of the exporters and importers may be different, thus there would be need for translating the basic text and its related implications.

Non-Payment: Exporting tends to entail a greater risk of non-payment than domestic sales. This risk is known as the buyer's risk.

IMPORTERS' RISKS

Delay in delivery of goods and settlement of funds: The time taken for goods to pass from the seller to the buyer is generally longer for exports than for goods sold to buyers at home. This poses a problem because buyers prefer not to pay until the goods have been inspected while suppliers want payment on or before shipment. What actually happens is often a compromise – the result of the relative bargaining powers of the two parties to trade.

Exchange Risks: Export trade involves a financial transaction in a foreign currency either to the buyer or to the seller, or sometimes to both, and hence entails exchange risks.

Exchange Control: Export trade may involve exchange control regulations, both in the seller's and the buyer's country, and a variety of further risks for the seller.

Political Risks: There are risks in the event of war or national disaster between countries. These risks are also known as country risks.

Manufacturing Risks: The buyer cancels or modifies the order unilaterally. In such a case the exporter has to find an alternative buyer who is willing to buy the goods. The exporter might be forced to accept a substantially lower price. A system well-developed by international banks ensures that contracts signed between two parties in the United Kingdom

(U.K.) are adhered to and that the parties fulfill their delivery or payment obligation.

The buyer/importer has concerns about the quality and quantity of goods. The buyer/importer, therefore, should be aware of the types of documents that are required to protect against these risks.

Export/Import Facilities: The sophisticated arrangements which surround exporting trade stem from the various risks, and a wide range of the available facilities and how to avoid these risks are described later in this book.

CHAPTER 2

Services Offered by Commercial Banks

The finance of international trade forms an important part of any major bank's services package. Many have specialised departments to handle the various aspects involved, comprising experienced staff able to cope up with the demands of customers with overseas business to transact.

Trade Enquiries: Banks with overseas branch networks or correspondent banking relationships are able to identify potential markets for their exporting customers, and assist to an extent with the introduction to their importing customers overseas.

Credit Information: By using the standard form of bank-to-bank status enquiry it is possible for banks based in the U.K. to obtain information on importers e.g. in respect of their creditworthiness, from banks overseas.

Economic and Political Reports: Many large international banks employ economists who provide reports on a number of countries, which are useful to exporters, particularly if the country concerned is politically unstable or its economy is weak.

Travel Services: In addition to the usual services available to the travelling business executive, such as travellers' cheques and foreign currency, the banks may also be able to provide a letter of introduction addressed to their overseas branch or correspondent. This letter introduces the customer and requests that all possible assistance is given so that local trading terms and conditions may be fully understood.

Exchange Control Regulations: Many countries have restrictions on the amount of local and/or foreign currency that can be taken into and out of the country at any one time. Consequently, an exporter who is unaware of the current situation may export goods to a country and then find that the importer is unable to transfer the funds due in settlement without the sanction of the Central Bank. Banks are able to provide their customers with advice to avoid such problems.

Exchange controls were lifted in the U.K. during October 1979, and U.K. residents are now free to transfer and receive funds as they see fit to do so, without the approval of the Regulators, provided money laundering and terrorist activities are not involved.

Sale and Purchase of Foreign Currencies/Exchange Contracts: Banks sell and purchase foreign currencies to and from their customers/non-customers and travellers. An exporter may find that before payment in foreign currency is received the exchange rate has reduced thus reducing profit on the transaction. It is possible for an exporter to enter into a forward exchange contract with a bank, which enables the bank to fix the exchange rate at which the currency will be converted on a specified date/period in the future. The exporter can then price goods safe in the knowledge that the rate will not change whatever happens in the foreign exchange markets. The bank covers its own commitment by matching deals in the market.

Collection of Bills: A British exporter who has drawn a bill of exchange on an overseas buyer is able to obtain reimbursement by asking their bank to send the bill to the importer's bank i.e. an exporter's bank will 'collect' the proceeds.

If the bill/cheque or draft is sent without any attached documents it is known as a 'clean' collection. More often, documents of title to the goods concerned are enclosed with the bill and it then becomes a 'documentary' collection. Unlike a documentary credit there is no guarantee of payment when the bill is presented for payment. Thus the bill routed through the bank remains at risk of non-payment.

When a bank is asked to collect a bill of exchange, with or without other documents, it acts as agent to the exporter. Careful note is taken of any instructions that the exporter may give, particularly concerning what action the bank is to take if the bill is not accepted (if usance) or unpaid. The risk of non-payment can be reduced if the documents are handed over against payment of the bill (a D/P bill). If an element of trust exists between the exporter and importer and the bill is a usance bill, documents may be released against the importer's acceptance (a D/A bill). The importer's bank in another country will be acting as an agent to the bank in the U.K. and will remit the proceeds to the U.K. when payment is made. The exporter's account will then be credited less the bank's charges for the collection, unless otherwise agreed.

In a manner similar to documentary credits, collections are subject to International Chamber of Commerce Uniform Rules for Collections (ICC Publication URC 522).

FINANCE FOR EXPORTS

Banks finance exporters in a number of ways, including:

Advances Against Shipping Documents: Often when handling bills and documents on a collection basis, banks are willing to allow overdrafts to the exporters subject to the bank's satisfaction about the financial standing of the parties. The documents of title can be used as a form of security pending receipt of the collection proceeds.

Export Credit Guarantee Department (ECGD) Insurance cover may be required. The exporter pays an insurance premium for the cover. The bank is then guaranteed by the ECGD for the repayment should the importer default. The ECGD policy is assigned to the bank so that any proceeds under the policy are paid directly to the bank and not to the customer.

Negotiation of Bills of Exchange: Bills drawn on, and usually accepted by, the importer can be 'negotiated' by the exporter's bank. The bank purchases the bill from the exporter paying over the proceeds before maturity, in return for an interest charge rather like discounting a bill. Negotiation is 'with recourse' that allows the bank to claim the amount paid back from the exporter if the bank is unable to collect the bill proceeds.

CHAPTER 3

Methods of Trade

In international markets the situation is often more complex than in local markets. In local markets it is possible that the parties may have known each other for some time and have built a certain level of trust. Trading risk in local markets is much less than in international markets. There are a number of methods of trade and settlement of trade accounts. Details of various methods of trade that are available to buyers and sellers for trading indicating the risks involved and the benefits are discussed in the following pages. Before importers and exporters decide to do business with each other they need to understand and adopt a method suitable to meet their specific needs.

The contract between buyer and seller will specify the way in which payment is to be made. The seller will ask: how will I be paid, when will I be paid and how can the risk of non-payment be minimised?

Certain methods of payment are less risky than others. It is up to the buyer and seller to agree on a method that suits them both.

CASH ON DELIVERY

It is a system where goods and all shipping documents are sent direct to the buyers who pay on delivery or after an agreed period. The system does not offer any security to the seller/exporter. The seller can face risks of non-receipt of payment or goods may be left in a distant port due to non-payment by the buyer/importer. A high degree of mutual trust and confidence must exist between the two parties.

ADVANCE PAYMENT

This is the safest way for an exporter to receive payment for goods shipped abroad because the funds are received before the goods are released. The risk has been transferred to the importer who must trust the exporter to actually deliver the goods paid for. The method of payment is usually by cheque, bank draft, mail transfer or telegraphic transfer/SWIFT. Due to various implications of this system, advance payments are rarely used. More common is the payment in advance of a cash deposit by the buyer, with the balance being paid in one of the following ways.

OPEN ACCOUNT

When the exporter and importer trust one another implicitly, perhaps because they have traded together for a number of years, they may agree to trade on open account terms. Goods are shipped to the importer and the documents of title are sent directly by the exporter. A set date for payment is given and the importer merely remits the necessary funds to the exporter as agreed. In transactions involving regular shipments the importer often makes payments at set intervals, paying for goods received during that particular period. The exporter has no control over the goods and cannot be guaranteed payment, so an open account is perhaps the riskiest method of trade available.

COLLECTIONS

Promissory Notes: A promissory note is simply a promise to pay. It is written out by the buyer, promising to pay the exporter (or bearer), an amount of money at a specified time. A bill of exchange is an instrument drawn by a seller on a buyer. The promissory note provides a degree of security similar to that afforded by an accepted bill of exchange.

Bills of Exchange: Another method of payment for exports is by means of bills of exchange which are drawn on the buyer by the seller. Bills of exchange provide a very flexible and popular method of settling international trade transactions. Such trade bills may be at sight or a term/at usance. In the former case, the drawee of the bill (the buyer) has to pay cash on presentation of the bill with a term/usance bill, a credit period (known as the tenor or usance bill) is allowed to the buyer, who signifies agreement to pay on the due date by writing an acceptance across it.

A British exporter who has drawn a bill of exchange on an overseas buyer is able to obtain reimbursement by asking his bank to send the bill to the importer's bank i.e. the exporter's bank will 'collect' the proceeds.

LETTERS OF CREDIT

Payment through the medium of a bill of exchange can be made still more secure by the use of a letter of credit (although a bill of exchange is not always necessarily required under a letter of credit, it is frequently called for under its terms).

A letter of credit is issued by the buyer's bank at the buyer's request in accordance with the payment terms of the underlying contract; and is a guarantee of payment by that bank. The beneficiary would be well advised to seek the advice of his own bankers on the value of the issuing bank's guarantee, as there may be exchange control problems, political risks, or even a question about the credit standing of the issuing bank.

If the credit is made irrevocable, the issuing bank is unable to amend or cancel its terms without the consent of all the parties, including the beneficiary. A further, security can be obtained by the exporter by making it a confirmed irrevocable letter of credit, where the bank through which the letter of credit is transmitted to the exporter adds confirmation.

METHODS OF PAYMENT/SETTLEMENT OF ACCOUNT

Cheque

The buyer could draw a cheque payable at his own domestic bank, and forward it to the exporter. It may take some weeks for such a cheque to be cleared through the banking system, though it is sometimes possible for the exporter to obtain funds against the cheque by having it purchased by his own bank.

Bank draft

This is an instrument drawn by the buyer's bank, normally on a correspondent bank in the exporter's country. The buyer sends the draft to the exporter, who then obtains payment via his own bank. It is possible for the buyer's bank to draw a draft on itself, which is less convenient to an exporter in the United Kingdom if payment is required in GB Pounds, and, in any case, will not finally be paid until it is presented to the bank on which it is drawn.

Mail transfer (MT)

In this case, the buyer's bank sends instructions by airmail to a correspondent bank, asking it to credit the exporter or his bank with GB Pound or foreign currency. Bank charges for remitting funds by MT are met by either the buyer or the exporter depending on what the parties have agreed. This method is slower than the other methods of transfer of funds between the banks in two different countries.

SWIFT

Swift Transfer: This is identical to Mail Transfer except that the instructions are conveyed by telex or cable or electronically. Transfers can also be made via the SWIFT (Society for Worldwide Inter-bank Financial Telecommunications) network.

CHAPS

Clearing House Automated Payment System is a private telecommunication and payment system for inter-bank clearing of British Pound payments, operated since 1984 by the Bankers Clearing House of London.

CHIPS

Clearing House Inter-bank Payment System is a computerized funds transfer system for international dollar payments linking over 140 depository institutions with offices or subsidiaries in New York. Funds transfers through CHIPS, operated by the New York Clearing House Association, account for over 90 per cent of all international payments relating to international trade. Final settlement occurs through adjustments in special account balances at the Federal Reserve Bank of New York.

Direct debit

It is a pre-authorised payment system used in collecting recurring bills by electronic means. Generally, the borrower signs a pre-authorisation agreement giving his bank the right to debit an account for the amount due on a designated day.

EFT

Electronic Funds Transfer between accounts by electronic means rather than conventional paper-based payment methods such as writing a cheque.

Fed wire

Federal Wire is a high-speed electronic communication network linking the Federal Reserve Board of Governors, the 12 Federal Reserve Banks and 24 branches, the U.S. Treasury Department and other federal agencies.

CHAPTER 4

Foreign Exchange Rates

INTRODUCTION

Both the importer and the exporter need to know what means are available to make payments overseas and to receive payments from foreign buyers. They may have the option to decide whether to trade in GB Pound or a foreign currency. Before they look at these important points, it would be better to consider the international financial system as this will help in the selection of the appropriate method of payment and/or settlement of funds due.

FOREIGN CURRENCY TRANSACTIONS

When payments are made between countries there is no physical movement of currency notes, but instead the transactions are accounted for and recorded in the books of accounts of the banks. Almost all the commercial banks operating in one country maintain accounts with other banks operating normally in the main cities of foreign countries.

BANK'S ACCOUNTING SYSTEM

For example, if a payment is to be made to a British exporter by a German buyer, depending upon the method of payment adopted, either the Euro account of the British (exporter's) bank will be credited or a GB Pound account of the German (importer's) bank will be debited. The exporter will be paid value of the exports in GB Pound, or in the GB Pound equivalent of the Euros by the exporter's bank in the UK.

Commercial banks are involved in thousands of foreign currency transactions each business day on behalf of their customers, in respect of visible and invisible trade. They maintain a careful check on the transactions made on their Nostro and Vostro accounts, and buy/sell foreign currency in the foreign exchange market as per their and their customers' need.

FOREIGN EXCHANGE MARKET

In the United Kingdom there is no foreign exchange market by way of physical structure or a building. Rather the foreign exchange market comprises the foreign exchange departments of a large number of banks and other authorised dealers. They have an efficient telecommunication network between one another and are able to maintain an up-to-date exchange rate.

EXCHANGE RATES QUOTATION

The exchange rate of a currency is in fact the price of one unit of currency against the other. In London this price is quoted or expressed as so many units of a foreign currency per Pound, i.e. on an indirect basis. The prices (rates) are quoted, one for buying and the other for selling currency. The dealer i.e. the bank, will buy at the higher quotation and will sell at the lower quotation, so as to receive as many units as possible of foreign currency for every Pound and when selling the dealer will want to give as few units of foreign currency as possible for every Pound. The maxim of foreign exchange dealers is 'BUY HIGH, SELL LOW', but for the customer the opposite is true.

GB Pound spot and forward rates

As an example, a table of spot and forward market exchange rates for some of the world currencies at a particular date at close of market against GB Pound is given in Table 4.1.

The left-hand column shows the currency of the country. Column "A" gives the range of movement of the exchange rate of a currency during the day. Column "B" indicates the exchange rate at the close of business of the exchange market. The closing exchange rates become the opening rates of exchange when the foreign exchange market opens the following business day. Columns "C" and "D" indicate forward exchange margins for one month and three months respectively.

FOREIGN EXCHANGE RATES

Table 4.1 Example of exchange rates spot/forward against GBP

Country/City	"A" Range	"B" Close	"C" 1 month	"D" 3 months
Copenhagen	11.102–11.126	11.119–11.121	192–63pr	494–260pr
Euro	1.4890–1.4926	1.4909–1.4917	7–10dis	23–27dis
Montreal	2.2698–2.2806	2.2724–2.2732	23–11pr	63–43pr
New York	1.9556–1.9679	1.9598–1.9603	2.45–4.45pr	3.0–8.0dis
Oslo	12.254–12.303	12.291–12.298	223–72pr	531–322pr
Stockholm	13.448–13.502	13.488–13.496	30–17pr	78–59pr
Tokyo	232.09–233.69	233.16–233.19	104–88pr	280–257pr
Zurich	2.3910–2.4023	2.3943–2.3956	75–59pr	200–171pr

Premium = pr   Discount = dis

SPOT EXCHANGE RATES

The spot exchange rate is a rate of exchange at a particular moment of time of the day. The exchange rate may fluctuate during the day as shown above in column "A". The settlement of these transactions takes place within 48 hours, i.e. two working days.

Let us assume the above rates are at the close of business, they are the rates that would apply as the market opens on the following business day. If a large transaction of a currency is involved an up-to-date/latest rate should be obtained from the bank dealer.

FORWARD EXCHANGE RATES

Forward rates apply to transactions for completion at an agreed future date beyond two working days. The Forward Exchange rates can be "Fixed Forward Rate" or "Option Forward Rate".

FIXED FORWARD EXCHANGE RATES

Fixed Forward Rate is for receipt or delivery of a foreign currency at a fixed date some time in the future i.e. after one month, three month or six months etc.

OPTION FORWARD EXCHANGE RATES

Option Forward Exchange Rate is for the receipt or delivery of a foreign currency sometime in the future between two agreed dates. For example an importer has to pay for goods in foreign currency and wishes to enter into a three months forward contract with one month's option. Here the customer has the option to buy the foreign currency any time during the third month. In this case the two dates in the future are after the end of the second month and before the end of the third month from the date of the forward contract.

For an example the spot rate is quoted (at close of business from the above table, column "B") in London Foreign Exchange Market, London as U.S.$1.9598 − 1.9603 = £1, it means that the Foreign Exchange dealer will buy from its customer(s) US$1.9603 for a Pound and will sell US$1.9598 for a Pound to the customer(s). The difference between the two rates 1.9603 − 1.9598 = 0.0005 points denotes the profit margin of the foreign exchange dealer.

HOW EXCHANGE RATES ARE DETERMINED

The price of a currency is determined by the rate of exchange of another currency. This rate of exchange is determined on the basis of demand and supply of a currency in the foreign exchange market. If the demand of a currency increases, its value will rise, and if the demand of the currency decreases, its value will fall. For example, let us take the value of GB Pound against US Dollar. If on a particular day the rate of exchange £/US$ is 1.9603 and the demand for Pound increases, then the rate might go up to US$ 1.9620. This means that the Pound is now worth more US Dollars than before. If the demand for Pound falls then the rate might move down to US$1.9500. This means GB Pound is now worth less US Dollars than it was earlier. This will indicate that the value of US Dollar has increased in comparison to GB Pound.

FACTORS INFLUENCING EXCHANGE RATE

There are many factors that influence the exchange rates and also demand and supply for a particular currency.

Balance of Payment: If the Balance of Payment of a country is in deficit, for example, if the UK's imports are more than the exports, payments for the imports have to be made in GB Pound. The foreign exchange market will be flooded by GB Pound. The increased supply of GB Pound will depress its value, this means the exporters to the UK will get less US Dollars and exporters in the UK will get more GB Pounds.

Capital Transactions: In addition to commercial transactions, the demand and supply situation in the Foreign Exchange Market is affected by Capital transactions in respect of short-term and long-term investment, both in the UK and from overseas government loans and International Monetary Fund.

Confidence in a Currency: The confidence in a currency influences exchange rates. The confidence will be affected by the political and economic conditions of a country.

FORWARD EXCHANGE RATES

When a person intends to make a transaction in a foreign currency at a future date, he may enter into a forward exchange contract with a commercial bank or an authorised dealer in foreign currency. You will notice that in the Table 4.1 "Euro" currency is quoted at discount, which means "Euro currency" is cheaper to buy forward than immediate delivery (spot) every pound will buy more units of Euro currency. Therefore, the rate of exchange margin quoted as discount must be added to the spot rate. Where a currency is quoted at a premium (pr) rate, the GB Pound will buy lesser units of foreign currency. Therefore, the premium rate quoted must be deducted from the spot rate of exchange.

In the case of currencies at premium, the exchange margin figure is higher on the left-hand side and for currencies at discount the exchange margin figure is higher on the right-hand side. The dealer will buy high and sell low, the left-hand spot quotation is the dealer's selling rate and the right-hand spot quotation is the dealer's buying rate. The dealer will deduct the premium margin when buying and selling currencies at premium in future and will add discount margins when buying and selling currencies at discount in future.

FOREIGN EXCHANGE SPOT TRANSACTION – MECHANISM

Let us take for an example a British importer XYZ & Company has imported goods from the United States of America and receives an invoice for the value of the goods in US Dollars. The importing customer XYZ & Co. does not maintain a bank account in US Dollars with their bank. Therefore, the company will have to request to their bank to buy US Dollars to make payment for the imports and sell equivalent amount of GB Pounds. Theoretically, the bank does not have dollars available and in turn it will have to go to the Foreign Exchange Market Dealer to buy US Dollars.

Example 1 Foreign exchange transaction – mechanism

A UK importer wishes to make payment in US $ to an American exporter

A UK importer imports goods from United States and receives an invoice in US Dollars. To pay in US Dollars the importer sells GB Pounds to his bank and buys US Dollars.

As mentioned earlier the bank would like to make some profit from each foreign exchange transaction. If the bank makes a profit of 5 points as before the bank will give 5 points less of US Dollars to the customer. This figure is calculated as follows:

Foreign Exchange Dealer's selling rate of US $ against GB Pounds is	US$1.9598
Bank will make profit 5 points (margin) by giving less amount	.0005 −
	1.9593

Example 2 Foreign exchange transaction – mechanism

A UK exporter receives payment in US Dollars from an American importer

An example of a British exporter ABC & Company who has exported goods to the United States of America, the company agreed to sell in US Dollars

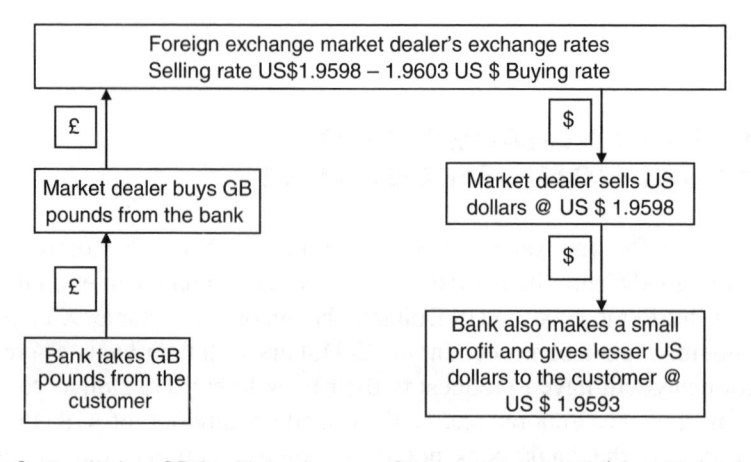

```
          Foreign exchange market dealer's exchange rates
          Selling rate US$1.9598 – 1.9603 US $ Buying rate

    [£]                                      [$]

 Market dealer buys GB              Market dealer sells US
 pounds from the bank               dollars @ US $ 1.9598

    [£]                                      [$]

                                    Bank also makes a small
 Bank takes GB                      profit and gives lesser US
 pounds from the                    dollars to the customer @
 customer                           US $ 1.9593

 Customer gives GB £ to his bank    Customer receives US $ from his bank
```

Figure 4.1 Action flow diagram customer sells GBP against USD

FOREIGN EXCHANGE RATES

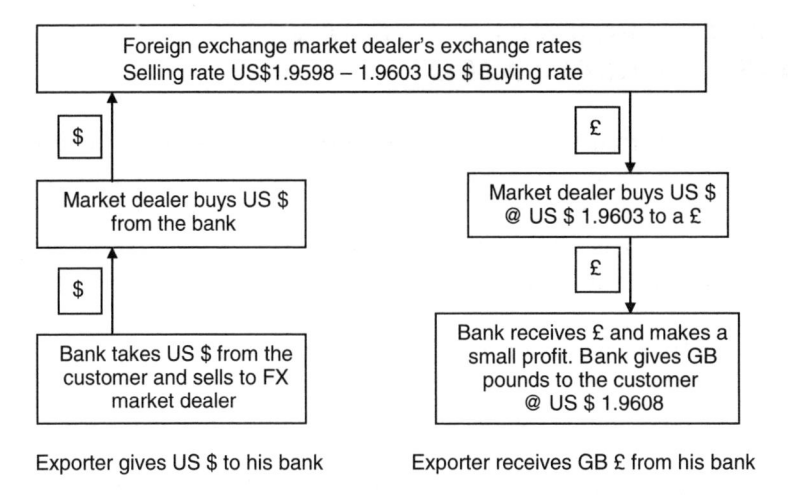

```
┌─────────────────────────────────────────────────────┐
│  Foreign exchange market dealer's exchange rates    │
│  Selling rate US$1.9598 – 1.9603 US $ Buying rate   │
└─────────────────────────────────────────────────────┘
         ▲                              ▲
       ┌───┐                          ┌───┐
       │ $ │                          │ £ │
       └───┘                          └───┘
         ▲                              ▲
┌──────────────────────┐   ┌──────────────────────────┐
│ Market dealer buys   │   │ Market dealer buys US $  │
│ US $ from the bank   │   │ @ US $ 1.9603 to a £     │
└──────────────────────┘   └──────────────────────────┘
         ▲                              ▲
       ┌───┐                          ┌───┐
       │ $ │                          │ £ │
       └───┘                          └───┘
         ▲                              ▲
┌──────────────────────┐   ┌──────────────────────────┐
│ Bank takes US $ from │   │ Bank receives £ and makes│
│ the customer and     │   │ a small profit. Bank     │
│ sells to FX market   │   │ gives GB pounds to the   │
│ dealer               │   │ customer @ US $ 1.9608   │
└──────────────────────┘   └──────────────────────────┘

Exporter gives US $ to his bank   Exporter receives GB £ from his bank
```

Figure 4.2 Action flow diagram customer sells USD against GBP

and sends an invoice for the value of the goods in US Dollars. ABC & Co. receives payment in US Dollars. The company does not maintain a bank account in US Dollars with the bank in the UK. Therefore, the company will have to request their bank to sell the amount of dollars to convert the amount in GB Pounds. Theoretically, the bank will have to buy those Dollars and sell them to the Foreign Exchange Dealer in Foreign Exchange Market to receive GB Pounds.

The bank's foreign exchange dealer wants to make some profit on each transaction. The dealer will sell lesser amount of US Dollars to the bank keeping a margin of 5 points. Whenever a bank dealer buys and sells foreign currencies some margin is kept as profit. Therefore, the bank's rate of exchange in the above examples is 1.9593 – 1.9608 i.e. bank sells US Dollars @ 1.9593 and bank buys US Dollars @ 1.9608 against one GB Pound. The bank dealer's exchange rate in the examples above will be US$1.9593 – 1.9608 against one GB Pound.

FORWARD EXCHANGE CONTRACT

A forward exchange contract is entered into between a bank and a customer, the bank fixes the rate of exchange at which a foreign currency will be bought or sold. The exchange rate may fluctuate during and at the time of maturity but it will not have any affect on the forward contract agreed between the bank and the customer. Through forward exchange contracts both the importer and exporter know the exact amount of their payables and receivable in foreign currency thereby covering against fluctuation of any exchange rates during the period. Forward exchange contract is a legal contract to receive or deliver foreign currency at the agreed date.

HOW THE FORWARD EXCHANGE RATE IS CALCULATED

If the foreign currency is at premium the exchange margin for the period is deducted from the spot rate of exchange, because the foreign currency will be stronger in future. If the foreign currency is at discount in future, the exchange margin is added to the spot rate. This is because the foreign currency will be weaker in future and Pound will be able to buy more of foreign currency.

Forward Exchange contract may be a "fixed forward contract" or "option forward contract". In case of a "fixed forward contract" foreign currency will be delivered or received on a fixed date in future e.g. at the end of one, two, three months or more as agreed. It is shown in Figure 4.3.

If a forward contract for three months is entered on 1st December it will mature on 1st March. The agreed amount of foreign currency must be delivered or received on the agreed fixed date i.e. 1st March.

Option forward contract: In an "option forward contract" the bank agrees to receive or deliver foreign currency any time between two different dates both in future. For example a customer enters into a three months "option forward contract" with a one month option. The option is in the last month of the option period. The customer will have the option to buy or sell foreign currency any time during the third month i.e. between the end of the second month and the end of the third month as shown in Figure 4.4 below.

An option forward contract for three months entered on 1st December with an option of one month will have an option period between 1st of February and 1st of March. The foreign currency may be delivered or received any time during the option period but it will definitely mature on 1st March. The agreed amount of foreign currency must be delivered or received on the agreed fixed date i.e. 1st March.

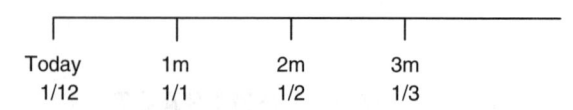

Figure 4.3 Fixed forward contract

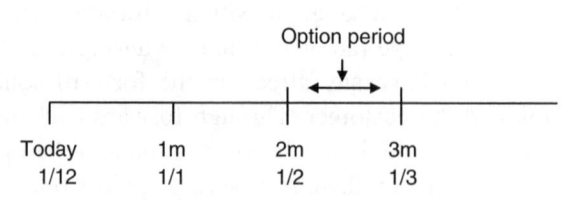

Figure 4.4 Forward contract with option over third month

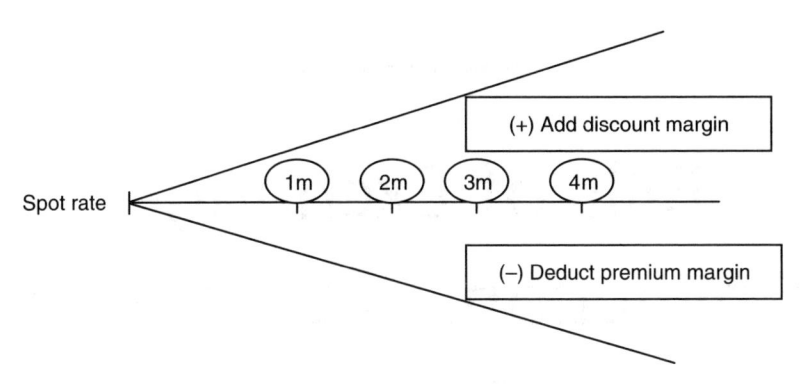

Figure 4.5 Exchange margins – premium and discount in forward contract

For example 3 months forward rate will be calculated as follows:

$$\begin{array}{r} \text{Spot Rate GB £} = \text{US \$ } 1.9598 - 1.9603 \\ \underline{0.0300 - 0.0800} \quad \text{Plus 3 months exchange margin} \\ 1.9898 - 2.0403 \end{array}$$

Exchange margin is added to the spot rate as the currency in future is at discount. Bank will buy US $ 2.0403 and sell US $ 1.9898 against £1, three months forward. The Gap between the buying and selling rates forward will never narrow.

CHAPTER 5

Bills of Exchange, Collections, Purchasing and Discounting

Bill of Exchange: Bills of exchange are widely used in international trade, partly since they are convenient methods of debt collection from traders abroad. Finance may be arranged in a number of ways against Bills of Exchange, both for the buyer (drawee) and for the seller (drawers). If a bills of exchange has been dishonoured the holder may sue the other parties to the bill.

DEFINITION OF A BILL OF EXCHANGE

"A Bill of Exchange is an unconditional order in writing addressed by one person to another signed by the person giving it requiring the person to whom it is addressed to pay on demand or at a fixed or determinable future time a sum certain in money to or to the order of a specified person or to bearer" (Sec 3, The Bills of Exchange Act 1882).

To ease understanding the definition is broken down into small segments and each segment considered individually:

1. "An unconditional order": The order to pay should not be subject to the fulfilment of any condition(s). It should simply say, "Pay". If a condition is set e.g. "Pay John Clark when he marries my daughter" it is not a bill of exchange but a conditional order.

    "In writing": It is not possible to have an oral bill of exchange. Evidence must be available, in writing, of its existence. What the bill is actually written on, or written with, is not important.
2. "Addressed by one person".

FINANCING AGAINST BILLS   21

Specimen of a bill of exchange

```
No. 0012345                                    (7)      £50,000.00
                                                      Date 4th July 2005
At 3 month After Sight (6)
              (1)                              (8)
Pay----------------Exporting Company Limited-------------------or to the order
GB pounds fifty thousand only--------------------------------------------------
                              (7)
For Value received

To                                      For and on behalf of
Importing Co Ltd                        Exporting Company Limited
123 New Road  (3 & 5)          (2)
Nairobi (Kenya)                         (sd)----------(4)---------Director
```

Figure 5.1 Bill of exchange – specimen

3. "To another person" (the drawee): A bill of exchange is usually written by the person selling goods or services (the drawer) and addressed to the person who is required to pay (the drawee).

4. "Signed by the person giving it": It is signed by the person who is owed money (the drawer).

5. "Requiring the person to whom it is addressed to pay": It is self-explanatory (the drawee).

6. "To pay on demand": The bill would say "at sight" requiring immediate payment to be made. "Or at a fixed or determinable future time" If the bill is not payable immediately then it may be payable "at 90 days sight" meaning that it is due 90 days from the day it is seen by the person to whom it is addressed. A bill payable "90 days from the date of docking of the s.s. Titanic" would not be valid, because the ship may sink!

7. "A sum certain in money": The exact amount must be stated. "About £1,000" would not be acceptable, although "£1,000 plus interest at 10%" would be because the extra amount can be calculated.

8. "To or to the order of a specified person (the Payee) or to bearer": An order bill payable to a specific person can be easily transferred to another by endorsement. A bearer bill is payable to the holder of the bill at the date of maturity (payment).

Most bills of exchange are written on specially printed forms available from all good business stationers. Such bills often have "for value received" printed on them to establish "valuable consideration", usually essential if legal action is proposed under contract law.

Parties to a bill of exchange

There are three main parties to a bill of exchange:

The Drawer is the person, who gives an order to pay the amount of the bill of exchange.

The Drawee is the person on whom the bill is drawn i.e. the person who is required to pay the amount of the bill of exchange.

The Payee is the person to whom the amount of the bill is payable. The drawer and payee of a trade bill are often the same person.

Other parties to a bill of exchange

The Endorser: When a person (the payee) transfers the bill of exchange to another person the payee writes his signature together with a statement on the reverse of the bill and is known as the endorser.

The Endorsee: The name of the person to whom the bill of exchange is transferred. The endorsee's name is written in the endorsement.

The Acceptor: An acceptor is the person (the drawee), who gives consent to comply with the order of the drawer to pay by signing across the face of the bill of exchange.

The Holder: The payee or any other person who for a valid reason or legally comes into actual possession of a bill of exchange.

The Holder for value: A person who gives "consideration" to obtain actual possession of the bill.

The Holder in Due Course: A person who obtains actual possession of the bill of exchange:

(i) When it is complete and regular on its face (i.e. properly completed with all information required);

(ii) Before it is overdue i.e. before its maturity date;

(iii) Without notice that it has been previously dishonoured (unpaid);

FINANCING AGAINST BILLS

(iv) In good faith and without notice of defect in the title of the person from whom obtained;

(v) After giving "consideration" for it.

Types of bills of exchange

Sight bill of exchange

A sight bill of exchange is one which is payable on sight, demand or presentation to the drawee. Acceptance of a sight bill is not required because the bill is payable on demand i.e. immediately the drawee has "seen" it.

Usance bill of exchange

A usance bill of exchange is one which is payable sometime in future i.e. after a number of days, months or years e.g. "90 days sight". It needs to be accepted by the drawee to make him liable to the bill. The drawee accepts the bill by signing on the face of the bill i.e. the drawee agrees to make payment on maturity. A usance bill is also known as Term or Tenor bill.

Clean bills of exchange

A clean bill of exchange is one that is not accompanied by the shipping documents. When the goods are shipped the documents are sent direct to the importer so that he can take delivery of the goods and the bill of exchange is handed over by the seller to his bank for collecting the payment from the importer.

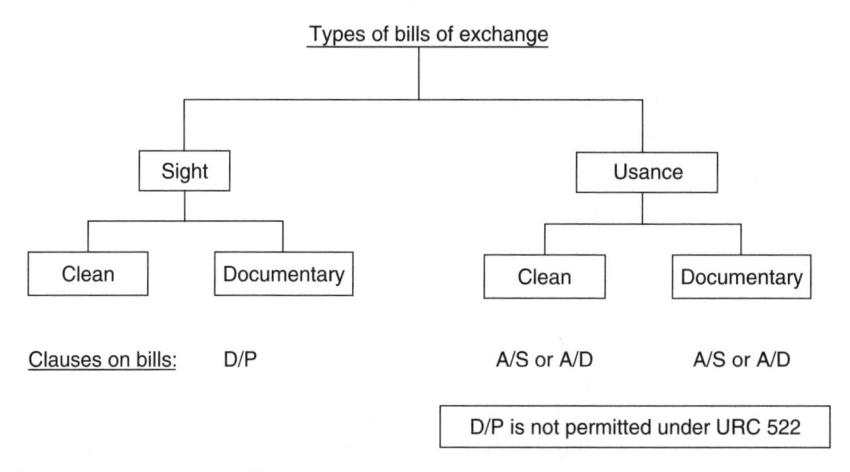

Figure 5.2 Types of bills of exchange

Documentary bill of exchange

A bill of exchange accompanied by shipping documents i.e. invoice, bill of lading, insurance policy and other documents, is called a documentary bill of exchange.

Accommodation bill of exchange

A bill to which a person, called an accommodation party, puts his name to oblige or accommodate another person without receiving any consideration for so doing. The position of such a party is, in fact, that of a surety or guarantor. Bills of this type are called "kites" or "windmills" or "windbills". "A" may accept a bill for the accommodation of "B" the drawer, who is in need of money. "A" receives no consideration and does not expect to be called upon to pay the bill when due.

Banks discourage the use of accommodation bills by the customers who may request finance against such bills.

CLAUSES ON BILLS OF EXCHANGE

D/P – The drawer/seller gives instructions to the remitting bank to deliver documents relating to the goods against payment of the bill. The remitting bank instructs the agent bank i.e. collecting bank to follow the same instructions. These instructions are in the case of a sight bill of exchange. The buyer makes payment and takes delivery of the documents, which need to be presented to the carrier to delivery of the goods.

A/S – This clause is used in the case of usance bill of exchange. The seller sells goods on a credit basis. The drawer/seller gives instructions to the remitting bank to deliver documents relating to the goods after the bill has been sighted i.e. accepted. This means the buyer agrees with the terms and conditions of the sale contract and undertakes to pay on the maturity date. The maturity date is calculated after the date of acceptance of the bill of exchange. The remitting bank instructs the agent bank i.e. collecting bank to follow the same instructions.

A/D – This is another clause also used in the case of usance bill of exchange. The seller sells goods on a credit basis. The drawer/seller gives instructions to the remitting bank to deliver documents relating to the goods after the bill has been sighted i.e. accepted and the maturity date is calculated, as instructed by the seller, e.g. after the date of the bill of exchange or the bill of lading. This means the buyer agrees with the terms and conditions of the sale contract and undertakes to pay on the maturity date. The remitting bank instructs the agent bank i.e. collecting bank to follow the same instructions.

The use of D/P clause on usance documentary bills of exchange is not allowed under the URC 522.

Acceptance of a bill of exchange

Meaning of Acceptance – Acceptance is a promise to pay creditor when the drawee of a usance or time bill of exchange writes the words "accepted" above their name and signature across a bill.

A bill may be accepted:

(i) Before it has been signed by the drawer, or while otherwise incomplete;

(ii) When it is overdue or after it has been dishonoured by a previous refusal to accept, or by non-payment.

Importance and requisites of acceptance

(i) The acceptance of a bill is signification by the drawee of his assent to the order of the drawer,

(ii) An acceptance is invalid unless it complies with the following conditions, namely
   (a) It must be written on the bill and signed by the drawee. The mere signature of the drawee without additional words is sufficient.
   (b) It must not express that the drawee will perform his promise by any other means than the payment of money.
   (c) The acceptance must be completed by delivery of the bill or notification that it has been accepted.

A holder with a "general acceptance" bill may present it to the acceptor, but, if there is a place of payment mentioned on the bill it must be presented at that place, otherwise the holder will lose recourse against all other parties to the bill.

Liability of acceptor

The acceptor of a bill, by accepting it:

(i) Engages that he will pay it according to the tenor of his acceptance,

(ii) It precluded from denying to a holder in due course –
   (a) The existence of the drawer, the genuineness of his signature, and his capacity and authority to draw the bill,

(b) In the case of a bill payable to drawer's order, the then capacity of the drawer to endorse, but not the genuineness or validity of his endorsement

(c) In the case of a bill payable to the order of a third person, the existence of the payee and his then capacity to endorse, but not the genuineness or validity of his endorsement.

Presentation for acceptance

Presentation of a bill of exchange for acceptance is legally necessary:

(i) Where the bill is payable after sight. Presentment for acceptance is necessary in order to fix the maturity of the instrument.

(ii) Where a bill expressly stipulates that it must be presented for acceptance, and

(iii) Where a bill is drawn payable elsewhere than at the residence or place of business of the drawee. Except in these three cases, it is not obligatory to present a bill for acceptance. The holder may await the maturity of the bill and then present it for payment. As a rule, however, it is presented for acceptance to secure the liability of the drawee. If the drawee refuses to accept the bill, the holder then has an immediate right of recourse against the drawer and endorsers, if the appropriate steps are taken.

TYPES OF ACCEPTANCES

There are two principal types of acceptance of a usance bill of exchange:

General Acceptance – It is to confirm the drawee's liability and agreement to the terms of the bill.

Qualified Acceptance – where the drawee, upon accepting bill, varies or alters its terms e.g. by partial acceptance of the amount. The holder's agreement to any alteration may discharge the liability of any previous parties to the bill.

Types of qualified acceptances

(i) Qualified as to a certain event: A conditional acceptance, which makes payment dependent upon the fulfilment of a stated condition e.g., on arrival of a ship, or the goods themselves,

(ii) Qualified as to amount; A partial acceptance, an acceptance to pay part of the amount for which the bill is drawn e.g. a bill drawn for £10,000 but the drawee accepts for a lesser amount i.e. £7,000 only.

(iii) Qualified as to tenor; where the usance period on the bill is changed e.g. extended from 90 to 180 days,

(iv) Qualified as to place of payment; an acceptance to pay at a particular specified place but unless the words "and not elsewhere" or "and there only" or their equivalent are inserted the acceptance is a general acceptance.

ENDORSEMENT OF BILLS OF EXCHANGE

Many bills are payable to a specific person "or order". This means that title to the bill can be transferred, or "negotiated" by the payee to another person. This is achieved by endorsement and delivery to the person concerned.

By law, a bill is an order bill when:

– It is expressed to be payable to order, or

– It is payable to the order of a particular person, or

– It is payable to a particular person and does not contain words prohibiting any transfer.

Endorsement is not required to transfer the title of a bearer bill, as it may be negotiated by mere delivery to the other person.

Types of endorsements

There are four common types of endorsement.
Note: Under the Cheques Act 1992 these endorsements do not apply to cheques in the UK, but may apply to cheques in other countries.

(i) Blank Endorsement: This is where the payee simply signs his name on the reverse of the bill without stating the name of any particular endorsee. The cheque becomes payable to bearer.

(ii) **Special Endorsement:** The payee, on signing his name, specifies the endorsee. The endorsee can either collect the proceeds of the bill or sign his own name i.e. blank endorse the bill, to make it payable to bearer. Similarly, a blank endorsement can be converted into a special endorsement by any holder signing it and stating the name of the person to whom it is to be payable.

No. 0012345   £50,000.00
                                                                                              Date 4th July 2005

At 3 month After Sight

Pay----------------------Exporting Company Limited------------------------------------or to the order

GB pounds fifty thousand only---

For Value received

To   For and on behalf of
Importing Co Ltd   Exporting Company Limited
123 New Road
Nairobi (Kenya)   (sd)-------------------------Director

Blank endorsement

    For and on behalf of:
    Exporting Company Limited

    Signed_____Director

Figure 5.3 Example of a blank endorsement of a bill of exchange

---

No. 0012345   £50,000.00
                                                                                              Date 4th July 2005

At 3 month After Sight

Pay----------------------Exporting Company Limited------------------------------------or to the order

GB pounds fifty thousand only---

For Value received

To   For and on behalf of
Importing Co Ltd   Exporting Company Limited
123 New Road
Nairobi (Kenya)   (sd)-------------------------Director

FINANCING AGAINST BILLS 29

```
Special endorsement
                    Pay XYZ Bank Limited
                    ┌─────────────────────────────────┐
                    │ For and on behalf of:           │
                    │ Exporting Company Limited       │
                    │                                 │
                    │ Signed_____ Director  │
                    └─────────────────────────────────┘
```

Figure 5.4 Example of a special endorsement of a bill of exchange

```
No. 0012345                                              £50,000.00
                                                    Date 4th July 2005
At 3 month After Sight

Pay---------------------Exporting Company Limited------------------------------------or to the
order

GB pounds fifty thousand only-----------------------------------------------------------------

For Value received

To                                       For and on behalf of
Importing Co Ltd                         Exporting Company Limited
123 New Road
Nairobi (Kenya)                          (sd)-------------------------Director
```

```
Restrictive endorsement
                    Pay XYZ Bank Limited only
                    ┌─────────────────────────────────┐
                    │ For and on behalf of:           │
                    │ Exporting Company Limited       │
                    │                                 │
                    │ Signed_____ Director  │
                    └─────────────────────────────────┘
```

Figure 5.5 Example of a restrictive endorsement of a bill of exchange

(iii) Restrictive Endorsement: A restrictive endorsement, as the name implies, prevents further endorsement of the bill.

The payee specifies the name of the endorsee and writes "only" at the end e.g. "Pay XYZ Bank Limited only".

(iv) Conditional Endorsement: The least important of the four, the payee states a condition that has to be fulfilled before negotiation e.g. "Pay XYZ Bank Limited after arrival of goods".

In practice, banks will ignore any conditional endorsement as they presume the condition has been satisfactorily fulfilled.

```
No. 0012345                                              £50,000.00
                                                    Date 4th July 2005

At 3 month After Sight

Pay---------------------Exporting Company Limited------------------------------------or to the
order

GB pounds fifty thousand only-----------------------------------------------------------------

For Value received

To                                       For and on behalf of
Importing Co Ltd                         Exporting Company Limited
123 New Road
Nairobi (Kenya)                          (sd)-------------------------Director
```

```
Conditional endorsement
            Pay XYZ Bank Limited after arrival of the goods

            For and on behalf of:
            Exporting Company Limited

            Signed_____Director
```

Figure 5.6 Example of a conditional endorsement of a bill of exchange

Negotiability of bills of exchange

An instrument, which is legally considered as "negotiable", has the following characteristics:

- It is transferable by delivery, or by endorsement and delivery.

- The legal title passes to the person who takes it in good faith, for value, and without notice of any defect in the title of the transfer.

- The legal holder can sue in his own name.

- Notice of transfer need not be given to the party liable on the instrument.

- The title passes free of all equities or counterclaims between previous parties of which the transferee has no notice.

When a negotiable instrument e.g. a bill is passed from one person to another all prior parties are liable to the final holder if the instrument is dishonoured. The last person in the chain is deemed to be a "holder in due course" if he can prove that he has fulfilled the requirements of s.29 of the

Bills of Exchange Act 1882; i.e.

- He has taken the bill in good faith
- The bill is complete and regular on the face of it
- For value
- Before it is overdue
- Without notice of any defect in the title of the transferor or any prior dishonour of the bill.

It follows that before giving value the new holder may look to see who has previously endorsed the bill and assess his creditworthiness in case the bill should be dishonoured. This is in line with the practice of the Acceptance Houses who add their own names to various bills, effectively guaranteeing payment to any future holder, charging commission in return.

Discharge of bills of exchange

The Bills of Exchange Act states that any liability on the bill is discharged:

- When the bill is paid by the acceptor on the due date
- Where the acceptor becomes the holder of the bill at or before maturity
- Where any material alteration has been made to the bill without the agreement of all parties liable on the bill. If the bill is altered without consent those liable prior to the alteration (but not after) will be discharged
- Where the holder gives up his right to receive payment, cancelling the bill itself
- Where the bill becomes statute-barred under the Limitations Acts e.g. the holder usually has only six years to take legal action in recovery of the debt.

The majority of bills are properly accepted and subsequently paid on maturity. However, bills may be dishonoured by non-acceptance where the drawee refuses to accept liability, or dishonoured by non-payment when the acceptor refuses to pay.

In the UK, presentation of a dishonoured bill to the court is usually considered sufficient proof of dishonour when taking legal action. For foreign bills i.e. those drawn in this country payable abroad, or bills drawn overseas and payable in the UK, certain legal steps must be taken immediately in the country of dishonour to preserve the liability of previous parties to the bill. Any delay could result in their being discharged.

The first step is the "noting" of the bill, which is official evidence that the bill has been dishonoured. A local legal official, called a "notary public", represents the bill for acceptance or payment as required. If the request is refused the bill is noted.

The next step is formal "protest", which is a document sealed by the notary public confirming that the bill has been dishonoured. The protest document is accepted in most countries as evidence of dishonour.

On occasions a "notary public" may not be available, so a householder may, with the aid of two witnesses, issue a certificate attesting the dishonour of the bill. The "householder's protest" is considered the same as a formal protest document.

COLLECTION OF BILLS

A seller sells the goods to a buyer and asks his banker to collect money on his behalf from the buyers. So the bank acts as agent of the seller in collecting money from the buyer. In this respect the seller must give clear instructions to the bank.

The seller/exporter hands over the bill of exchange together with the relative documents for collection of payment by giving the instructions to his bank (by completing the application form for collection of bills) from the buyer/importer through the banking system/channel. The remitting bank records the information in its books and forwards the bill with the documents to the collecting bank with its schedule for collection with instructions as requested by the seller.

When the seller asks his bank to collect money against a clean/documentary bill on his behalf, this instructs the bank to release documents against acceptance of the bill, the bill is known as a D/A bill (Documents against Acceptance). If the documents are to be released against payment the bill is known as a D/P bill (Documents against Payment). If a sight bill is drawn the documents will be handed over to the buyer against payment only.

To avoid misunderstandings/difficulties and delay that might arise through acting as an agent to the customer, a set of rules has been developed by ICC called Uniform Rules for Collections, International Chamber of Commerce Publication (URC 522). The Rules are the basis on which the customer should instruct the bank. Banks use formats (application for collection of bills of exchange) given on the next page. It is required to be completed before accepting requests for collection of bill. The seller gives instructions to his bank (remitting bank) on the format by marking (X) against the appropriate statement/instructions.

FINANCING AGAINST BILLS 33

From:

Our Reference _____

Account No. _____

Date: ---------------------

Dear Sir,

Bills for collection drawn on ----------------------------- Amount ---------------------------------------

We enclose the first and second of exchange of our bill for collection/negotiation with recourse to us, subject to Uniform Rules for Collection (1995 (revision)) Publication number 522. Please follow instructions marked "✓":

( ) Documents to be released against payment/acceptance.
( ) Please airmail advise acceptance stating maturity date. Retain the accepted draft for presentation on due date.
( ) Payment/acceptance may be deferred at drawee's request pending arrival of the relative goods.
( ) In case of non-payment/non-acceptance on presentation please advise us by AIRMAIL/TELEX stating reasons.
( ) If unpaid/unaccepted, please Note/Protest the drafts and advise us by AIRMAIL/TELEX stating reasons.
( ) On arrival of goods, if documents remain unpaid/unaccepted, please attend to the warehousing and insurance of the goods and advise us by TELEX.
( ) Recover all charges, including your charges from drawees. Charges may not be waived.
( ) Please collect interest ---- % p.a. from the date of draft to approximate arrival of return remittance in London. Interest may not be waived.
( ) If unpaid on due date, overdue interest to be charged @ ---- % p.a. from due date to approximate arrival of return remittance in London. Interest may not be waived.
( ) In the event of foreign currency cover not being available at the time of maturity of the Bill, you may instruct your correspondent to accept deposit in local currency to the full equivalent of the value of the draft amount together with interest and charges at the rate ruling on the date of deposit and remit the same when foreign currency cover is provided by the Central Bank.
( ) Please obtain an undertaking from the drawees to hold themselves responsible for any difference due to fluctuations in exchange rates which may arise between the date of deposit in local currency and foreign currency allocation by the Central Bank.
( ) Please disburse the proceeds as under-
( ) Credit our account with you under advice to us.
( ) Send us your cheque for the amount due.
( ) Details of documents enclosed.

Documents	Draft	Invoice	Bill of lading/ air waybill	Insurance	Packing list	Cert. of origin	Others	
Original								
Duplicate								

( ) In case of need refer to:

Yours faithfully

_____
Authorised Signature

Figure 5.7 A specimen of customer's instructions for collections of bills of exchange

MECHANISM – SIGHT BILL FOR COLLECTION

1. Negotiations between the seller and the buyer

2. The buyer places an order

3. The seller makes goods ready and despatches through transporters/shippers

4. The seller prepares shipping documents and hands over to his bank (remitting bank) with instructions to collect money from the buyer

5. The seller's bank (remitting bank) records in its books and sends the documents to its agent's bank (collecting bank) in the place of the buyer with instruction to collect money from the buyer and remit to them

6. The collecting bank sends advice of receipt of documents to the buyer and asks for payment

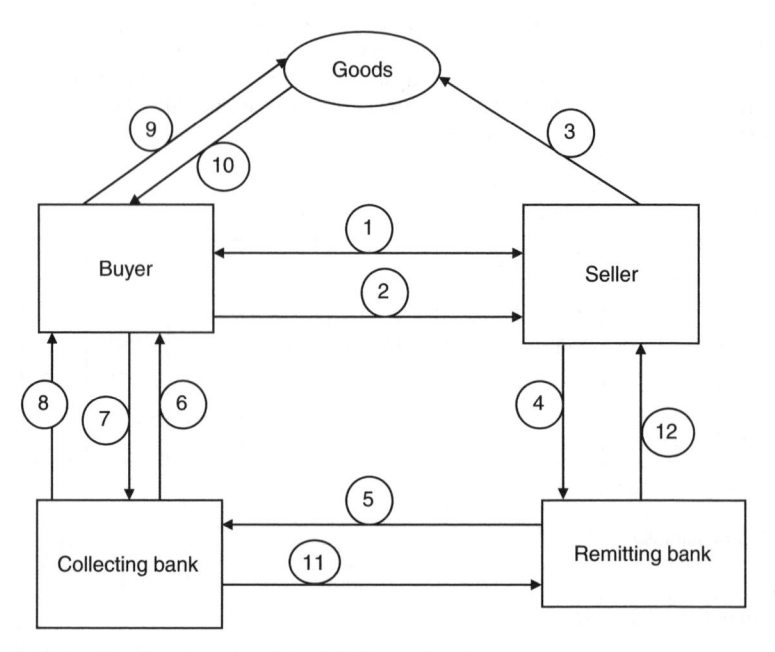

Figure 5.8 Mechanics of a sight bill for collection

7. The buyer makes payment

8. The buyer collects documents from the bank

9. The buyer presents the transport document to the transporters/shippers

10. The buyer collects the goods

11. The collecting bank remits funds to the (remitting bank) seller's bank

12. The remitting bank credits the seller's account and sends payment advice to the seller

MECHANISM – DOCUMENTARY USANCE BILLS FOR COLLECTION

Action steps – collection of bill of exchange

Once the buyer and seller have negotiated and agreed terms and conditions of sale then;

1. The buyer places an order to the seller

2. The seller makes goods ready, despatches them to the buyer through transporters and forwards the bill of exchange together with the relative documents to his bank, known as remitting bank (for example on 1st January).

3. The remitting bank receives the documents, records them in its books/registers, prepares a collection schedule on the basis of instructions received from the seller (for example on 5th January). The remitting bank forwards the collection schedule with bill and the documents to the collecting bank.

4. The collecting bank records the details in its books/registers and advises to buyer of having received the documents (for example on 10th January).

5. The buyer (if it is a usance bill) accepts the bill and takes the documents. The buyer then presents the transport document to the transport agent and collects the goods.

6. The collecting bank sends advice of acceptance and maturity date to the remitting bank.

7. The remitting bank makes note of maturity date against the original entry made in its register and forwards an advice to the seller.

8. On maturity (1st April) the buyer makes payment to the collecting bank (if the buyer is a customer of collecting bank it debits the buyer's account).

9. The collecting bank remits funds to the remitting bank through their bank's accounting system/arrangements.

10. The remitting bank records payment in its register, credits the seller's account and sends payment advice to the seller (1st April).

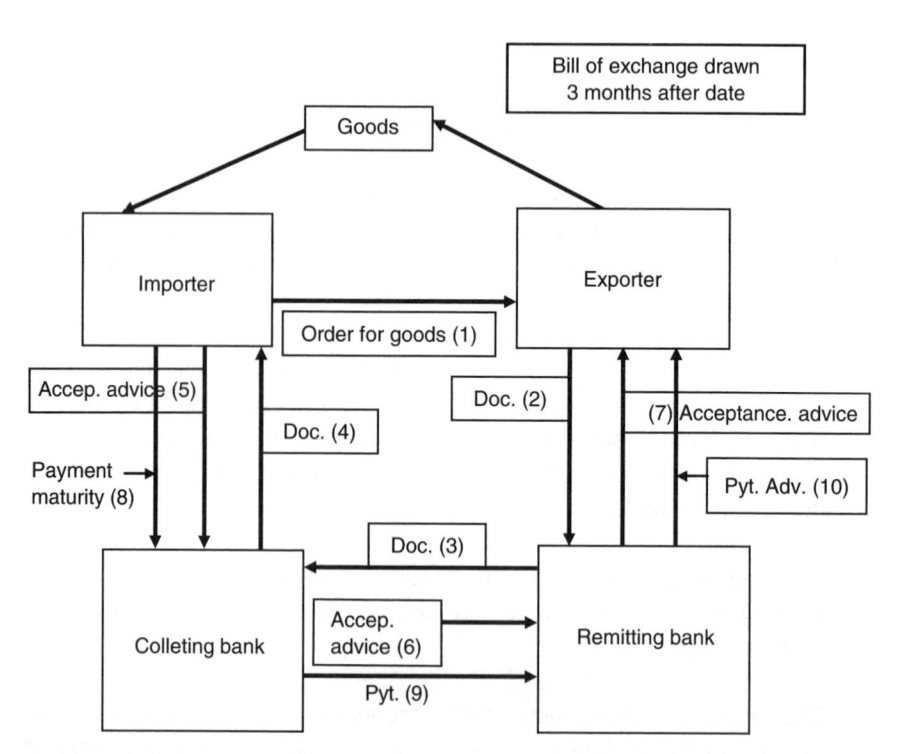

Figure 5.9 Mechanics of a documentary usance bill for collection

BILLS PURCHASED

The bills which are purchased by banks are usually Sight/Demand trade bills drawn on sound parties and the banks have up-to-date status reports on the drawees of bills of exchange.

The face value of a bill is credited to the customer's account at the time of purchase (some banks keep a x% margin of the amount). Interest on the amount is deferred until receipt of payment from the drawee or the collecting bank is received. The interest on the amount is calculated for the period from the date of purchase of the bill until receipt of payment (funds) by the bank.

BILLS DISCOUNTED

Banks discount trade bills, which are drawn on financially sound parties. The discount (interest) and commission (postage etc.) are deducted from the face value and the net amount is credited to the customer's account. Bank's Assets for Local Bills Discounted (LBD) and for Foreign Bills Discounted (FBD) account is debited with the face value of the bill. Bank's income accounts are credited with the appropriate amounts. On maturity/on receipt of payment (funds) from the drawee or the collecting Bank, Bills Discounted account is credited and appropriate (Cash or Agency account) *account is debited*.

Precautions to be taken

- The bills must be genuine trade bills

- The drawers and the drawees must be of sound financial position

- Bank must obtain status reports periodically (quarterly) on parties

- Facility amount must not exceed credit limits

- Finance must not be provided against bills for longer periods

- The bills must not be an accommodation bills

Accommodation Bill: A Bill of exchange to which a person, called accommodation party, puts his name to oblige or accommodate another person without receiving any consideration for doing so. Bills of this type are also called "windmills" or "windbills" or "kites". It is risky to provide a finance facility against these types of bills. Banks, therefore, do not provide finance facility against such bills.

MECHANISM – BILLS DISCOUNTED

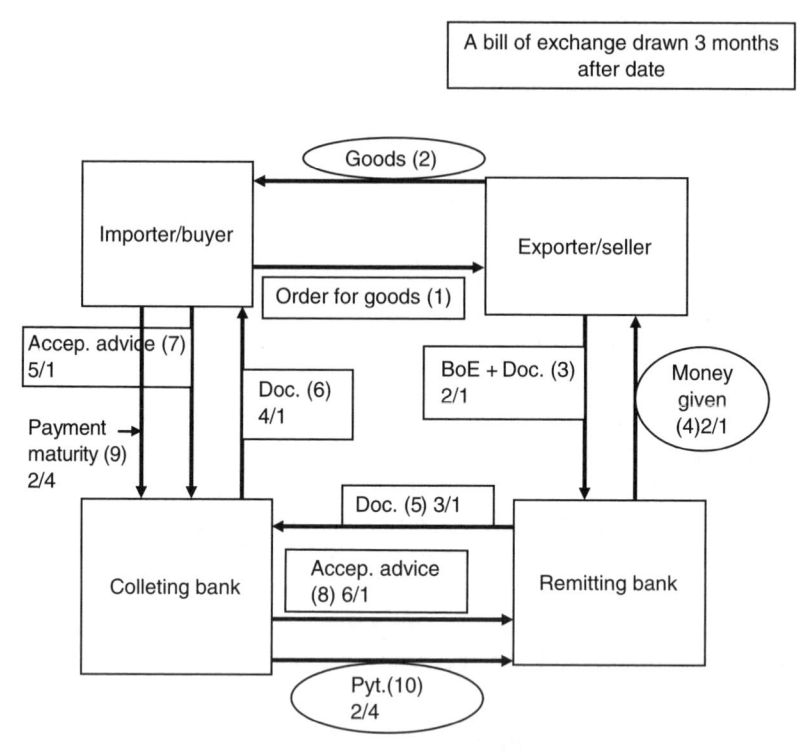

Figure 5.10 Mechanics of a bill discounting

BILLS PROCESSING COST (INDICATIVES)

The following is an example of the cost of processing of Bills for Collection. The scale of charges may vary from one bank to another.

Table 5.1 Bill of exchange indicative processing cost

Activity	Scale of charges	Amount
Outward bills		
Documentary bills	0.25% Minimum £20/US$ 5, Maximum £100/US$160. Exclusive of postage	
Clean bills/foreign currency bills/cheques/travellers cheques	0.25% Minimum £20/US$35 Maximum £50/US$80	

Continued

Table 5.1 Continued

Activity	Scale of charges	Amount
Postage/courier charges	Courier charges – UK/Europe £10/US$20 Other countries	
SWIFT/Telex charges	Maximum £20/US$35. Per collection	
Inward collections		
Documentary bills	0.2% – Minimum £20/US$35 Maximum £100/US$160. Exclusive of postage etc.	
Clean bills	0.2% – Minimum £20/US$35 Maximum £100/US$160 Exclusive of postage etc. Per collection Schedule	
Handling charges	Sight Bills 1 per mille on the bill amount Minimum £20/US$35 per month, or part thereof, if bill not paid within 30 days if intimation Usance bills 1 per mille on the bill amount Minimum £20/US$35 per month, or part thereof, if bill not paid within 30 days if intimation	
Issue of delivery order	£25/US$40 per order	
Issue of delivery order for taking delivery of pledged goods	£5/US$10	
Advise of due date/status/payment	£20/US$35 Postage/telephone per bill	
Postage/courier charges	UK and Europe: £10/US$20 Other countries $20/US$35	
Any other out of pocket expenses		
Total	(Total cost can be arrived at based on the above factors)	

CHAPTER 6

Documentary Letters of Credit

There is always an underlying agreement between the principal parties to a trade transaction, often a buyer and a seller. The agreement may be verbal or written in a formal or informal language. Its terms may be simple or complex, as the parties may feel necessary. Such an underlying agreement is referred to as a "sale contract".

A bank may grant a credit facility against a tangible security or without it. It depends on various factors. Sometimes banks may fix limits on various types of uses, such as, term loan, overdrafts, letters of guarantee etc. It helps the banks to monitor the use of each type of facility utilized by the customer. A letter of credit is also a credit facility like a loan or overdraft but its nature operation is different from a loan or overdraft facility.

Genesis: It is the safest and probably the fastest method of obtaining payment for goods exported. The documentary credit achieves a commercially acceptable compromise between the conflicting interests of buyer and seller by matching time of payment for the goods with the time of their delivery. It does this, however, by making payment against documents representing the goods rather than against the goods themselves.

A letter of credit is not only a method of obtaining payment but it also assures buyers of receiving documents relating to goods through their bank, provided they ask for the required type of documents.

Definition of Letter of Credit: (UCP 600 Articles 1 & 2) "For the purposes of the Article, the expressions "Documentary Credit(s)" and "Standby Letter(s) of Credit" (hereafter referred to as "Credit(s)"), mean any arrangement, however named or described, whereby a bank (the "Issuing Bank") acting at the request and on the instructions of a customer ("the Applicant") or on its own behalf,

(i) is to make a payment to or to the order of a third party ("the Beneficiary"), or is to accept and pay bills of exchange (Draft(s)) drawn by the Beneficiary,

or

(ii) authorizes another bank to effect such payment, or to accept and pay such bills of exchange (draft(s)),

or

(iii) authorizes another bank to negotiate, against stipulated document(s), provided that the terms and conditions of the Credit are complied with.

For the purposes of these articles, branches of a bank in different countries are considered another bank".

An irrevocable documentary credit (especially a confirmed one) is, therefore, an excellent instrument of payment. Also, if appropriate documents are called for and provided reliance can be placed on the integrity of the seller – it is an effective means of obtaining delivery of the goods.

It is nevertheless, a precision instrument, and must be properly handled by all concerned. Thus, both buyer and seller should observe certain rules of commonsense and understand their responsibilities.

It is an important instrument for the exporter to secure payment.

Parties to a letter of credit and their responsibilities

(a) Applicant's/Buyer's Responsibilities: Applicant to a letter of credit is a buyer or importer of goods. The applicant makes a request in writing to their bank to issue a letter of credit in favour of the seller/exporter of the goods or beneficiary. Their instructions to the issuing bank must be clear and precise and free from excessive detail. The bank cannot be expected to guess what is wanted: nor can it check complicated, and often technical, specifications, etc.

The purpose of the credit is to pay for the purchase not to "police" the commercial transaction. Its terms and conditions, and the documents called for, should, therefore, be in agreement with the sales contract on which it may be based.

Any examination of the goods prior to, or at the time of shipment must be evidenced by a document. The precise nature and issuer of such document must be stated in the credit.

The credit should not call for documents that the seller cannot provide, nor set out conditions that cannot be met. (This is particularly important with changes in traditional documentation resulting from trade facilitation developments and changes in transport technology.)

(b) **The Issuing Bank:** The issuing bank is the opening bank of a letter of credit on behalf and at the request of the applicant, the buyer/importer of the goods. Letter of credit is a legal contract between the seller/ beneficiary and the issuing bank. It is an independent undertaking of the issuing bank to pay or accept the bill of exchange and make payment, on presentation of the documents according to the terms and conditions stated in the letter of credit. If the documents do not satisfy the requirements of the letter of credit the issuing bank is not liable to act in any way i.e. to pay or accept the bill of exchange and make payment.

Letters of credit may be issued by mail, telex, cable or by SWIFT (Society for Worldwide Inter-bank Financial Telecommunication) in accordance with the requirements of the applicant and the beneficiary. Using SWIFT system is becoming more popular these days. Authentication of the letter is the responsibility of the advising bank by verifying authorised signatures on the letter, in case of mail, test key number in case of telex and cable etc.

(c) **The Advising Bank:** The advising bank is an agent bank of the issuing bank in the country of the exporter. The advising bank forwards the letter of credit to the beneficiary in accordance with the instructions of the issuing bank. Being an agent of the issuing bank, it has a list of signatories of the issuing bank. Therefore, it is advising bank's responsibility to ensure that the letter of credit is signed by the authorised signatories of the issuing bank before forwarding it to the beneficiary.

If the advising bank forwards the letter without any undertaking on its part it must say clearly when advising the letter of credit to the beneficiary, i.e. it (the advising bank) is under no obligations to make payment or incur any liability to make deferred payment etc.

(d) **The Seller's/Beneficiary's Responsibilities:** Although considerable time may elapse between the receipt of a credit and its utilization, the seller should not delay studying it and requesting any necessary changes, if required.

The seller should satisfy him that the terms, conditions and documents called for are in agreement with the sales contract. (Banks are not concerned with such contracts. Their examination of the documents will take into consideration only the terms of the credit and any amendments to it.)

When it is time to present the documents the beneficiary should:

(i) present the required documents exactly as called for by the credit. The documents must be in accordance with the terms and conditions of the credit and not on their face inconsistent with one another.

(ii) present the documents to the bank as quickly as possible and in any case within the validity of the credit and within the period of time after the date of issuance of the document specified in the credit or as applicable under Article No.14 (c) U.C.P. 600.

(iii) must remember that non-compliance with the terms stipulated in the credit or irregularities in the documents, oblige the bank to refuse settlement.

(e) A confirming bank: A confirming bank is the one, which adds its independent guarantee to the letter of credit. It undertakes the responsibility to make payment/acceptance of bills of exchange and pay on maturity or negotiate under the letter of credit in addition to the issuing bank. A confirming bank is usually the advising bank. If the issuing bank requests the advising bank to add its confirmation to the credit the advising bank does so. If the advising bank does not wish to do so, it must advise the issuing bank immediately of its intention of not doing so. Once the advising bank adds it confirmation, it is known as confirming bank. The confirmation is an independent undertaking between the confirming bank and the beneficiary.

(f) Nominated Bank: A nominated bank is the bank authorised by the issuing bank to pay, incur deferred payment liability, to accept bill of exchange and pay on maturity, or to negotiate the letter of credit.

(g) Reimbursing Bank: A reimbursing bank is a bank authorised by the issuing bank to honour the reimbursement claim made by the negotiating/ paying bank in settlement of negotiation/payment under a letter of credit. This is the bank with which the issuing bank has agency/accounting arrangements.

(h) The Carrier: The carrier is the company who take possession of the cargo with an undertaking to transport and deliver it safely at a place of destination agreed by the buyer and the seller. The cargo carrier is a shipping company, an airline or another type of transporter by road i.e. lorries etc. The cargo carrier supplies a transport document indicating receipt of goods and the terms of carriage of the goods.

(i) The Insurer: The insurer is an insurance company with prime responsibility for insuring the cargo as required under the terms and conditions of the letter of credit. The insurer indemnifies the holder of the insurance document i.e. insurance policy or insurance certificate against any loss or damage to the cargo.

WHO DOES WHAT?

The buyer and the seller conclude a sales contract for payment by documentary credit. The buyer requests his bank, the "issuing bank" to issue a letter of credit in favour of the seller/beneficiary specifying the instructions according to the agreed terms and conditions with the seller.

The issuing bank issues a letter of credit incorporating the terms and conditions agreed with the seller and asks another bank, usually the bank of the seller or another bank who is the correspondent of the issuing bank, to advise and/or confirm the credit, if so requested by the buyer/applicant.

The advising or confirming bank checks the authenticity of the letter of credit and informs the seller that the credit has been issued in their favour.

As soon as the seller receives the credit and is satisfied that he can meet its terms and conditions, he is in a position to load the goods and dispatch them. The seller then sends the documents evidencing the shipment to the bank where the credit is available (the bank). It may be the issuing bank, or the confirming bank, or any bank named (nominated bank) in the credit as the paying, accepting or negotiating bank, or it may be the advising bank or a bank willing to negotiate under the credit.

The advising bank/confirming bank scrutinises carefully the documents received under a credit. If the documents are in conformity with the terms of the credit it will process them accordingly. Any other bank, including the advising bank if it has not confirmed the credit, may negotiate, but with recourse to the beneficiary.

The bank, if other than the issuing bank, sends the documents to the issuing bank.

The issuing bank also scrutinises the documents and, if the documents are found as per terms of letter of credit it:

(a) effects payment in accordance with the terms of the credit, either to the seller if he has sent the documents directly to the issuing bank or to the bank that has made funds available to the beneficiary in anticipation, or

(b) reimburses in the pre-agreed manner the confirming bank or any bank that has paid, accepted or negotiated documents under the credit.

When the documents have been scrutinised by the issuing bank and found to meet the credit requirements, they are released to the buyer upon payment of the amount due, or upon other terms agreed between the buyer and the issuing bank.

The buyer will present the transport document to the carrier who will then release the goods.

ADVANTAGES AND DISADVANTAGES OF LETTERS OF CREDIT

Advantages to exporter

Assurance of Payment: The beneficiary is assured of payment as the issuing bank is bound to honour the documents drawn under the letter of credit.

Ready Negotiability: The exporter, if he needs money immediately can secure payment by having the documents, drawn under the letter of credit, discounted (post shipment advance).

Compliance With Regulations: Letter of credit is evidence that the exchange control regulations, if applicable in the country of the importer, have been complied with.

Pre-Shipment Facility: The exporter can secure an advance from his bank against a letter of credit received for export of goods (pre-shipment advance).

Advantages to importer

Credit facility from the Issuing Bank: The issuing bank lends its own credit facility to the importer against a letter of credit, if the importer cannot avail any credit facility from the exporter.

Assured delivery of goods: The issuing bank honours the documents drawn under a letter of credit only when all the terms and conditions of the credit have been complied with. Therefore the importer is assured not only of obtaining the goods, but also, if proper care is taken, obtaining the specified goods in time. In this respect the buyer and seller should negotiate the date of shipment of the goods from named ports of shipment and destination.

Disadvantages to applicant/importer

Fraudulent Documents: The beneficiary wants to sell goods against a letter of credit and lays down the terms and conditions, regarding payment for the goods, suitable to him. He is going to supply certain documents as an evidence of shipment of goods and, if bent upon defrauding, he may succeed in obtaining payment by supplying poor quality goods or falsifying the documents.

Expensive: Issuing banks charge fees for issuing a letter of credit and such fees are not required to be paid in case of an open account system. The charges recovered by banks under an open account system are much less than under a letter of credit.

Credit Line: A certain amount/portion of the buyer's/applicant's credit line with their bank gets tied up in an outstanding letter of credit. It will not be available for any more pressing credit needs, which may develop in the applicant's business operations.

Cash flow: The applicant may have to tie up his cash as collateral security against the letter of credit, which will cause deficit in his cash flow.

Documents Delayed: It often happens that the documents of title to goods do not reach the importer on time because those are processed by different banks in different countries.

Goods Delayed: Sometimes the goods are delayed in transit because of various reasons. If the importer had committed him or herself with another party to supply those goods on or before a pre-determined date delay may cause damage to his reputation and/or financial loss.

Disadvantages to the beneficiary

Discrepancies in documents: If the exporter is not familiar with the proper procedures for processing documents, the documents may be presented with discrepancies and the bank will send those on collection basis.

Difficult terms and conditions of L/C: Terms and conditions relating to certain documents may not be easy to fulfill or those documents may be difficult to obtain.

Different Language: Letters of credit may be received in the importing country's language and may not be understood by the exporter. It will be costly to get the documents translated.

Competitive Terms: Letters of credit payment terms are so restrictive that sellers may lose sales to competitors who quote less restrictive terms.

Documents Delayed: It often happens that the documents of title to goods do not reach the importer on time because documents have been processed by different banks in different countries.

Goods Delayed: Sometimes the goods are delayed in transit because of various reasons. If the exporter has committed by issuing a performance bond etc in favour of the importer to supply those goods on or before a pre-determined date, the delay may cause damage to his reputation and also financial lossif a claim is made by the importer.

LETTER OF CREDIT – MECHANISM

1. Proforma invoice

2. Firm order placed by importer

3. L/C application

4. Foreign currency forward contract

5. L/C. Advice sent through AB/CB

6. L/C. Confirmation advice to beneficiary

7. L/C. Confirmation advice

8. Exporter hands goods to the carrier

9. The carrier issues bill of lading/transport document

10. Insurance company issues insurance policy

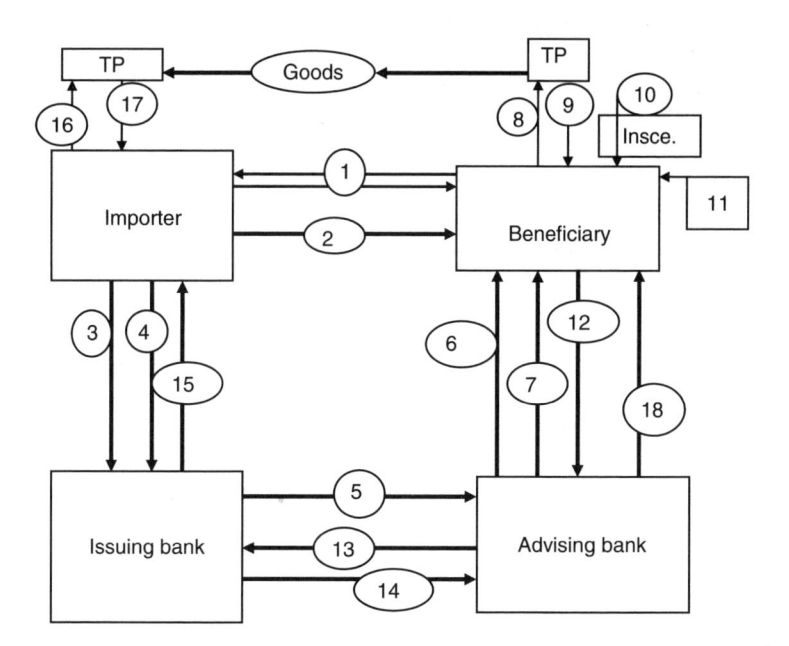

Figure 6.1 Letter of credit – mechanism

11. Other documents as required

12. Documents forwarded by the beneficiary to AB/CB and documents checked and/or negotiated by AB/CB/NB

13. Documents forwarded by the AB/CB/NB to the issuing bank in accordance with reimbursement clause

14. The issuing bank provides reimbursement to the AB/CB/NB

15. Payment/Acceptance of documents/Bills of Exchange and other documents forwarded to the importer

16. The importer hands transport documents to the carrier

17. The carrier delivers goods to the importer

18. Funds credited to the beneficiary's account.

LETTER OF CREDIT CONTRACTS AND REGULATIONS

Contracts and regulations

1. Sale contract between buyer and seller

2. L/C. Contract between the importer and the issuing bank

3. Foreign currency forward contract between the importer and the issuing bank

4. L/C. Contract between the issuing bank and the beneficiary

5. L/C. Contract between AB/CB/NB

6. L/C. Contract between the exporter/beneficiary and AB/CB/NB

7. Pre-shipment finance contract between AB/CB/NB and the beneficiary

8. Counter indemnity between AB/CB and the beneficiary – performance bond

DOCUMENTARY LETTERS OF CREDIT

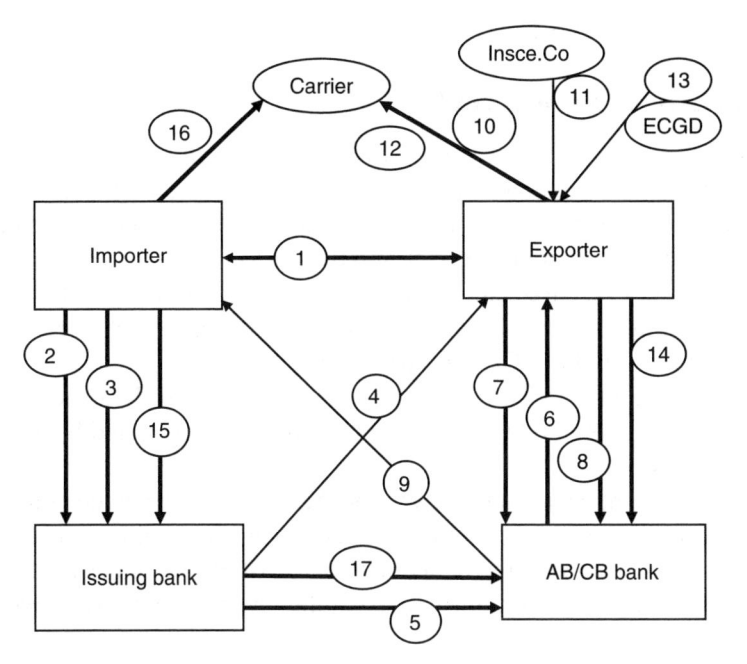

Figure 6.2 Letter of credit – contracts and regulations

9. Performance bond between the AB/CB and the importer

10. Contract of freightment – the exporter and the carrier company

11. Contract of insurance – between the beneficiary and the carrier company

12. Risk cover contract – between the exporter and the carrier company

13. Export finance guarantee – NCM and ECGD etc.

14. Seller's indemnity for negotiation of documents under reserve – between the beneficiary and the negotiating bank

15. Loan contract for L.I.M. between the importer and the issuing bank

16. Shipping guarantee – between issuing bank and carrier company

17. L/C. confirmation contract between IB & CB.

SALE CONTRACT

What is a sale contract?

A sale contract is an agreement between the buyer and the seller in which various terms and conditions of the transaction are specified. One need not get confused with the terms "sale contract" and "letter of credit". Credits, by their nature, are separate transactions from sales or other contract(s) on which they may be based and banks are in no way concerned with or bound by such contract(s), even if any reference whatsoever to such contract(s) is included in the credit (UCP. 600 Art. 4(a)).

The sale contract, in its simplest form, is an accepted order to buy or offer to sell a certain commodity or service that has been negotiated between the buyer and the seller.

The agreement between the buyer and the seller may be made orally or in writing. Although an oral contract is in general legally binding, it may cause some problems due to different understandings of its provisions by different parties. Therefore, to avoid misunderstanding, a verbal contract is required to be confirmed in writing.

Contents of a sale contract

A properly negotiated sale contract should include the following points:

- Description of goods

- The price of the goods

- Payment terms i.e. Sight/Usance (term period)

- Trade terms

- Packing and marking

- Shipping instructions i.e. date shipment

- Ports of shipment and discharge

- Insurance of goods

- Inspection and warranties

- Methods of payment

- Additional documents or conditions

The terms used will determine which party is to bear the costs involved in shipping the goods abroad, and are subject to international rules for their interpretation. They are known as "Incoterms" and are published by the International Chamber of Commerce, commonly known as ICC Publication "Incoterms 2000".

CHAPTER 7

Letters of Credit – Types

Let us understand letter of credit and its various types with the help of a grid as under.

TYPES OF LETTERS OF CREDIT

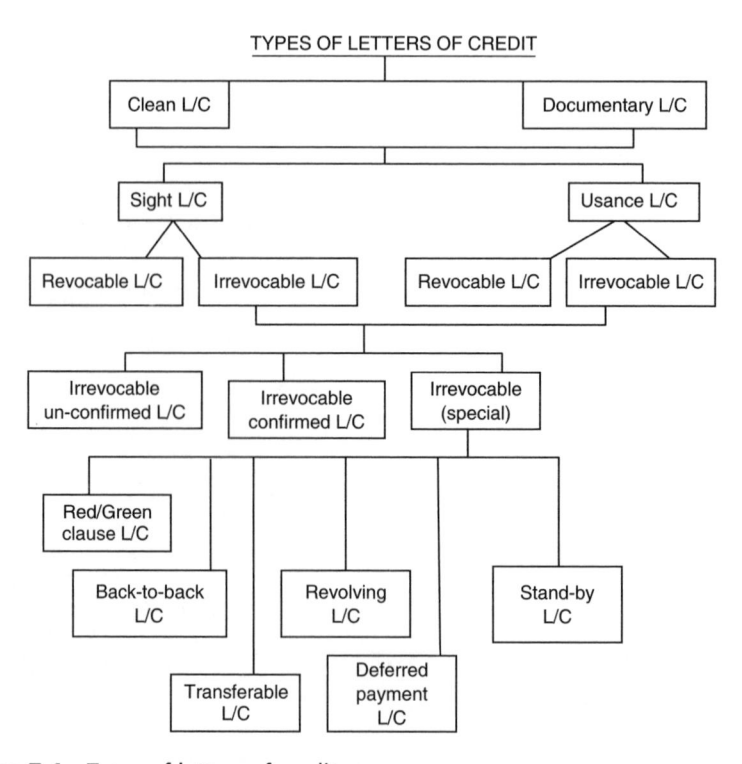

- Clean L/C
  - Sight L/C
    - Revocable L/C
    - Irrevocable L/C
      - Irrevocable un-confirmed L/C
      - Irrevocable confirmed L/C
        - Red/Green clause L/C
        - Back-to-back L/C
        - Transferable L/C
        - Revolving L/C
        - Deferred payment L/C
      - Irrevocable (special)
        - Stand-by L/C
- Documentary L/C
  - Usance L/C
    - Revocable L/C
    - Irrevocable L/C

Figure 7.1 Types of letters of credit

CLEAN LETTER OF CREDIT

A clean letter of credit does not specify the documents of title to goods or terms and conditions to be complied with before effecting payment. In such cases goods are sent direct to the importer (buyer) and payment is made without the production of financial documents. It is not safe for a bank to establish such a type of letter of credit as neither the goods nor the documents of title to goods come into the possession of the bank and the bank issuing a clean letter of credit may suffer a loss if the applicant fails to make the payment. Such types of letters of credit could only be established where both parties i.e. the importer and exporter are of undoubted integrity.

DOCUMENTARY LETTER OF CREDIT

A documentary letter of credit is one which specifies certain terms and conditions to be satisfied in respect of documents of title to goods and other documents required together with the bill(s) of exchange if required to be drawn under a letter of credit. The interest of the issuing bank is safeguarded as the documents of title to goods remain in the bank's possession. The importer cannot take the delivery of the goods unless the importer (applicant) accepts the bill of exchange or makes payment there-against.

CIRCULAR OR TRAVELLER LETTER OF CREDIT

It is risky for travellers to carry cash when they wish to visit several places. It was the practice among banks to issue a letter called circular letter of credit, requesting their branches, agents and correspondents to pay, up to a certain amount of money by a fixed date (date of expiry of the letter) to the person named in the letter. Another letter called a letter of introduction was also issued, addressed to their branches, agents and correspondents bearing the specimen of signature of the beneficiary i.e. applicant. Both of these documents were required to be presented to the bank/agent making the payment against the letter.

REVOCABLE LETTER OF CREDIT

All letters of credit issued by banks are irrevocable unless specifically mentioned as revocable. A revocable letter of credit can be amended or cancelled by the issuing bank at any moment and without prior notice or notification to the beneficiary.

- The buyer (importer) has maximum flexibility as he/she is able to amend or cancel the credit without prior notice to the seller up to the moment of payment, acceptance or negotiation by the bank at which the issuing bank has made the credit available.

- The seller is at risk because the credit may be amended or cancelled while the goods are in transit and before the necessary documents have been presented.

- The seller may face the problem of obtaining payment direct from the buyer

- However, the issuing bank must:

    (i) Reimburse another bank with which a revocable credit has been made available for sight payment, acceptance or negotiation for any payment, acceptance or negotiation made by such bank prior to receipt by it of notice of amendment or cancellation, against documents which appear on their face to be in compliance with the terms and conditions of the credit;

    (ii) Reimburse another bank with which a revocable credit has been made and proceeds available for deferred payment, if such bank has, prior to receipt by it of notice of amendment or cancellation, taken up documents, which appear on their face to be in compliance with the terms and conditions of the credit.

The beneficiaries, usually, do not like this type of L/C. This type of L/C may be used by the parties having utmost trust or to complete a legal formality of a country to transfer funds. It is important to note that there is no mention of a revocable letter of credit in the UCP 600.

A revocable L/C does not carry a definite undertaking of the issuing bank and is advised by the advising bank without any undertaking on its part. It does not carry the issuing bank's request for confirmation. The advising bank is required to verify and ensure legality of the signature appearing on a letter of credit.

IRREVOCABLE LETTER OF CREDIT

An irrevocable letter of credit cannot be amended or cancelled without the agreement of the applicant, issuing bank, the confirming bank (if a letter of credit has been confirmed) and the beneficiary (UCP 600 Article No. 10).

An irrevocable credit constitutes a definite undertaking of the issuing bank, provided that the stipulated documents are presented and that the terms and conditions of a credit are complied with:

(i) If a credit provides for sight payment to pay, or that payment will be made;

(ii) If a credit provides for deferred payment – to pay, or that payment will be made, on the date(s) determinable in accordance with the stipulations of the credit;

(iii) If a credit provides for acceptance – to accept drafts drawn by the beneficiary if a credit stipulates that they are to be drawn on the issuing bank, or to be responsible for their acceptance and payment at maturity if a credit stipulates that they are to be drawn on the applicant for the credit or any other drawee stipulated in a credit;

(iv) If a credit provides for negotiation – to pay without recourse to drawers and/or bonaafide holders, draft(s) drawn by the beneficiary, at sight or at a tenor, on the applicant for the credit or on any other drawee stipulated in the credit other than the issuing bank itself, or to provide for negotiation by another bank and to pay, as above, if such negotiation is not effected.

(v) Note: Under a letter of credit the bill of exchange should not be drawn on the applicant but must be drawn on the issuing bank. This is because a letter of credit is an undertaking of the issuing bank with the beneficiary. If a bill of exchange is required to be drawn on the applicant, then it will be considered as an additional document required under a credit.

Examples of "Irrevocable Clauses" on a letter of credit:

A. "We undertake to honour such draft(s) on presentation provided that they are drawn in conformity with the terms of a credit" or

B. "We hereby engage that payment(s) will be duly made against documents presented in conformity with the terms of a letter of credit"

It may be advised to the beneficiary direct, if appropriate, or through an advising bank. When it is advised through an advising bank:

- The advising bank may add its confirmation, if required by the beneficiary.

- The issuing bank may request the advising bank to add confirmation. If the advising bank is not prepared to add its confirmation it must inform the issuing bank without delay unless otherwise specified by the issuing bank

- When the advising bank adds its confirmation to it, it is called "irrevocable Confirmed Letter of Credit"

IRREVOCABLE CONFIRMED LETTER OF CREDIT

An irrevocable letter of credit may be advised to the beneficiary through another bank without any undertaking on its part, but where the issuing bank requests or authorises another bank to add its confirmation to the credit and the other bank does so, then the letter with this additional clause of confirmation is called a "confirmed" letter of credit: this confirmation is a definite undertaking of the bank doing so in addition to the undertaking of the issuing bank. Provided the terms and conditions of a letter of credit are complied with, such confirmation or undertaking cannot be cancelled or amended without the consent of all parties to the letter of credit.

Where a letter of credit bears a confirmation of another bank it will assume the same liabilities as the issuing bank.

When an issuing bank authorises or requests another (advising) bank to confirm its irrevocable credit and the latter has added its confirmation, such confirmation constitutes a definite undertaking of that bank (known as confirming bank) in addition to that of the issuing bank, provided that the stipulated documents are presented and that the terms and conditions of the letter of credit are complied with.

Example of "confirmation clause"

"This credit bears our confirmation and we engage to:

(i) Pay – if the credit provides for sight payment to pay, or that payment will be made;

(ii) if the credit provides for deferred payment – to pay, or that payment will be made, on the date(s) determinable in accordance with the stipulations of the credit;

(iii) if the credit provides for acceptance, to accept drafts drawn by the beneficiary if the credit stipulates that they are to be drawn on the confirming bank, or to be responsible for their acceptance and payment at maturity if the credit stipulates that they are to be drawn on the applicant for a letter of credit or an other drawee stipulated in a letter of credit;

(iv) if a letter of credit provides for negotiation – to negotiate without recourse to drawers and/or bona fide holders, draft(s) drawn by the beneficiary, at sight or at a tenor, on the issuing bank or on the applicant for a letter of credit or on any other drawee stipulated in a letter of credit other than the confirming bank itself".

If a bank is authorised or requested by the issuing bank to add its confirmation to a credit but is not prepared to do so, it must so inform the issuing bank without delay. Unless the issuing bank specifies otherwise in its confirmation authorisation or request, the advising bank will advise a letter of credit to the beneficiary without adding its confirmation.

Such undertakings can neither be amended nor cancelled without the agreement of the issuing bank, the confirming bank (if any) and the beneficiary. Partial acceptance of amendments contained in one and the same advice of amendments is not effective without the agreement of all the above named parties.

An irrevocable letter of credit which has been confirmed by another independent bank (confirming bank) gives the seller a double assurance of payment as a bank in the seller's country has added its own undertaking to that of the issuing bank.

Silent confirmation

The request to confirm a letter of credit is made by the issuing bank to the advising bank on behalf of the applicant. This is a separate contract between the issuing bank and the advising/confirming bank.

Silent confirmation: Sometimes, the issuing bank does not ask the advising bank to add confirmation but for some reason the beneficiary approaches the advising bank to add its confirmation to a letter of credit without the knowledge of the issuing bank. This is known as silent confirmation. This is a separate contract between the beneficiary and the confirming bank. Under these circumstances, the issuing bank takes no liability in this respect. The issuing bank will have no obligation to inform the confirming bank of:

- any amendment to the letter of credit or
- in case of instances of fraudulent or falsified documents presented, the issuing bank will refuse to honour its commitments under the letter of credit.

REVOLVING LETTER OF CREDIT

A revolving letter of credit is one where, under the terms and conditions thereof, the amount is renewed or reinstated without specific amendment to the letter of credit being needed.

A revolving letter of credit may be revocable or irrevocable. It can revolve in relation to time or value.

REVOLVING LETTER OF CREDIT – MECHANISM

Revolving letter of credit is used when the same goods are to be imported or purchased on a repeat basis over a period of time without any changes/amendments to the terms and conditions of a letter of credit:

- The amount of the credit is available again for the stated credit amount after each drawing.

- The credit may revolve in either time or value.

- Time is the most common.

- Credit revolving in the time e.g. monthly means that the credit is available every month until the expiry date.

- May be automatically re-available or subject to the receipt of the issuing bank's instructions at each cycle.

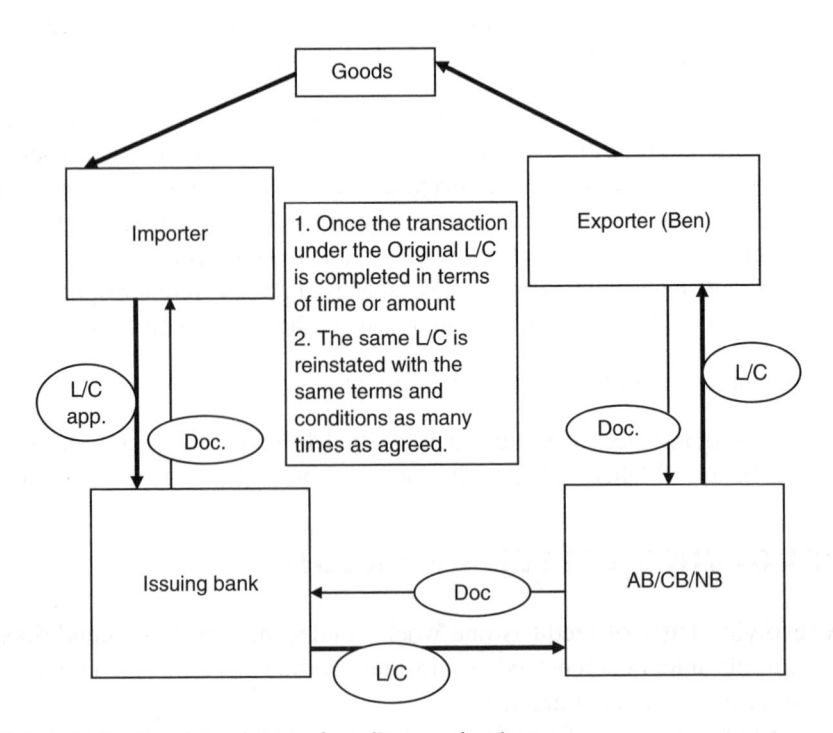

Figure 7.2 Revolving letter of credit – mechanism

A revolving credit may be cumulative: this means shipment missed in one cycle can be carried forward into the next cycle and non-cumulative means shipment missed in one cycle cannot be carried forward into the next cycle.

This type of credit permits the beneficiary to ship the good and make periodic drawing up to the value of the credit until the expiry date of the revolving letter of credit. If such a credit revolves in time it is also called a "periodic letter of credit".

RED CLAUSE LETTER OF CREDIT

A red clause letter of credit is a credit with a special clause incorporated into it that authorises the advising bank to provide a credit facility by way of advance against the letter of credit for the purchase of raw material or for working capital e.g. preparation of the goods to be exported by the beneficiary. The clause also stipulates the cover i.e. security for such advance and is incorporated at the specific request of the applicant.

To draw the attention of the beneficiary this clause was written in red or green ink. Thus it derived the name as "red clause" letter of credit.

The red clause: It is a special clause added, (see mechanics of red clause for example of wording of red clause) at the request of the importer, in red ink or a red border to the clause, to an irrevocable credit to draw attention to the special clause on the credit. The clause contains an authorisation by the issuing bank to the advising or confirming bank to make funds available to the beneficiary before presentation of documents.

It is often used as a method of providing the seller with funds prior to shipment of goods. Therefore, it is of great value to middlemen that require pre-shipment finance where the buyer would be willing to meet this special request from the seller/beneficiary. It originated, for example, so that a wool importer in England could enable a wool shipper in Australia to obtain funds to pay the actual suppliers (either by direct purchase or through the wool auctions) by obtaining a loan from the Australian bank, either on an unsecured basis or against the security of interim documents.

The finance facility is arranged between the buyer and the seller. The advising or confirming bank provides the beneficiary loan or overdraft facility up to the amount authorised or percentage of the value of the credit and would get repayment of the facility plus interest, from the proceeds due to the beneficiary when the goods are shipped and documents presented in accordance with the terms and conditions of a letter of credit. If the seller fails to ship the merchandise, the advising or confirming bank recovers the amount advanced plus interest from the issuing bank, who in turn recovers from the buyer (applicant).

The issuing bank ensures to take cash deposit or mark a lien on the applicant's deposit to protect itself from any loss for claim made by the advising/confirming bank in case the beneficiary fails to ship the goods and submit the documents under a letter of credit, as it is the liability of the applicant to pay for such a facility to the exporter.

RED CLAUSE LETTER OF CREDIT – MECHANISM

Example of a standard Red Clause addressed to the advising/confirming bank

You are authorized to advance up to ------ % of the credit amount to the beneficiary, and we undertake to repay on demand any amounts so advanced with or without presentation of shipping documents called for in this credit

Example of advance payment red clause (RC)

The negotiating bank is hereby authorized to make advance to the beneficiary to the extent of £ --- or the unused balance of this credit, whichever is less, against the beneficiary's receipt for the amount advanced which must state the advance to be used to pay for the purchase and shipment of the merchandise for which this credit is opened and accompanied by the beneficiary's written undertaking to deliver documents in conformity with the credit terms to the negotiating bank on or before the latest date for negotiation. The advance, with interest, is to be

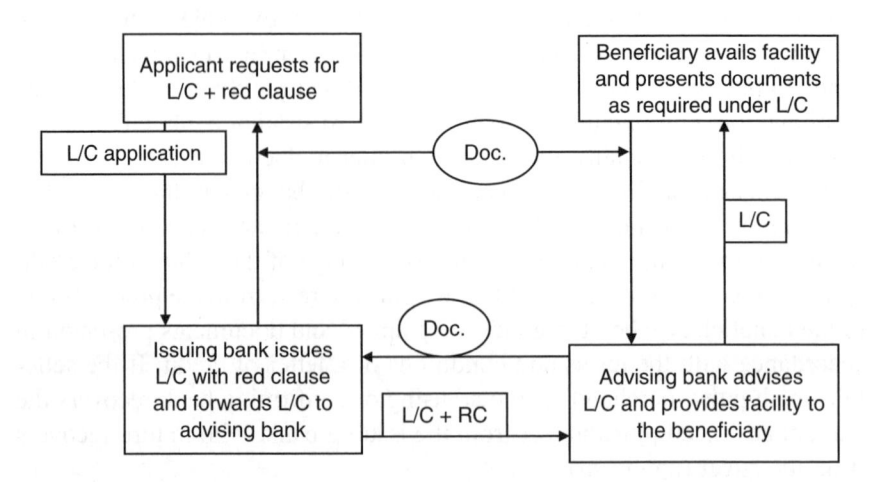

Figure 7.3 Red clause letter of credit – mechanism

deducted from the proceeds of the draft(s) drawn under this credit. We (the issuing bank) hereby undertake the repayment of such advances, with interest, should they not be repaid to the negotiating bank by the beneficiary on or before the latest date for negotiation.

Example of anticipatory drawing red clause

You are authorized to draw clean sight draft(s) on the issuing bank to the extent of £ --- accompanied by your signed statement that the amount drawn to be used for the purchase and shipment of the merchandise for which this credit is opened and your written undertaking to deliver documents in conformity with the credit terms to the negotiating bank on or before the latest date for negotiation.

Risk Factors: A foreign exchange risk may accrue to either party, depending upon the currency of a letter of credit. If payment is to be made in the currency of the beneficiary, the buyer will incur the foreign exchange risk. If a letter of credit is in the buyer's currency, the foreign exchange risk will accrue to the seller/beneficiary.

Before the beneficiary avails this facility from the advising/confirming bank he will be required to give two undertakings in writing to the bank:

(1) That the amount drawn or advanced under a letter of credit will be used only for the purchase and/or shipment of the merchandise for which the credit is opened;

(2) That the documents in conformity with requirements of a letter of credit will be delivered to the bank on or before the latest date for negotiation.

Example of red clause payment at maturity

The negotiating bank is hereby authorized to make advance to the beneficiary to the extent of ------ % of the amount of this credit, against the beneficiary's receipt for the amount advanced which must state that the advance is to be used to pay for the purchase and shipment of the merchandise under the credit and written undertaking to deliver the documents in conformity with the credit terms to the negotiating bank on or before the latest date for negotiation. The advance, with interest, is to be deducted from the proceeds of the draft drawn under this credit. We (the issuing bank) hereby undertake the payment of such advances, with interest, should they not be repaid by the beneficiary or by negotiation/payment on presentation of the documents strictly in terms of this credit at maturity.

Green Clause: This clause is distinct to Red Clause and primarily covers in a degree to which each one ties up the applicant's funds and exposes the applicant to a foreign exchange risk. The merchandise is taken as collateral security against the advance of funds allowed by this clause. The advance funds may be given against warehouse receipts. Such clauses are not common these days and are of academic interest.

TRANSFERABLE LETTER OF CREDIT

A transferable letter of credit is a credit under which the beneficiary (first beneficiary) may request the bank authorised to pay, incur a deferred payment undertaking, accept or negotiate (the "transferring bank"), or in the case of a freely negotiable credit, the bank specifically authorised in a letter of credit as a transferring bank, to make the credit available in whole or in part(s) to one or more other beneficiary(ies) (second beneficiary(ies)) (UCP 600 Article 38).

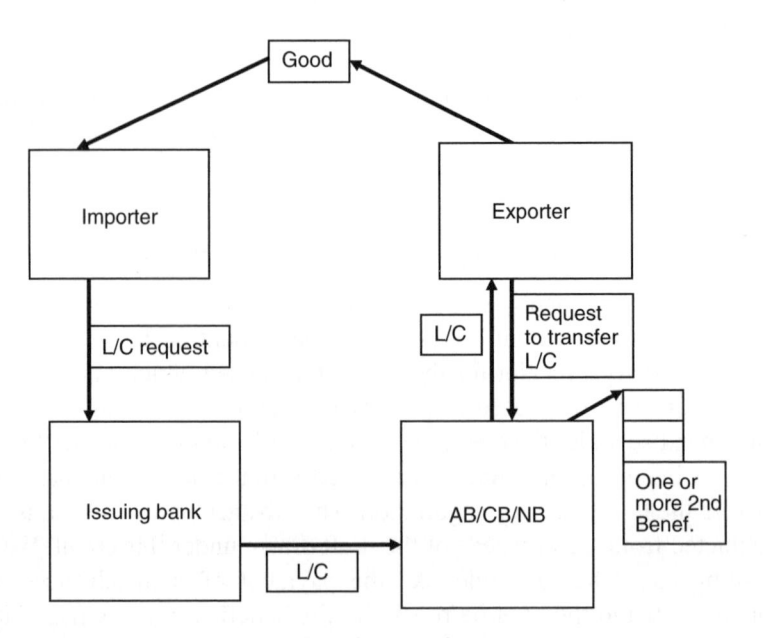

TRANSFERABLE LETTER OF CREDIT – MECHANISM

Transferable Letter of Credit: A transferable credit is one that can be transferred by the original (first) beneficiary to one or more second beneficiaries

Figure 7.4 Transferable letter of credit – mechanism

(Article 38 UCP 600). It is normally used when the first beneficiary does not supply the merchandise him or herself, but is a middleman and thus wishes to transfer part, or all, of his rights and obligations to the actual supplier(s) as second beneficiary(ies).

It should be noted that a letter of credit would only be issued as a transferable one on the specific instructions of the applicant. This would mean that both the credit application form and the credit itself must clearly state that the credit is transferable. (Only an irrevocable credit would be issued in this form and a letter of credit can be transferred once only.) A suggested format in this regard is given on the next page.

TRANSFERABLE CREDIT – LIMITATIONS

This type of letter of credit can only be transferred once i.e. the second beneficiary(ies) cannot transfer to a third beneficiary. The transfer must be affected in accordance with the terms of the original credit, subject to the following exceptions:

- The name and address of the first beneficiary may be substituted for that of the applicant for the credit.

- The amount of the credit and any unit price may be reduced: this would enable the first beneficiary to allow for profit.

- The period of validity and the period for shipment may be shortened.

- The transfer is affected on the instructions of the first beneficiary by the bank where the credit is available (the advising bank).

Thus, it permits a letter of credit to be arranged by the first beneficiary in favour of one or more second beneficiaries, while allowing the first beneficiary to substitute his invoices for those presented to the bank by the second beneficiary or beneficiaries. The bank must, of course, correlate and check both invoices with the other documents called for and ensure that all documents are in accordance with the terms of the original (prime) credit.

It is normally used when the first beneficiary does not supply the goods him or herself and requests to transfer part or all of his rights and obligations to the actual suppliers of the goods.

The transfer must be made by a named bank, and effected using exactly the same wording as the original credit, with only three (3) possible exceptions:

- The transferee's name and address is substituted for the beneficiary's.

- The amount of the credit may be reduced (by the beneficiary's profit).

- The expiry date may be brought forward to allow movement of documents between the transferring and the issuing banks.

The issuing bank must be informed of the transfer(s), name(s) of the second beneficiary and the amount(s).

Limitations

- Goods obtained must be the same as those required by the original credit.

- Only one level of transfer can be made (from first beneficiary to second beneficiary(ies).

- If "partial shipment" is not permitted it cannot be transferred to more than one transferee (second beneficiaries).

- Total value of transfers cannot exceed the value of a original letter of credit.

(Suggested Specimen of Request to Transfer Transferable L/C)

(Amend to suit the Bank's-----------------------------requirement)

The Manager,

Bank ----------------------------

Address ------------------------.

Dear Sir,

    Re: Transferable Irrevocable Credit No. ------------ for £ ----------- in our favour.

We refer to the above letter of credit issued by ------------ and request you to transfer the benefit of the credit to: --

of --
to the extent of £ -------------- upon the same terms and conditions, with the following variations:

The transferred credit is to be available until -------- and we shall be glad if you will advise the transferee(s) of this and the above variations by / cable/ swift or letter accordingly. No amendment of the terms of the original credit may, however, be advised to them without reference to us. The original credit is enclosed for endorsement, together with our cheque for £ ------- being your commission @ ----% for effecting the transfer, correspondents charges, if any, being for our account.

In consideration of your so transferring the credit we undertake to deliver to you, on or before your payment/negotiation of drafts drawn under the transferred credit, our own drafts, invoices for amounts equal to or exceeding those of the transferee(s) and other documents (if any) as required by and drawn in accordance with the original credit.

On our compliance with the above undertaking you will deliver the transferees invoices to us and will pay us the amount, if any, by which the total of our invoices exceeds theirs but if we should fail to deliver to you our drafts or invoices or any other requisite document forthwith, as agreed above, you are hereby authorised at your discretion and without notification to us to forward the transferees documents to your principals and without responsibility for any consequential disclosure of the transferee's names and prices or any other particulars.

It is understood that neither you nor your correspondents shall be under any responsibility for the description, quality, quantity or value of the merchandise covered by the documents against which you have paid/negotiated in accordance with the transferred letter of credit or for the correctness, genuineness or validity of the documents themselves, nor shall you be under any obligation to notify us of the failure of the transferees to tender any documents to you: and we hereby indemnify you in respect of all loss, damage and expense of any kind which you may incur as a direct; or indirect result of your acting on these instructions.

Yours faithfully,

AUTHORISED SIGNATURE
(Authorised signature should be confirmed by the beneficiary's bank)

PROCEDURE FOR EFFECTING TRANSFER OF A LETTER OF CREDIT

A transferable letter of credit usually attracts the attention of the advising bank. The advising bank, before forwarding such a letter of credit to the beneficiary, will attach its usual covering letter and any forms, which the beneficiary may need to complete to effect the transfer, if so wished.

The beneficiary of the original letter of credit may decide:

(a) Not to use the option to transfer a letter of credit or

(b) To transfer a part of a letter of credit amount or

(c) To transfer the whole amount of a letter of credit to one or more second beneficiaries.

If the original beneficiary decides to transfer a complete or partial letter of credit the beneficiary must complete the appropriate form, as required under a letter of credit. The beneficiary's signatures on the transfer form need to be verified by his bank before informing the issuing bank of the transfer. The advising bank will transcribe appropriate (full) details of the transfer(s) from the original letter of credit on its own letter(s) and forward to the second beneficiary(ies).

On receipt of the completed transfer form(s) the issuing bank will make note of the changes in the name(s) of the beneficiary(ies) and the amounts, as necessary.

BACK-TO-BACK LETTER OF CREDIT

It may happen that the credit in favour of the seller is not transferable, or, although transferable, cannot meet commercial requirements by transfer in accordance with (Article 38 of UCP 600) conditions. The seller, however, is unable to supply the goods and needs to purchase them from another supplier. The other supplier of the goods is prepared to sell to him on the basis of a letter of credit. In this case, it may be possible to use a "back-to-back credit". This concept involves the issue of a second credit by the seller in favour of his supplier.

Under the back-to-back concept, the seller, as beneficiary of the first credit, offers it as "security" to the advising bank for the issuance of the second credit. As applicant for this second credit the seller is responsible for reimbursing the bank for payments made under it, regardless of whether or not payment has been received under the first credit. There is, however, no compulsion for the bank to issue the second credit, and, in fact, some banks may not do so.

In the case of a counter credit, the procedure is the same except that the seller requests his own bank to issue the second credit as a counter to the first one. The seller's bank may agree to issue such a credit if the transaction falls within the seller's existing credit line or if a special facility is granted for the purpose. The bank will, of course, have rights against the seller in accordance with the term of a credit line or special facility.

With both the back-to-back credit and the counter credit, the second credit must be worded so as to produce the documents (apart from the commercial invoice) required by the first credit – and to produce them within the time limits set by the first credit – in order that the seller, as beneficiary under the first credit, may be entitled to be paid within those limits.

It is usually a domestic letter of credit issued on the strength of a foreign letter of credit, by the bank notifying/negotiating a foreign letter of credit. A back-to-back letter of credit is issued in favour of the suppliers of raw materials or finished products/goods to the beneficiary of a foreign letter of credit, which are to be exported under a foreign letter of credit.

It may happen that the credit in favour of the seller is not transferable, or, although transferable cannot meet commercial requirement by transfer in accordance with Article No.38 of the UCP 600 conditions. The seller, however, is unable to supply the goods and needs to purchase them from, and make payment to, another supplier.

Under the above circumstances the beneficiary of a letter of credit (foreign letter of credit is also known as Prime letter of credit) offers it as "security" to the advising bank for issuance of a second letter of credit matching the commercial requirements. The second letter of credit is known as "back-to-back" L/C.

Banks have special preference for trade related business. In order to develop such business, they keep on exploring different avenues, and back-to-back letter of credit is one of them.

It is, however, imperative that before focusing on back-to-back credit business, banks should be fully aware of the inherent risks involved in this type of business. The objective of these guidelines is to assist banks in exercising proper care in developing back-to-back letter of credit business, so that the banks' interest is safeguarded.

Back-to-back L/C: Salient features

Certain aspects of back-to-back transactions requiring further clarification are:

- Overall Risk
- Issuing Bank of Prime Letter of Credit
- Credit Check on Letter of Credit Openers

- Assignment of Prime Letter of Credit
- Cash Margin
- Pricing
- Technical details
- Prime Letter of Credit
- Bank's Appropriate Credit Approval

Back-to-back transactions risks

If the advising bank of the original credit does not add its confirmation to the original credit, it does not become a party to such credit and will thus be unable to reject an amendment that the opening bank of the original credit will issue.

The bank will, therefore, stipulate in its credit agreement with the intermediary that amendments will have to be approved by the bank.

If the advising bank of the original letter of credit does not wish to add its confirmation to the original credit, it has to be certain about the credit standing of the bank issuing that credit and the situation in the country of that bank. After all, this credit serves as collateral for the issuance of the back-to-back credit. Normally, the bank issuing the back-to-back credit will be prepared to accept the credit without confirmation if the issuing bank is a first class bank located in a reputable or low or no risk country. In all other cases, the bank will insist on adding its confirmation. In any case, the bank will have the credit exposure to the opening bank no matter whether it confirms the credit or not. After all, the credit serves as security for the commitment it enters into. This means that the overall commissions charged to the client should be identical. If the credit is confirmed, the bank will charge a confirmation commission and a lower issuance fee for a back-to-back letter of credit. If the credit is not confirmed, the issuance commission will be higher, as it has to compensate for the credit risk of the opening bank.

In transactions with different purchase and sale terms, e.g. Free on Board (FOB) purchase and CFR (cost and freight) or CIF (cost, insurance and freight) sale, there are additional risks involved relating to transportation and/or insurance.

It is important that the freight is paid and insurance is effective. So there should be sufficient cash and credit line in place to cover the freight and insurance charges.

Risk factors

It is important to understand that a back-to-back letter of credit is essentially a self-liquidating transaction. A bank opening back-to-back credit sometimes may not have collateral security or comfort to rely upon, except prime letter of credit.

Inherently, back-to-back credit is a straightjacket transaction, which requires extreme precision in handling. Prime letter of credit is not collateral as it has no intrinsic value, but it is a perfect source of repayment, provided its terms are respected in back-to-back letter of credit. In case of even a slight variation, a back-to-back letter of credit opening bank could be left to bear the loss without any support from the opener of the prime letter of credit.

Consequently, back-to-back letter of credit can be a safe and rewarding business if terms of the prime letter of credit are strictly adhered to, and could be disastrous if proper care is not taken of.

BACK-TO-BACK LETTER OF CREDIT – MECHANISM

Important points to consider

The customer (beneficiary) requests his bank to take the foreign (prime) L/C as security for another (back-to-back) L/C that he wishes to be issued.

Certain terms and conditions of the back-to-back (second) L/C must be modified according to the circumstances.

The back-to-back L/C should have an early expiry date to allow the customer time to:

(i) Manufacture goods

(ii) Make goods ready for despatch

(iii) Substitute his own shipping documents

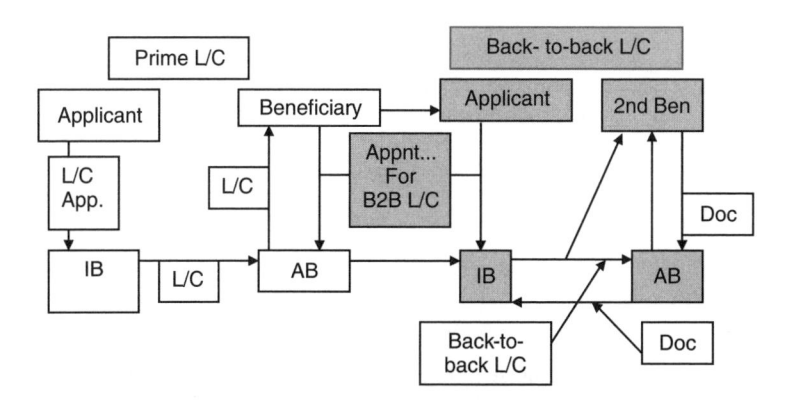

Figure 7.5 Back to back letter of credit – mechanism

Back-to-back L/C must be for a smaller amount because the supplier wants to make a profit on the transaction.

The supplier (beneficiary of prime L/C) must substitute documents showing his own name. If the beneficiary of back-to-back (second) L/C is to be paid before the beneficiary of prime L/C receives payment the bank must consider credit limit (credit worthiness) of the customer (first beneficiary) carefully.

The issuing bank should not permit the advising/negotiating bank to negotiate documents against second L/C with discrepancies, however minor those discrepancies may be.

Intermediary supplier's and ultimate buyer's names must not be disclosed. If any amendment(s) to the prime (first) L/C is/are received, it must be checked whether such amendment(s) affect the back-to-back (second) L/C in any way. If necessary, appropriate amendment(s) must be made in time.

If any amendment(s) is/are to be made to back-to-back L/C the terms and conditions of the prime L/C must be checked for whether such amendment(s) affect the prime L/C in any way. If necessary, appropriate amendment(s) must be made before any amendments to the back-to-back L/C.

The bank which, issues back-to-back L/C is responsible to scrutinise the documents in respect of both L/Cs.

The bills of lading under back-to-back letter of credit should be to the order of the bank issuing back-to-back L/C.

The bank issuing back-to-back L/C must take care of accounting aspect of liabilities and record necessary entries.

First or prime L/C must be assigned to the bank issuing back-to back L/C.

The bank must create a charge on the customer's stock and book debt (i.e. General Letter of Pledge or Hypothecation).

Transferable and Back-to-Back Credits – Comparison

TRANSFERABLE L/C	BACK-TO-BACK L/C
Involves one credit	Involves two separate credits
Credit only transferable at the applicant's request	Credit may be used as security to create a back-to-back credit without the knowledge of the applicant of prime L/C
Subject specifically to UCP 600 Art. 38	No specific article of UCP 600

STATUS OF ISSUING BANK OF THE PRIME LETTER OF CREDIT

As the entire transaction is structured on the basis of prime letter of credit it is important to establish the credentials of the issuing bank, and also the genuineness of the instrument. In this connection, the following points require special attention:

- The issuing bank should be reputable.

- The bank handling back-to-back credit must be holding and control documents vis-à-vis test keys and specimen signatures of prime letter of credit issuing bank so that genuineness of the instrument could be established.

- It is suggested that before getting involved in serious negotiations, the bank should know the status of the bank issuing prime letter of credit issuing bank. It is also equally important to clearly understand the country risk of the country where the prime letter of credit issuing bank is domiciled. Once the status, risks and relationship with the bank and country involved are cleared, detailed negotiations should be undertaken.

- Even a prime letter of credit opened by banks in locations of high-risk area countries require prior clearance for undertaking cross-border risks, and should be referred to the competent authority of the bank before making any commitments.

CREDIT CHECK ON LETTER OF CREDIT APPLICANT

The nature of back-to-back letter of credit transactions is such that at times, the bank is required to deal with a new customer without having the benefit of a previous track record. It is, therefore, important that before undertaking the transaction, the bank should check the credit worthiness of the applicant.

It is also more important to check the credit worthiness of the applicants of back-to-back letter of credit as they are usually middlemen/brokers, who undertake transactions which may be far in excess of their capacity, and may be unknown to the dealing bank.

However, if the back-to-back letter of credit applicant is a regular customer of the bank or a known entity in the market with an established track record, then the bank may exercise its own judgement.

A satisfactory credit report on the beneficiary of the back-to-back letter of credit to be opened by the bank should be obtained.

Assignment of prime letter of credit

Sometimes the prime letter of credit may be a final source of repayment of the bank's obligations under their back-to-back letter of credit. It is important to perfect their interest in the prime letter of credit. The following steps will be useful.

- When back-to-back letter of credit is opened, a lien should be marked on the prime letter of credit, showing details of the back-to-back letter of credit.

- Where prime letter of credit is restricted for negotiation to another bank or confirmed by a third bank, it is necessary to obtain a Letter of Authorisation from the beneficiary assigning the proceeds of negotiation under the prime letter of credit to the bank (issuing back-to-back L/C), which must be reported to the letter of credit advising/confirming bank and their acknowledgment obtained.

- If this assignment request is addressed to the advising/confirming bank of the. prime letter of credit it should be obtained before establishing the back-to-back letter of credit.

- The assignment must be obtained for the total amount of the prime letter of credit, and if this is not possible, at least for an amount sufficient to cover the back-to-back letter of credit including estimated bank charges.

- Prime letter of credit should be held in custody, together with the assignment of letter of credit duly completed.

Cash Margin: The back-to-back credit usually resists the idea of providing a cash margin. However, the issuing bank should endeavour to negotiate a cash margin, especially where the opener is a newly established company and/or is a relatively unknown party.

In this respect, it is important to understand that cash margin will not provide any comfort if there is a problem in carrying out the transaction caused by negligence of the bank opening back-to-back credit.

Cash margin is always desirable as it ensures a continued commitment and involvement of the applicant of the letter of credit.

There is no rule of thumb regarding the margin amount, but there has to be a stake by way of a reasonable cash margin. It varies between 20 to 30 per cent or more of the face value of back-to-back letter of credit.

Pricing: As discussed earlier, a back-to-back letter of credit is a self-liquidating transaction. Therefore, pricing of each transaction should depend on the risk and complexities involved.

Besides applying a regular schedule of charges for a letter of credit charges, a bank may negotiate a handling fee, depending upon the market practice in their area of operation.

In the case of the prime letter of credit opening bank being domiciled in a country of high-risk, branches of the bank should get clearance from the competent authority, as the transaction may require confirmation of prime letter of credit at a fixed price, which will be advised on a case-by-case basis. Hence, the bank's charges will include:

- Confirmation Commission

- Handling Fee

- Regular schedule of charges for Letter of Credit

It is always advisable to negotiate pricing before undertaking the deal as the parties are inclined to know and accept or otherwise pricing before initiating the transaction.

Technical Details: It is not possible to provide exhaustive guidelines on technical details as to the accurate opening and handling of back-to-back credit. However, a few points are hereunder:

Prime letter of credit should first be examined thoroughly to ensure that the terms and conditions could be honoured under back-to-back letter of credit. However, if there is any clause in prime letter of credit, which could not be transcribed in back-to-back credit, a suitable amendment/deletion should be obtained from the bank issuing prime letter of credit before opening back-to-back letter of credit.

A letter of credit, containing clauses providing for reimbursement on receipt of documents or on inspection at the port of discharge, is not acceptable as prime letter of credit.

The amount of back-to-back letter of credit should always be less than the amount of prime letter of credit.

The shipping and negotiation dates of back-to-back credit should expire earlier than the corresponding expiry dates of prime letter.

The issuing bank may incorporate a clause in back-to-back credit as "documents must be presented for negotiation within (x number of) days after the date of issuance of the transport document, but within the validity of the expiry date of a Letter of Credit" In this case it must be ensured that the date for presentation of documents be reduced accordingly when issuing back-to-back credit. Negotiations, in any case, must be within validity period of the back-to-back letter of credit.

If for any reason the time limit is not sufficient in the prime letter of credit to cover back-to-back letter of credit, it must be ensured that a suitable amendment extending its validity is received before issuing a back-to-back letter of credit.

In some cases, a prime letter of credit may require certain documents, such as an Inspection Certificate – or Certificate of Origin or Sanitary Certificate, etc, to be issued by a particular organisation, for example a government agency, and consequently back-to-back letter of credit require exactly the same documents.

Since quality and specification of goods to be shipped under prime letter of credit are of utmost importance, the bank should incorporate a suitable inspection document, if such requirement was not provided for in the prime letter of credit.

In the case of CIF shipments, the prime letter of credit requires insurance policy/certificates. It must be ensured that the insurance coverage and value of both letters of credit must be identical. If, for example, prime letter of credit calls for the coverage of "invoices value plus 10%", and in view of the lesser value of the relative back-to-back letter of credit, it would not be possible to comply with the identical terms of the prime letter of credit.

Where prime letter of credit is advised through another bank, it is important to ensure that complete control over all subsequent amendments is maintained. The beneficiary should not accept any amendment in the prime letter of credit without the bank's knowledge and consent.

In cases where prime letter of credit is restricted to the bank (issuing back-to-back letter of credit), it must be ensured that all subsequent amendments are suitably matched with back-to-back letter of credit, after obtaining written consent to this effect from the beneficiary. Where a particular amendment cannot be honoured, it is necessary that prime letter of credit opening bank should be informed immediately after obtaining written consent from the applicant.

Once a prime letter of credit has been advised to the beneficiary (your customer), amendments thereto can be effective only if accepted by the beneficiary and the bank. Banks should ensure that their customers do not accept any amendments without their approval. Before accepting any amendments to the prime letter of credit it should be ensured that the corresponding amendments to the back-to-back letter of credit are acceptable to the beneficiary of the letter of credit.

To identify a back-to back letter of credit transaction from any other regular letter of credit, it is necessary to mark a "Cross Reference Caution" on the related files, i.e., prime letter of credit and back-to-back letter of credit, so that the transaction can be carefully monitored and the possibility of an amendment being advised without reference to the prime letter of credit is avoided.

The back-to-back credit must be made restricted, as far as possible, for negotiation at the issuing bank's counters. In this way, the bank would be able to ensure that negotiation takes place within a reasonable time before expiry date of the prime letter of credit.

However, if it is not possible, then a suitable clause should be incorporated in the back-to-back letter of credit instructing negotiating bank to send all shipping documents in one lot through a reputable courier service, as well as to advise the issuing bank by a tested telex the details of negotiation including the name of the courier service, airway bill number, date documents despatched, etc. In this way, the bank could monitor movement and the timely delivery of the documents.

In back-to-back transaction, drafts and commercial invoices are commonly replaced before the documents are presented at the counter of prime letter of credit issuing bank. In this connection it is suggested that bank should obtain pre-signed documents before opening back-to-back letter of credit. It is important to observe this procedure where the branch is dealing with a relatively unknown or new customer and also if the cash margin is not provided by the applicant of the back-to-back letter of credit. If blank documents are obtained beforehand, then prime letter of credit would be negotiated even if the letter of credit opener declines to co-operate or is unable to provide the documents when required.

A letter of assignment must be obtained from the applicant of back-to back letter of credit before a credit is established.

Documents under back-to-back letter of credit bearing discrepancies must not be accepted. Any request from the back-to-back letter of credit applicant for accepting documents with the discrepancies should not be entertained unless secured by 100 per cent plus bank charges etc. as cash margin.

Shipping guarantees should under no circumstances be issued for shipment made under back-to-back letter of credit. Once a shipping guarantee is issued, the bank will be obliged to accept documents regardless of discrepancies.

Prime letter of credit: While considering proposals for opening letters of credit against the cover of a prime letter of credit, it is necessary to take additional safeguards as under:

Where prime letter of credit is on CIF terms, and back-to-back letter of credit is on C&F terms, a corresponding insurance cover of adequate value should be obtained from the customer, identical to that of support letter of credit.

Where prime letter of credit is on CIF terms and back-to-back letter of credit is required on FOB terms, in addition to the insurance requirement specified above, it should be ensured that the back-to-back letter of credit provides for the bills of lading to evidence "Freight Prepaid".

Similar terminology would apply in the case where a prime letter of credit calls for C&F terms whereas back-to-back letter of credit is on FOB basis, except that the requirement of insurance coverage would not apply.

A prime letter of credit may call for a particular "Transport Document" whereas the customer may require the bank to issue a back-to-back letter of credit. This sort of transaction evolves when a customer cannot arrange with his proposed buyer to either, have the goods shipped on similar terms and conditions as arranged with the ultimate buyer or the customer would not like to disclose the name of the actual buyer.

To illustrate, support letter of credit may call for "Marine Bill of Lading", while the back-to-back letter of credit may require "Truck Bill of Lading". Alternatively, a support letter of credit may call for shipment of goods from Toronto to Egypt, while a back-to-back letter of credit may call for despatch of goods from USA to Toronto.

Safeguards

Considering the involvement of two modes of carriage in these transactions, the following safeguards are suggested:

The related goods must be under the bank's control, at all times.

- The documents, when received, should be handed over only to the clearing agent/shipping company approved by the bank for this purpose.

- The clearing agent/shipping company would be responsible to ensure that the goods are cleared and shipped under their supervision, and proper documentation made out strictly in terms of prime letter of credit and is delivered directly to the bank.

- While handing over documents to the clearing agent/shipping company, it should be ensured that they are accompanied by a proper letter giving detailed and specific instructions regarding documents required, such as, what date should appear on the transport document, the exact descriptions of merchandise, as well as proof of shipment and port of discharge etc.

- The letter must clearly stipulate that these documents would be delivered to the bank directly. The documents must correspond with the requirements as called for in the prime letter of credit.

- Proper insurance with "bank" clause should be obtained before back-to-back letter of credit is opened.

- Trans-shipment must not be allowed. Such transactions, may delay delivery under prime letter of credit.

- Proper documentation required for customs clearance must be incorporated in the back-to-back letter of credit wherever necessary.

- Since goods under the support letter of credit would involve payment of customs duty, sales tax, ocean freight (if applicable) and inland freight, etc. It should be ensured that prime letter of credit amount would cover all these costs.

- The back-to-back letter of credit must also include a clause requiring an inspection certificate so as to evidence that the merchandise conform with specification, quality, quantity, etc. as stipulated in the prime letter of credit. To inspect the goods the Inspection Agency required to be approved by the bank and any cost invoiced would be on the account of the customer.

In handling back-to-back letter of credit transactions, it must always be borne in mind that prime/support letter of credit is only a source of repayment, provided of course the documents there-under are absolutely in order. Otherwise the prime/support letter of credit does not form a security.

Credit approval by the competent authority, as per internal guidelines of the bank, may be required in dealing with this type of letter of credit.

THIRD COUNTRY OR TRANSIT LETTER OF CREDIT

Mechanics of Third Country or Transit Letter of Credit

Sometimes a London bank may be asked by a bank(s) overseas to open letters of credit in favour of beneficiaries in another overseas country. The exporter may request the importer to have a letter of credit issued by a bank in a country other than the country of the importer. This is done through an overseas correspondent bank. The bank in London may be requested to issue a letter of credit by an overseas bank for various reasons such as:

- The importer and exporter would like to settle in a currency which is acceptable to both parties e.g. in GB Pounds or any other currency. This is done through Nostro and Vostro accounts held in London by most of the overseas banks.

- The financial standing of UK banks and financial stability of the UK in the eyes of the world as regards integrity, experience/expertise in handling documentary letter of credit transactions with absolute impartiality.

- The UK government is most unlikely to declare a moratorium.

- Finance under the letter of credit may be arranged in London from time to time, exchange control regulations permitting, where local finance in either of the two countries is more expensive or not available (e.g. by term drafts drawn on and accepted by the London bank and then discounted by them on thc London money market at the fine rate for bank bills).

- Where the opening bank is unknown in the seller's country (i.e. its signatures cannot be verified). Where direct communication between the buyer's and seller's countries is not possible for political reasons.

Additionally, sellers sometimes require a credit to be confirmed by a bank in the UK and passing the credit through such a bank (provided they

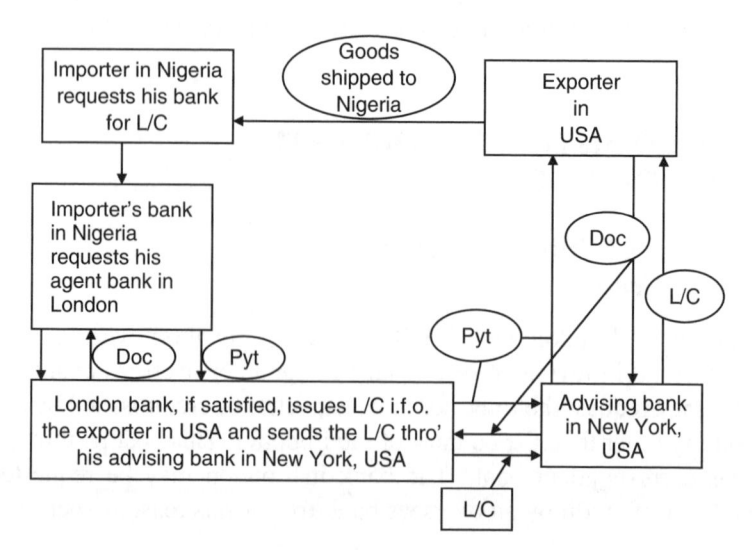

Figure 7.6 Third country/transit letter of credit – mechanism

have arranged a credit line) is a convenient way of providing such confirmation. This occurs more frequently when the buyer's country is considered by the seller to be politically unstable, or its currency to be weak, or the buyer's bank to be other than first class. The London bank's confirmation, in such cases, makes the credit as good as that of the London bank.

Banks in the UK are requested to advise or open transit credits for various reasons, such as:

(i) Settlement being effected in GB Pounds, a major trading currency often acceptable to both buyer and seller, which can conveniently be arranged through the GB Pound (Vostro) accounts maintained by UK banks for the hundreds of different banks abroad; transit credits need not be expressed in GB Pound since settlement may be arranged by UK banks in other currencies.

(ii) The opening bank may be unknown in the seller's country (i.e. signatures appearing on a letter of credit cannot be verified).

(iii) There may not be direct communication between the buyer's and seller's country. This may be due to political reasons.

(iv) The settlement may be effected easily in most trading currencies like GB Pounds and U.S. Dollars etc.

Additionally, sellers sometimes require a credit to be confirmed by a bank in the U.K. and passing the credit through such a bank (provided they have arranged a credit 'line') is a convenient way of providing such confirmation. This occurs more frequently when the buyer's country is considered by the seller to be politically unstable, or its currency to be weak, or the buyer's bank to be other than first class. The London Bank's confirmation, in such cases, makes the credit as good as that of the London bank.

DEFERRED PAYMENT LETTER OF CREDIT – MECHANICS

Deferred Payment L/C: The deferred payment letter of credit was developed in early 1950s in the Far Eastern Trade practice, where a negotiable instrument was not commonly used. The goods are delivered to the buyer before the date of payment or receipt of payment. If the goods prove

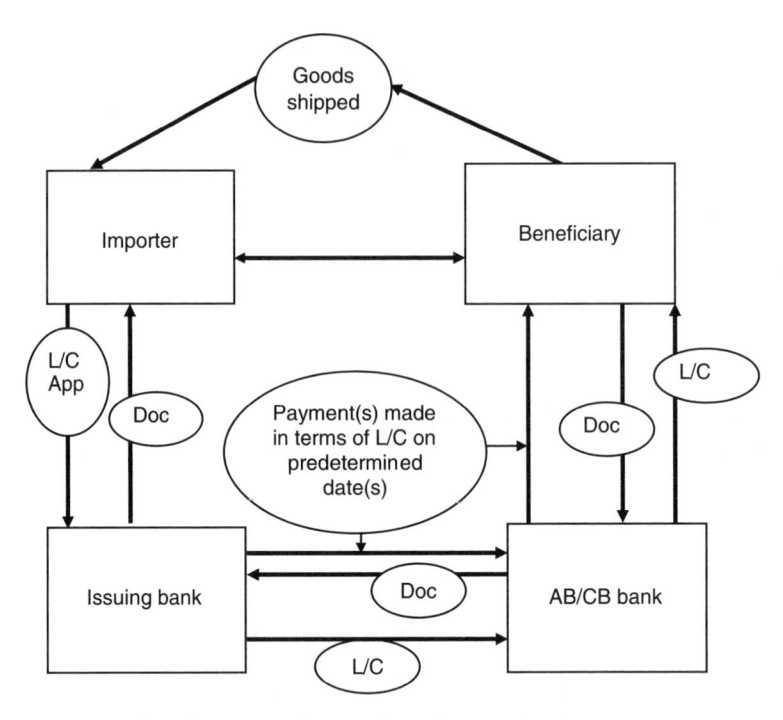

Figure 7.7 Deferred payment letter of credit – mechanism

defective the buyer may resort to any appropriate legal action. When documents under the credit are received, they are to be checked as the normal practice of banks but no bill of exchange is drawn under deferred letter of credit.

Under this type of letter of credit the payment to the beneficiary is made at pre-agreed future date(s) which may be after a specified number of days or months from the date of shipment or presentation of documents. Sometimes this type of credit is referred to as deferred sight letter of credit. The issuer of this letter of credit undertakes to the beneficiary on pre-agreed date(s). Payment may be made in periodic instalments.

UCP 600 Article 2(b) states if a credit provides for deferred payment to pay on the maturity date(s) determinable in accordance with the stipulations in the credit.

This deferred credit should not be confused with a usance letter of credit. In the case of a usance credit there must be a bill of exchange but in the case of a deferred payment letter of credit a bill of exchange is not drawn.

STANDBY LETTER OF CREDIT

The role of the traditional documentary credit (commercial credit), issued at the request of the buyer in favour of the seller, has been to enable the seller to obtain the payment due from the buyer when he, the seller, has fulfilled their part in the commercial contract and "evidenced" this fact by presenting "stipulated documents".

The role of a standby credit is different, although it possesses all the elements of a documentary credit subject to UCP 600. It is often used in lieu of the performance guarantee, for example in respect of major construction contracts or major long-term sales. But it may sometimes be used for other purposes, such as a form of guarantee by, for example, a parent company's guarantee of loans granted to a subsidiary. A standby letter of credit may be issued in favour of the seller to ensure that if payment is not received under some other pre-agreed method it will be made under a standby credit upon the seller fulfilling his part of the standby credit.

A standby credit may be issued at the request of the applicant (usually seller or contractor) directly in favour of the beneficiary (usually buyer or employer), or it may be issued in favour of a bank in the beneficiary's country to cover a guarantee issued by that bank in favour of the beneficiary.

A standby letter of credit is one whose value is held in reserve or only paid as a penalty for non-compliance with some other contract, or on failure of other payments to be forthcoming. Standby letters of credit are mostly used to prove a commitment to honour a contract.

Basically, however, a standby credit is intended to cover a "non-performance" (default) situation instead of a "performance" situation, as with the traditional documentary credit. This affects both the position of the issuing bank and the type of documentation called for. Even if the applicant has claims that he "performed" the bank must pay under the terms of the credit if the specified documentation is presented – usually a sight draft on the issuing bank accompanied by a statement of claim issued by the beneficiary. (This position has been upheld in a number of cases where the courts have ruled against an applicant seeking an injunction to prevent the issuing bank from honouring its undertaking).

The type of documentation referred to above gives some indication of the "extent to which they may be applicable" to standby credits. Thus, many articles dealing with "Documents" would seem likely to not to be applicable.

A standby letter of credit operates just like any other letter of credit except that:

- It is not secured by goods in trade.
- Its value will be paid out only on non-performance.
- Its purpose is to prove financial ability and commitment to honour a contract, not to pay for specific goods/services, because it is used to secure contracts, not for payment in full for anything.
- Value of standby letter of credit rarely exceeds more than 10 per cent of the value of the contract.

STANDBY LETTER OF CREDIT – MECHANISM

This type of credit was first mentioned under UCP regulations in 1983 revision of ICC and since then it is recognised under ICC regulations. It performs a similar function to a "performance bond". It provides a "guarantee" that payment will be made by the issuer (via the opening bank) if the buyer fails to render

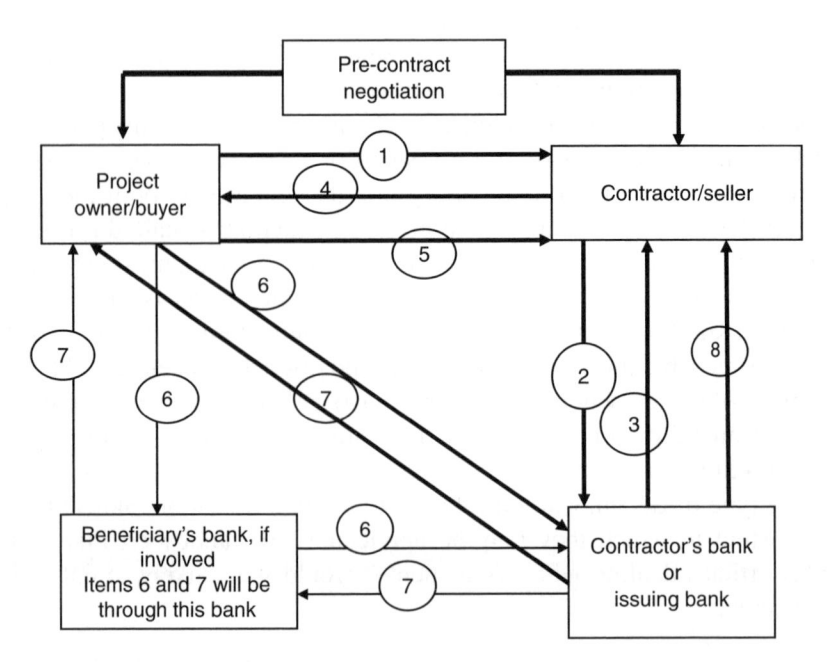

Figure 7.8 Standby letter of credit – mechanism

payment or performance to the beneficiary. The payment may be evidenced by documentation or, possibly, by a simple demand from the beneficiary.

1. Invitation for Bid. The project owner sends a tender to bid on a project to a contractor. The tender requires a bid bond and permits the bid bond to be in the form of a standby letter of credit.

2. The contractor applies to the bank for the issuance of a bid bond.

3. The contractor's bank (issuing bank) issues a bid bond and forwards it to the contractor.

4. The contractor forwards his bid together with the bid bond to the project owner.

5. The project owner accepts the contractor's bid and sends a contract to the contractor.

6. If the contractor fails to sign the contract or fails to obtain and forward to the project owner a performance bond, the project owner will demand payment under the bid bond.

7. When the contractor has signed the contract and obtained a performance bond, or whatever else the contract may require, the project owner will return the bid bond to the contractor to be cancelled.

8. The issuing bank informs the contractor of his action.

Distinction between a commercial letter of credit and a standby letter of credit

Table 7.1 Comparison of commercial and standby letter of credit

Basic concept	Commercial L/C	Standby L/C
Performance	It is a payment device	It is a security instrument
Documentation	All parties expect the beneficiary to draw documents,	Does not expect the beneficiary to draw documents. Claim is made only if something goes wrong.
	Involves third party's Documents i.e. B/L, insurance and other commercial documents	May involve only a declaration
Security	Third party documents of title provide security to bank	No inherent security, an additional security or margin may be required by the bank

A specimen of Standby Letters of Credit

(Specimen 1)

Name and full address of Issuing Bank

Name and full address of the beneficiary

Gentlemen,

Date:

OUR IRREVOCABLE STANDBY LETTER OF CREDIT NO ------- FOR GB POUNDS --------- IN YOUR FAVOUR --------------------------------------

In consideration of your having entered into an agreement with --- (Full name and address) hereinafter referred to as the applicant to supply a consignment of ----------------------- for a total value of GB Pounds ------- (amount in word)

We, the Bank -----------------, hereby issue our Irrevocable Standby Letter of Credit No:------ in your favour, which is available to you ---------days after the date of Bill of Lading/Airway Bill upon your written demand which must be accompanied by the following documents and must reach us at our Counter, ------------------ within the validity of this Standby Letter of Credit.

1. *Our written statement signed by your two authorised signatories, whose signatures must be certified by your bankers, stating that the goods as detailed herein above have been shipped to ----------------------- in accordance with your agreement with ----------------------- and you have not received payment for the same from ------------- after --------- days from the date of Bill of Lading/Airway Bill.*

2. *Copy of the unpaid invoice made out to ---------------------- evidencing the shipment of the abovementioned goods, consigned to ----------------- and the amount due from the applicant.*

3. *Copy of the Clean on Board Bill of Lading/Air Waybill evidencing the shipment of the above mentioned goods consigned to ----------------------*

4. *This original Standby Letter of Credit expires on ---------- in London, UK*

We undertake that documents drawn under and in strict compliance with this Standby Letter of Credit shall be duly honoured upon presentation to us at our counter in London on or before the expiry date.

This Standby Letter of Credit is subject to the Uniform Customs and Practice for Credits (2007 Revision) International Chamber of Commerce No.600.

Authorised Signature   Authorised Signature

PLEASE NOTE: The text may require modification according to the circumstances
Specimen of a Standby Letter of Credit
****

(Specimen 2)

FROM: XYZ BANK PLC

We herewith issue our irrevocable standby letter of credit No. ----------
which is subject to the Uniform Customs and Practice for Documentary
Credits (2007 Revision) ICC Publication No. 600, as follows:

Applicant: Name and address of the buyer

Beneficiary: Name and address of supplier

For an amount of: (Currency and amount)

Date/Place of expiry: (Latest date of credit validity) --------- (Place)---------

Available with XYZ BANK PLC, London at sight, but not prior to 30 days after shipment date, against presentation of the following documents:

1. Beneficiary's statement, purportedly signed by an authorised/signatory, reading to the effect that:
   (a) Goods have been delivered in accordance with the contractual terms
   (b) The invoice and any relevant payment documents have been presented to the applicant
   (c) The amount claimed has not been paid and is now past due by the applicant in accordance with the contract terms;

2. Copy of unpaid invoice addressed to the applicant by beneficiary.

3. Copy of bill of lading covering: Goods

The amount available for drawing under this standby letter of credit will be automatically reduced by the amount of any payment(s) made in favour of (beneficiary) whether under and/or outside this standby letter of credit, if such payment is effected by XYZ Bank PLC and if reference is made to this standby letter of credit.

Special Conditions: Documents presented later than 21 days after the issuance date of the transport document(s) are acceptable.

Bank charges: All banking charges outside of the Issuing Bank are for the beneficiary's account.

Method of Reimbursement: After receipt of strictly credit conform documents at our counters in London we will remit funds to the presenting bank in accordance with their instructions.

Instructions to the Advising Bank: Please advise the beneficiary without adding your confirmation.

-------------------------   ------------------------   Date: --------------------
Authorised Signature   Authorised Signature

SKELETON LETTER OF CREDIT

This type of letter of credit does not specify the goods to be shipped but state "General Merchandise" which allows the beneficiary's freedom to ship any goods up to the amount of the credit. It is particularly important when a transferable credit is issued to agents of the applicant company allowing them freedom to shop around while abroad.

OMNIBUS LETTER OF CREDIT

This type of credit does not specify the port of loading, which implies the applicant's acceptance of specific goods from any port or anywhere in the world.

STRAIGHT LETTER OF CREDIT

It is a letter of credit, which expires for payment or acceptance at the counters of the issuing bank. The issuing bank gives the following type of undertaking, "We engage with you that the drafts drawn under and in compliance with the terms and conditions of this credit will be honoured upon presentation of documents to us as specified not later than. Date)".

CHAPTER 8

Methods of Payment Settlement

There are different methods of payment settlement. The following statement if made by the issuing bank, "We hereby engage that payment will be duly made against documents presented in conformity with the terms of this credit".

PAYMENT L/C

The following action steps take place:

(a) The seller/beneficiary send the documents evidencing the shipment of the goods to the bank where the credit is available (issuing bank or advising/confirming bank)

(b) The bank examines the documents and if the documents meet with the requirements of the letter of credit, makes payment.

(c) This bank, if other than the issuing bank, then sends the documents to the issuing bank and claims reimbursement in accordance with the bank's agreed settlement procedures.

CHANNELS OF PAYMENT SETTLEMENT

Payment

(a) Requires only 2 parties – (buyer and seller)

(b) May or may not involve a bill of exchange

(c) Where a bill of exchange is involved it must be a sight bill of exchange

(d) Payment is always without recourse

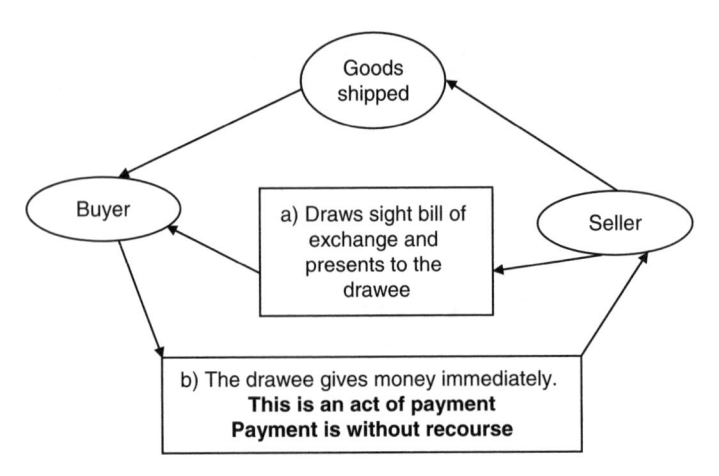

Figure 8.1 Channels of payment settlement

Diagram nodes: Buyer, Seller, Goods shipped; a) Draws sight bill of exchange and presents to the drawee; b) The drawee gives money immediately. **This is an act of payment. Payment is without recourse**

PAYMENT L/C – BILL ON ISSUING BANK

Payment settlement – method/acceptance letter of credit

The issuing bank usually gives the following undertaking, "We hereby engage that drafts drawn in conformity with the terms of this credit will be duly accepted on presentation and duly honoured at maturity".

The following action steps take place:

(a) The seller/beneficiary sends the documents evidencing the shipment of the goods to the bank where the credit is available (issuing bank or advising/confirming bank) accompanied by a usance bill of exchange drawn on the bank with the specified tenor.

(b) The bank examines the documents and if the documents meet with the requirement of a letter of credit, the bank accepts the bill of exchange and returns it to the seller/beneficiary.

(c) This bank, if other than the issuing bank, sends the documents to the issuing bank, stating that it has accepted the bill and maturity date. At maturity reimbursement will be made in accordance with the bank's agreed procedures

METHODS OF PAYMENT SETTLEMENT

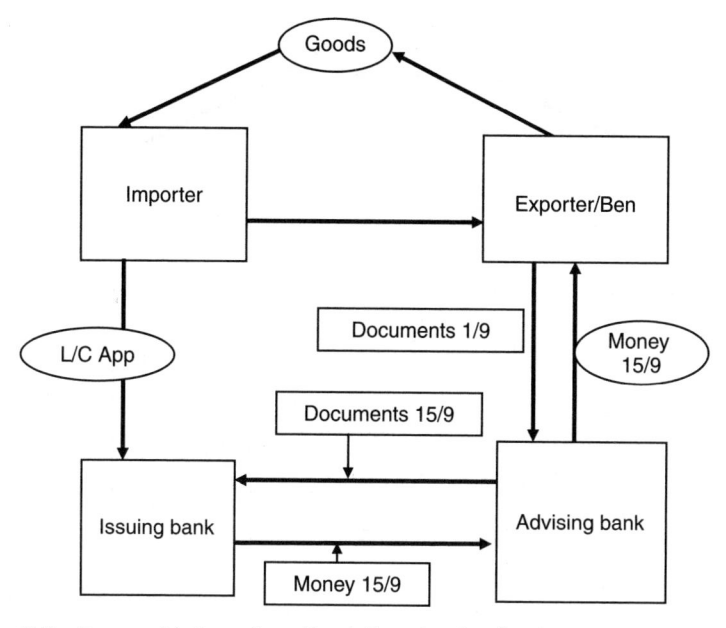

Figure 8.2 Payment letter of credit – bill on issuing bank

MECHANISM OF SETTLEMENT – ACCEPTANCE L/C

ACCEPTANCE

Involves 2 Stages

Stage 1. Requires Minimum of 2 Parties

(a) Requires a bill of exchange

(b) It must be a usance bill of exchange

(c) Acceptance is an undertaking of liability of the drawee to pay on maturity

Stage 2.

(a) Presentation of the Bill of exchange on maturity

(b) Money is given at maturity Act of Payment (without recourse)

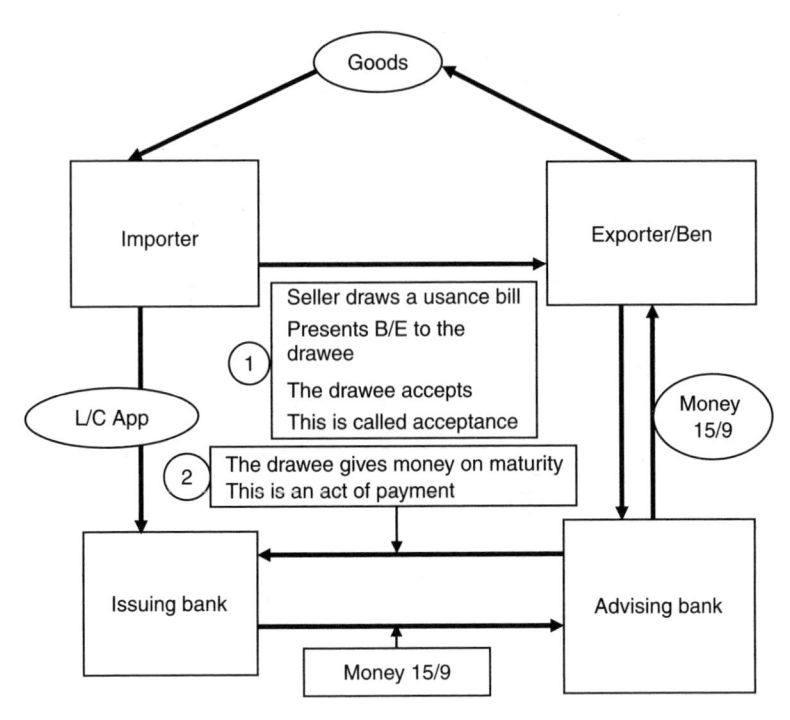

Figure 8.3 Acceptance letter of credit – mechanism of settlement

METHOD OF SETTLEMENT – USANCE BILL ON ISSUING BANK

Bankers' acceptances

The rules under UCP 600 Article No. 2(c) "if the credit provides for acceptance:

(a) By the issuing bank – to accept Draft(s) drawn by the Beneficiary on the Issuing Bank and pay them at maturity. Or
(b) By another drawee bank – to accept and pay at maturity Draft(s) drawn by the Beneficiary on the Issuing Bank in the event the drawee bank stipulated in the Credit does not accept Draft(s) drawn on it, or to pay Draft(s) accepted but not paid by such drawee bank at maturity;"

It means that where a bill of exchange is required it should be drawn on the issuing bank or on "AB" or "CB" if authorised in the letter of credit. A bill of exchange is an order for payment. When it is a sight bill the order to pay is made by the drawee payable on demand but a usance/time bill of exchange orders for payment sometime in future. This is one of the most common methods of giving the drawee/buyer longer time to settle the account. A usance/time bill of exchange which meets the terms and conditions of the letter of credit, requires the drawee (buyer) to give an

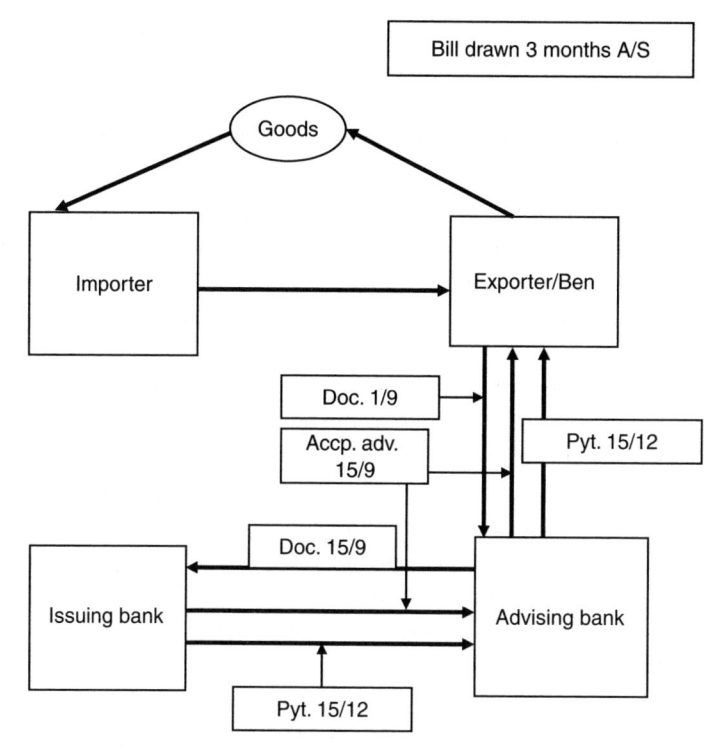

Figure 8.4 Usance bill on issuing bank – mechanism of settlement

undertaking to make payment on due date and to receive the documents of title to goods in order to collect the goods. A letter of credit is a legal contract between the issuing bank and the seller/beneficiary, the latter draws the bill on the issuing bank. If documents under a letter of credit meet its requirement the bank has no alternative but to accept the bill of exchange by signing on the face of the bill with or without adding the word "accepted" thereon. This is known as bank's or banker's acceptance. By adding this statement, the bank acknowledges it legal obligation to pay the face value of the bill of exchange on its maturity date.

A bill of exchange accepted by a bank is a negotiable instrument, and can be sold or transferred by one party to another merely by endorsement and delivery. Whoever holds the instrument until its maturity actually finances the underlying transaction, whether the holder is a seller, an investor or a bank.

Advantages of discounting bankers' acceptances

A bankers' acceptance can be discounted when the holder sells it. The party, which discounts such a bill must ensure that it is a trade bill of exchange and relating to current shipment of goods and that it is correctly drawn. The advantage of discounting such a bill is that (1) bankers' acceptances are considered safe and sound, (2) it is a self-liquidating transaction and the bank will make payment on maturity.

METHOD OF SETTLEMENT – NEGOTIATION

Meanings of Negotiation: There are several meanings of the word "negotiation". In general, the term is applied to arranging a contract or discussing the terms and conditions of a contract. The legal meaning of the word "negotiation" particularly in connection with cheques, bills of exchange is when such instruments are transferred from one person to another. Negotiation is a means of financing an outward collection or funding the payee of a cheque, bill of exchange or the beneficiary of documents under a letter of credit payable abroad.

We refer the term in relevance to the specific meaning of the beneficiary of documents under a letter of credit payable abroad. When a bank negotiates an outward collection it is buying its customer's bills and/or documents drawn on an overseas buyer. It is a convenient method of providing the exporter with working capital. The bank in buying the bill and/or documents will look to the overseas buyer as a source of repayment. In the event of non-payment or delayed payment, the negotiating bank exercises the right of recourse to its customer, the drawer. Therefore, if payment does not arrive within a reasonable time, the negotiating bank will debit its customer's account with the amount advanced plus interest. The cost of negotiation is similar to loan interest when provided by a bank.

When a bank negotiates, it pays its customer straight away and sends the bill and/or documents to the issuing bank.

Under English law the negotiating bank may become a holder in due course of the bill of exchange when it negotiates, and as such it gets a right of action against the drawer in the event of default by the drawee.

Negotiation of a Letter of Credit: The issuing bank usually gives the following undertaking on the letter of credit, "We hereby engage with the drawers and/or bonafide holder that drafts drawn and negotiated in conformity with the terms and conditions of this credit will be duly honoured on presentation and that drafts accepted within the terms of this credit will be duly honoured at maturity".

Negotiation – Sight Bill of Exchange Drawn on Issuing Bank

The following action steps take place:

(a) The seller/beneficiary sends the documents evidencing the shipment of the goods to the bank (advising bank/confirming bank) accompanied by

METHODS OF PAYMENT SETTLEMENT 93

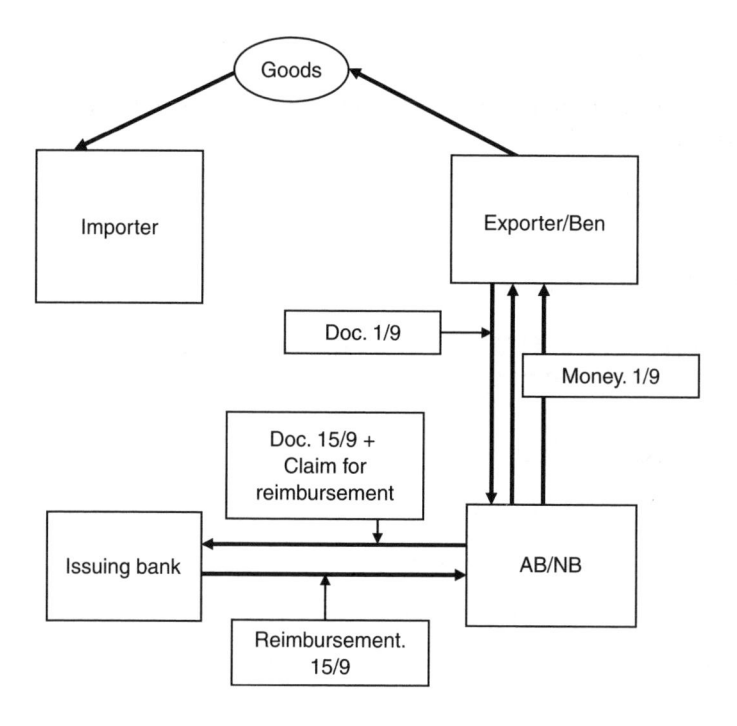

Figure 8.5 Negotiation sight letter of credit – bill drawn on issuing bank

a bill/draft drawn on the issuing bank as specified in the credit (at sight or at a tenor)

(b) The bank (AB/NB) examines the documents and if the documents meet the requirements of a letter of credit, may negotiate i.e. make payment. This bank, if other than the issuing bank, then sends the documents to the issuing bank and claims reimbursement in accordance with the bank's agreed procedures.

(c) Negotiation by advising bank is with recourse to the beneficiary and negotiation by confirming bank is without recourse to the beneficiary.

Negotiation

(a) Requires at least three parties

(b) In case of sight negotiation, there may or may not be a bill of exchange

(c) If there is no bill of exchange pure documents drawn under a sight l/c may be negotiated

(d) If there is a bill, it must be a sight bill of exchange

(e) The act of negotiation by a bank, other than the issuing bank, is with recourse

(f) Negotiation by the confirming bank is without recourse

SITUATION NO. 2

NEGOTIATION UNDER 3 MONTHS USANCE L/C BILL ON ISSUING BANK

Usance Negotiation

(a) Requires at least three parties

(b) There must be a bill of exchange

(c) It must be a usance bill of exchange

(d) The act of negotiation by a bank who is not a confirming bank is with recourse

(e) Negotiation by the confirming bank is without recourse to the beneficiary

Procedure for advising/confirming bank

The seller may sometimes present documents that do not meet letter of credit requirements. In such a case, the bank may act in one of the following ways:

1. Return the documents to the beneficiary (seller) to have them amended for re-submission within the validity of the credit and within the period of time after date of issuance specified in the credit, or applicable under Article number 16 UCP 600). Or

2. Send the documents for collection. Or

3. Return the documents to the beneficiary for sending through his own bankers, if the confirming or advising bank is not the beneficiary's bank. Or

4. If authorised by the beneficiary, cable or send message by SWIFT or write to the issuing bank for authority to pay, accept or negotiate. The bank must provide a full list of irregularities to the issuing bank. Or

5. Call for an indemnity from the beneficiary or from a bank, as appropriate, i.e. pay, accept or negotiate on their undertaking that any payment made will be refunded by the party giving the indemnity, together with

METHODS OF PAYMENT SETTLEMENT 95

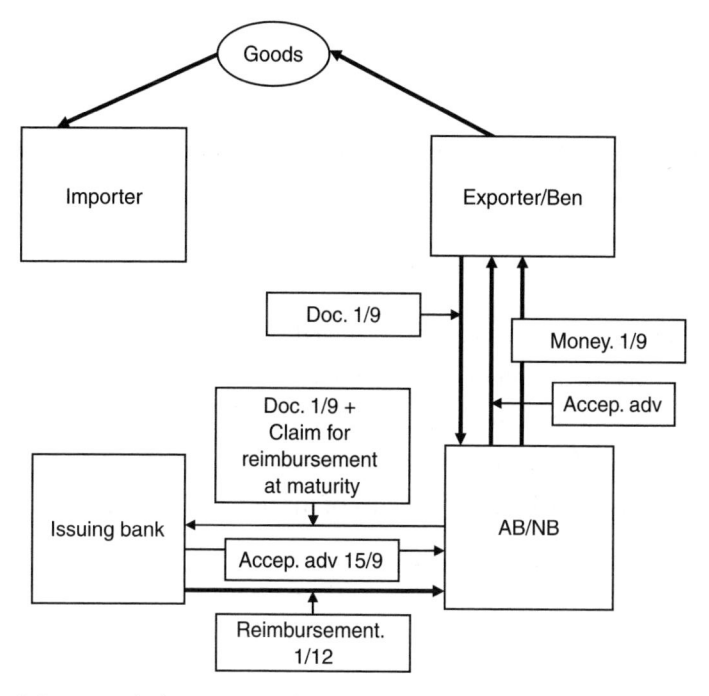

Figure 8.6 Negotiation – 3 months usance L/C bill on issuing bank

interest and all charges, if the issuing bank refuses to provide reimbursement against documents that do not meet the credit requirement.

6. Based on practical experience, and with the agreement of the beneficiary, pay, accept or negotiate "under reserve", i.e. retain the right of recourse against the beneficiary if the issuing bank refuses to provide reimbursement against documents that do not meet the credit requirement.

A suggested format for indemnity when undertaking negotiation under reserve is as following:

NEGOTIATION OF DOCUMENTS UNDER RESERVE

(A suggested form of an indemnity bond in case of discrepancies)

The Manager   Date _____

Bank's name _____

Address _____

_____

Dear Sir,

Re: _____

In consideration of your *negotiating/accepting/paying on presentation a Bill of Exchange (*delete as appropriate)

Dated_____for_____amount in words_____
_____

Drawn under letter of credit No._____dated_____Issued by_____
_____Notwithstanding that the documents tendered therewith fail to conform with the requirements of the said letter of credit by reasons of (state here specifically the irregularities in documents tendered together with the relative precise requirements of the letter of credit)

_____

_____

_____

We undertake to indemnify you from and against all losses or damage, which you may incur or sustain because of the above irregularities in the documents. Provided that any claim upon us hereunder shall be made before _____ (date).

Yours faithfully

Signature(s) _____

NEGOTIATION OF DOCUMENTS UNDER RESERVE

(A suggested form of an indemnity bond in case discrepancies)

The Manager   Date _____

Bank's name _____

Address _____

_____

Dear Sir,

Letter of Credit No. _____ issued by_____

In consideration of you paying us the sum of (amount in words and figures) _____

under the above-mentioned credit we hereby indemnify you from all consequences which may arise notwithstanding the following discrepancies in the documents.

-----------------------------------   --
Signed by the beneficiary   Signed by the beneficiary's bank
                                             or third party

ADVISING/CONFIRMING BANK – PROCEDURAL ASPECT

The seller may sometimes present documents that do not meet the credit requirements.
In such a case, the bank may act in one of the following ways:

- Return the documents to the beneficiary (seller) to have them amended for re-submission within the validity of the credit and within the period of time after date of issuance of bill of lading specified in the credit, or

- Inform the advising/negotiating bank immediately of the irregularities

- Contact the buyer/applicant and seek his instructions

- If the buyer/applicant is not ready to accept the documents, inform the advising/negotiating bank immediately of non-payment or non-acceptance of the documents

CHAPTER 9

Financial Load Variations – Eight Types of Letters of Credit

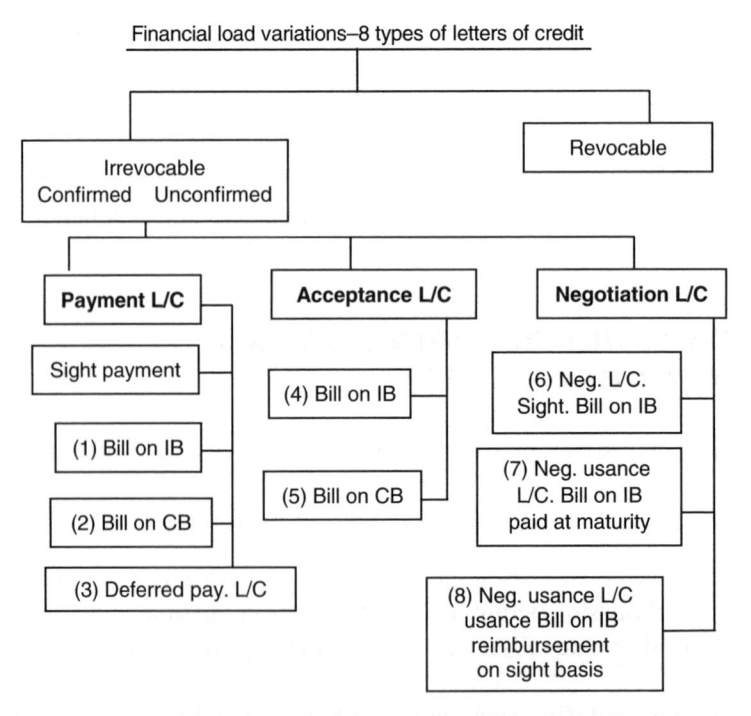

Figure 9.1 8 types of letters of credit – financial load variations

PAYMENT LETTER OF CREDIT – BILL DRAWN ON ISSUING BANK

Financial load is for transit time only and borne by the beneficiary.

1. The importer applies for a letter of credit to his bank – issuing bank (IB).

2. The IB issues a sight letter of credit with Bill on IB and forwards it to an agent (advising bank) (AB) bank in the exporter's country with a request to forward it to the beneficiary.

3. The AB forwards a letter of credit to the beneficiary, if satisfied with the terms and conditions the beneficiary makes goods ready, despatches the goods and prepares the documents.

4. The beneficiary forwards the documents to the advising bank (AB).

5. AB forwards the documents to the IB.

6. IB checks the documents, if satisfied, debits the importer's account and remits funds to the AB for the credit of the beneficiary's account.

7. The IB forwards the documents to the importer.

8. The AB credits the beneficiary's account and forwards payment advice. Payment by the issuing bank is without recourse.

In this case the beneficiary finances the transaction for the whole period until he receives payment. The financial load is borne by the beneficiary.

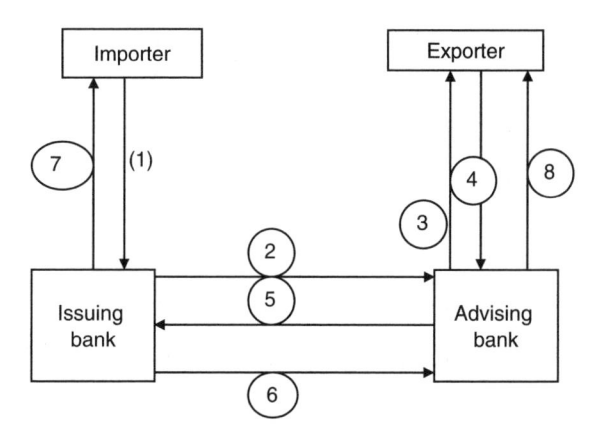

Figure 9.2 Payment L/C – bill of issuing bank

PAYMENT LETTER OF CREDIT – BILL DRAWN ON CONFIRMING BANK

Financial load is for transit time only and borne by the confirming bank

1. The importer applies for a letter of credit to his bank – issuing bank (IB).

2. The IB issues a sight letter of credit with a Bill on the confirming bank and requests to AB to confirm the latter and forward it to the beneficiary.

3. The AB confirms the letter (now the AB has become CB) and forwards the confirmed letter of credit to the beneficiary, if satisfied with the terms and conditions, the beneficiary makes goods ready, despatches the goods and prepares the documents.

4. The beneficiary forwards the documents to the advising bank (AB/CB).

5. CB checks the documents and, if satisfied, makes payment to the beneficiary.

6. CB forwards the documents to the IB and claims reimbursement from the IB.

7. IB checks the documents, if satisfied, debits the importer's account and remits funds to the CB as reimbursement.

8. The IB forwards the documents to the importer.

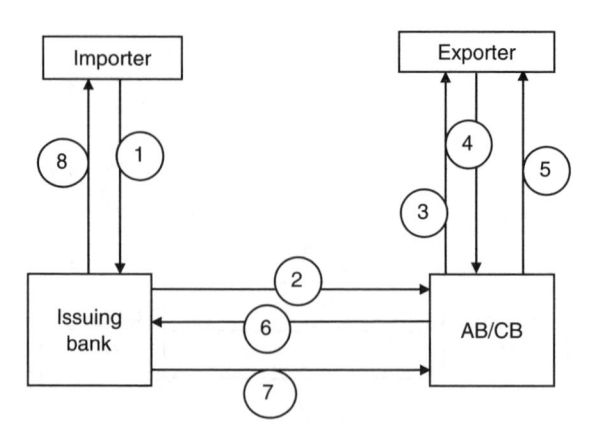

Figure 9.3 Payment L/C – bill on confirming bank

In this case the CB finances the transaction for the whole period until funds are received from the IB. The financial load is borne by the confirming bank.

DEFERRED PAYMENT LETTER OF CREDIT

Financial load is for transit time plus usance time and borne by the beneficiary.

1. The importer applies for a letter of credit to his bank – issuing bank (IB).

2. The IB issues a deferred payment letter of credit and forwards it to an agent (advising bank) (AB) bank in the exporter's country with a request to forward it to the beneficiary.

3. The AB forwards a letter of credit to the beneficiary, if satisfied with the terms and conditions the beneficiary makes goods ready, despatches the goods and prepares the documents.

4. The beneficiary forwards the documents to the advising bank (AB).

5. AB forwards the documents to the IB.

6. IB checks the documents, if satisfied, forwards the documents to the importer.

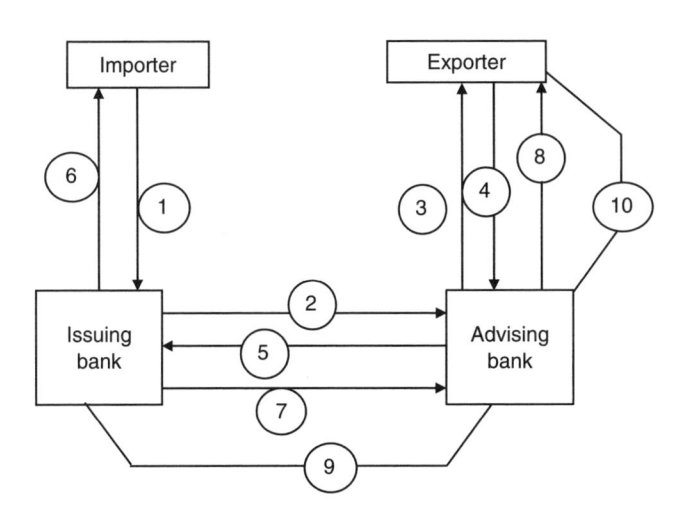

Figure 9.4 Deferred payment L/C

7. The IB acknowledges the receipt of documents to AB.

8. AB informs the beneficiary of safe receipt of the document.

9. On the due date IB debits the importer's account and remits funds to the AB for the credit of beneficiary's account.

10. AB credits the beneficiary's account and forwards payment advice.

In this case the beneficiary finances the transaction for the whole period until he receives payment. The financial load is borne by the beneficiary.

ACCEPTANCE LETTER OF CREDIT – BILL DRAWN ON ISSUING BANK

Financial load is borne by the beneficiary for the whole period.

1. The importer applies for a letter of credit to his bank -issuing bank (IB).

2. The IB issues a usance letter of credit with a Bill on IB and forwards it to an agent (advising bank) (AB) bank in the exporter's country with a request to forward it to the beneficiary.

3. The AB forwards a letter of credit to the beneficiary, if satisfied with the terms and conditions the beneficiary makes goods ready, despatches the goods and prepares the documents.

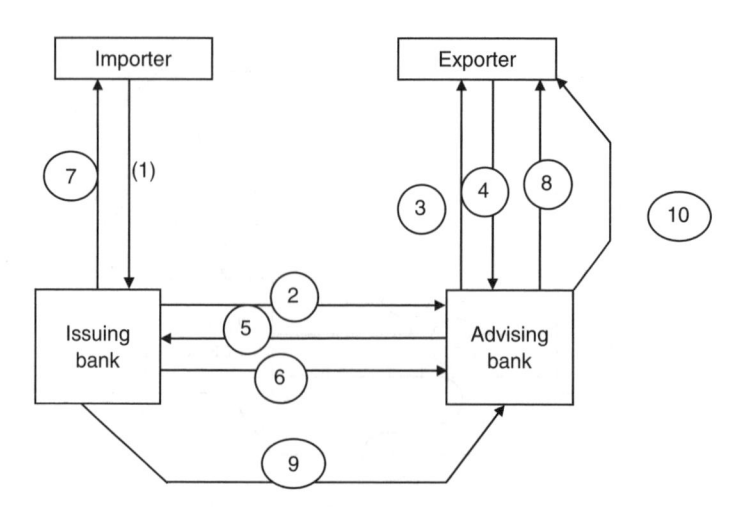

Figure 9.5 Acceptance L/C – bill on issuing bank

4. The Beneficiary forwards the documents to the advising bank (AB).

5. AB checks documents, if satisfied, forwards the documents to the IB.

6. IB checks the documents, if satisfied, accepts the bill of exchange and forwards acceptance advice with maturity date to AB.

7. IB forwards the documents to the importer.

8. AB forwards the acceptance advice with maturity date to the beneficiary.

9. On due date IB debits the importer's account and remits funds to the AB for the credit of the beneficiary's account.

10. The AB credits the beneficiary's account and forwards payment advice.

In this case the beneficiary finances the transaction for the whole period until he receives payment. The financial load for the whole period is borne by the beneficiary.

ACCEPTANCE LETTER OF CREDIT – BILL DRAWN ON CONFIRMING BANK

Financial load is borne by the beneficiary for the usance time and CB for transit time period.

1. The importer applies for a letter of credit to his bank – issuing bank (IB).

2. The IB issues a usance letter of credit with a Bill on CB and forwards it to an agent (advising bank) bank in the exporter's country with a request to allow the bill to be drawn on him (CB) and confirm the letter of credit and forward it to the beneficiary.

3. The AB/CB confirms the letter of credit and forwards it to the beneficiary.

4. The beneficiary, if satisfied with the terms and conditions makes goods ready, despatches the goods, prepares the documents and forwards the documents to the confirming bank (CB),

5. CB checks documents and, if satisfied, accepts the bill and gives the accepted bill, if required, to the beneficiary.

6. CB forwards the documents to IB with an advice of maturity date.

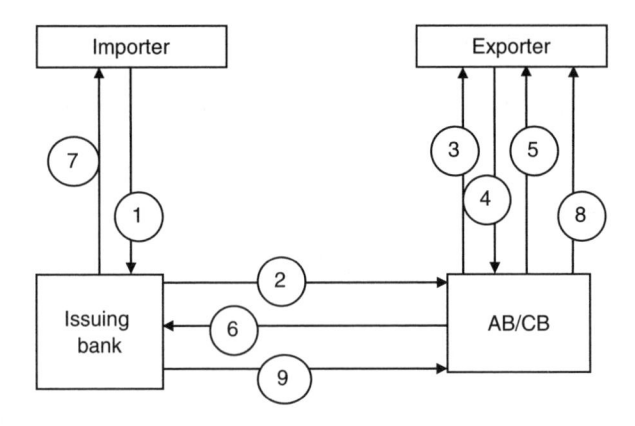

Figure 9.6 Acceptance L/C – bill on confirming bank

7. IB checks documents, if satisfied, forwards them to the importer.

8. On due date CB credit to the beneficiary's account and claims reimbursement from the IB.

9. On due date IB debits the importer's account and remits funds to the CB in reimbursement.

In this case the beneficiary finances the transaction for the usance period and CB for transit time until CB receives reimbursement. Both beneficiary and confirming bank share the financial load.

SIGHT NEGOTIATION LETTER OF CREDIT – BILL DRAWN ON ISSUING BANK

Financial load is borne by the negotiating Bank.

1. The importer applies for a letter of credit to his bank – issuing bank (IB).

2. The IB issues a sight negotiation letter of credit with a Bill on IB and forwards it to an agent (advising bank) (AB) bank in the exporter's country with a request to forward it to the beneficiary.

3. The AB forwards the letter of credit to the beneficiary, if satisfied with the terms and conditions the beneficiary makes goods ready, despatches the goods and prepares the documents.

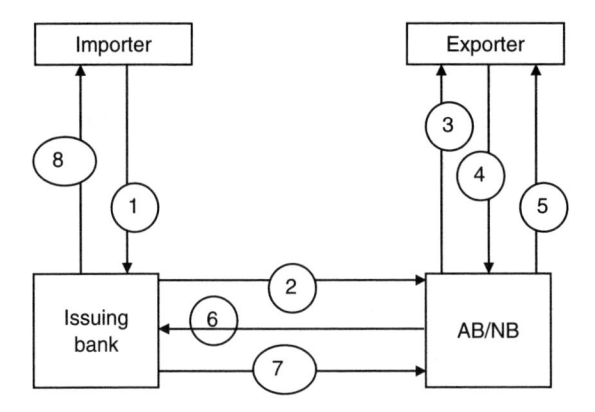

Figure 9.7 Sight negotiation letter of credit – bill drawn on issuing bank

4. The beneficiary forwards the documents to the advising bank (AB), and requests to AB to negotiate documents i.e. to provide him with funds against the documents until receipt of money from the issuing bank.

5. AB checks documents, if satisfied with documents and the beneficiary's business etc. AB agrees to negotiate documents with a condition of recourse that if, negotiating bank (NB) does not receive funds from the IB the beneficiary will give money back. This negotiation is with recourse as the NB is a third party and the bill is drawn on IB.

6. NB forwards the documents to the IB and claims reimbursement.

7. IB checks the documents, if satisfied, debits the importer's account and remits funds to the NB in reimbursement.

8. IB forwards the documents to the importer.

USANCE NEGOTIATION LETTER OF CREDIT – BILL DRAWN ON ISSUING BANK PAID AT MATURITY

Financial load is borne by the negotiating Bank.

1. The importer applies for a letter of credit to his bank – issuing bank (IB).

2. The IB issues a usance negotiations letter of credit with Bill on IB and forwards it to his AB in the exporter's country with a request to forward

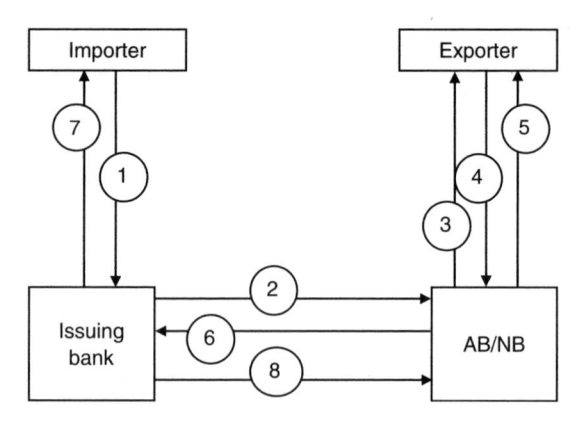

Figure 9.8 Usance negotiation L/C – bill drawn on issuing bank paid at maturity

it to the beneficiary and authorising to negotiate documents till maturity of the bill.

3. The AB forwards the letter of credit to the beneficiary, if satisfied with the terms and conditions the beneficiary makes goods ready, despatches the goods and prepares the documents.

4. The beneficiary forwards the documents to AB and requests to provide funds until the IB pays against the letter of credit.

5. AB checks the documents, if satisfied, negotiates the documents and credits the beneficiary's account. This act of negotiation is with recourse to the beneficiary.

6. NB forwards the documents to the IB informing having negotiated them under a letter of credit and claims reimbursement at maturity.

7. IB checks the documents, if satisfied, accepts the bill of exchange and forwards the documents to the importer with an advice of maturity date for payment.

8. On due date IB debits the importer's account and remits funds to the negotiating bank.

In this case the negotiating bank finances the transaction for the whole period until payment is received. The financial load is borne by the negotiating bank.

USANCE NEGOTIATION LETTER OF CREDIT – BILL DRAWN ON ISSUING BANK REIMBURSEMENT ON SIGHT BASIS

Financial load is by issuing Bank.

1. The importer applies for a letter of credit to his bank – issuing bank (IB).

2. The IB issues a usance negotiation letter of credit with Bill drawn on IB and forwards it to AB authorising AB to negotiate documents and claim reimbursement immediately.

3. The AB forwards the letter of credit to the beneficiary, if satisfied with the terms and conditions the beneficiary makes goods ready, despatches the goods and prepares the documents.

4. The beneficiary forwards the documents to the advising bank (AB) and requests to provide funds until the IB pays against a letter of credit.

5. AB checks the documents and if satisfied, negotiates documents and credits the beneficiary's account. AB is now NB, negotiating bank.

6. NB forwards the documents to IB and claims reimbursement immediately.

7. IB checks documents, if satisfied provides reimbursement to NB by debiting its assets account.

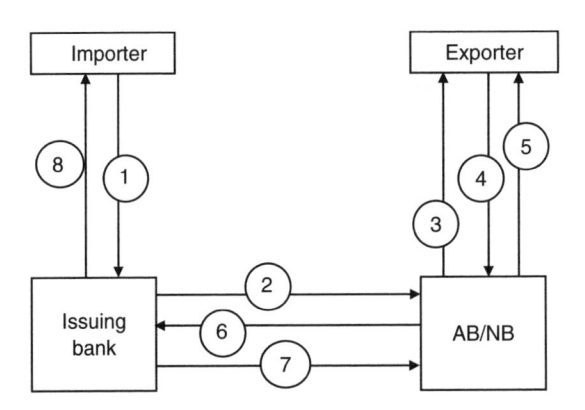

Figure 9.9 Usance negotiation L/C – bill on issuing bank re-imb. on sight basis

8. IB forwards the documents to the importer.

9. On maturity date IB debits the importer's account and credits its assets account.

In this case the beneficiary gets finances immediately and the IB finances the transaction for the whole period until it receives payment from the importer.

The financial load is borne by the issuing bank.

CHAPTER 10

Incoterms

BACKGROUND

The term INCOTERMS means International Commercial Terms for the use of buyers and sellers of goods. When a contract is made between a buyer and seller or between an importer and exporter the terms of sale and purchase for delivery of goods must be clarified to avoid any dispute at a later stage. Very often this is not done in the initial stage and oversight or lack of knowledge of the INCOTERMS on the part of the parties involved can cause difficulty to them and also their bankers.

These terms were established by the ICC (International Chamber of Commerce), after discussions with various interested parties. The value of the INCOTERMS is universally recognised. The utility and practical nature of these terms is clearly established and enables distribution of cost through application of INCOTERMS.

To avoid or minimise disputes and difficulties in trade the ICC introduced these rules in 1933. These rules have been revised periodically, keeping in mind the developments taking place from time to time and the revisions in the systems and procedures to handle international trade. These rules were last revised in 1999 and became effective from 1st January 2000.

A contract comes into being when two parties reach an agreement on a transaction. It is fairly universal principal that when one party accepts all the terms offered by the other party a valid contract is established. In principle these two parties are free to decide between themselves how the contract will be fulfilled, what price will be charged, how and when the payment will

---

* The text reproduced here is valid at the time of reproduction. As amendments may from time to time be made to the text, readers are requested to refer to the website www.iccwbo.org for the latest version and for more information on this ICC service.

Source: ICC Publication "Incoterms 2000".

be effected, who will carry out which functions, who will bear which costs of delivery, who will support which risks etc.

At times there are governments of countries who have certain regulations restricting international trade, which are required to be observed before entering into such transactions.

Purpose

The purpose is to provide a set of international rules for the interpretation of the most commonly used trade terms in local, national and international trade to:

- avoid misunderstanding the meaning of certain terms, disputes and litigation

- to adapt the terms to the increasing use of electronic data interchange (EDI)

- accommodate the changes in the use of technology and transportation systems for example

    - unitisation of cargo

    - use of containers

    - multimodal transport

    - roll on-roll off (ro-ro) traffic with road vehicles

    - railway wagons in "short-sea" marine transport

In every international trade transaction there are certain questions that must be asked by the parties concerned. Answers to such questions and assurance need to be satisfied before entering into a sale contract.

(a) Who will arrange to pay for the carriage of goods from one point to another?

(b) Who will bear the risk if these operations cannot be carried out?

(c) Who will bear the risk of loss of or damage to the goods in transit?

Structure of incoterms

For ease of understanding, the terms are grouped in four basically different categories: namely starting with the term whereby the seller only makes the goods available to the buyer at the seller's own premises (the "E" term – ex works); followed by the second group whereby the seller is called upon to deliver the goods to a carrier appointed by the buyer (the "F" terms – FCA (Free Carrier – shipping), FAS (Free Alongside Ship) and FOB (Free on Board)); continuing with "C" terms where the seller has to contract for the carriage, but without assuming the risk of loss or damage to the goods or additional costs due to events occurring after shipment and despatch (CFR (Cost and Freight), CIF (Cost, Insurance and Freight), CPT (Carriage Paid to) and CIP (Carriage and Insurance Paid)); and, finally, the "D" terms destination (DAF (Delivered at Frontier), DES Delivered ex Ship), DEQ (Delivered ex Quay), DDU (Delivered Duty Unpaid) and DDP (Delivered Duty Paid)).

The rights and obligations of the parties to the contract of sale with respect to the delivery of goods can be explained with the help of "INCOTERMS 2000" as under:

EX WORKS (......NAMED PLACE. "EXW")

"Ex Works" means that the seller fulfills his obligation to deliver when he has made the goods available at his premises (i.e. works, factory, warehouse etc) to the buyer in particular, the seller is not responsible for loading the goods on to the vehicle provided by the buyer or for clearing the goods for export, unless otherwise agreed.

The buyer bears all costs and risks involved in taking the goods from the seller's premises to the desired destination.

This term thus represents the minimum obligation for the seller. This term should not be used when the buyer cannot carry out directly or indirectly the export formalities. In such circumstances, the FCA term should be used.

FREE CARRIER (......NAMED PLACE. "FCA")

"Free Carrier" means that the seller fulfills his obligation to deliver when he has handed over the goods, cleared for export, into the charge of the carrier named by the buyer at the named place or point. If no such precise point is indicated by the buyer, the seller may choose within the place or range stipulated where the carrier shall take the goods into his charge. When according to commercial practice, the seller's assistance is required in making the contract with the carrier (such as in rail or air transport) the seller may act at the buyer's risk and expense.

This term may be used for any mode of transportation, including multimodal transport. "Carrier" means any person who, in a contract of carriage undertakes to perform or to procure the performance of carriage by rail, road, sea, air, inland waterway or by a combination of such modes. If the buyer instructs the seller to deliver the cargo to a person e.g. freight forwarder who is not a "carrier", the seller is deemed to have fulfilled his obligation to deliver the goods when they are in the custody of the person.

"Transport terminal" means the railway terminal, a freight station, a container terminal or yard, a multipurpose cargo terminal or any similar receiving point.

"Container" includes any equipment used to utilize cargo, e.g. all types of containers and/or flats, whether ISO accepted or not, trailers, swap bodies, ro-ro equipment, igloos, and applies to all modes of transport.

FREE ALONGSIDE SHIP (...NAMED PORT OF SHIPMENT. "FAS")

"Free Alongside Ship" means that the seller fulfills his obligation to deliver when the goods have been placed alongside the vessel on the quay or in lighters at the named port of shipment. This means that the buyer has to bear all costs and risks of loss or damage to the goods from that moment.

The FAS term requires the buyer to clear the goods for export. It should not be used when the buyer cannot carry out directly or indirectly the export formalities.

This term can only be used for sea or inland waterway transport.

FREE ON BOARD (...NAMED PORT OF SHIPMENT. "FOB")

"Free on Board" means that the seller fulfills his obligation to deliver when the goods have passed over the ship's rail at the named port of shipment. This means that the buyer has to bear all costs and risks of loss of or damage to the goods from that point.

The FOB term requires the seller to clear the goods for export. This term can only be used for sea or inland waterway transport. When the ship's rail serves no practical purpose, such as in the case of roll-on/roll-off or container traffic, use of the FCA term is more appropriate.

COST AND FREIGHT (..NAMED PORT OF DESTINATION. "CFR")

"Cost and Freight" means that the seller must pay the costs and freight necessary to bring the goods to the named port of destination but the risk of loss or damage to the goods, as well as any additional costs due to events occurring after the time the goods have been delivered on board the vessel, is transferred from the seller to the buyer when the goods pass the ship's rail in the port of shipment.

The CFR requires the seller to clear the goods for export. This term can only be used for sea and inland waterway transport. When the ship's rail serves no practical purpose, such as in the case of roll-on/roll-off or container traffic, use of the CPT term is more appropriate.

COST, INSURANCE AND FREIGHT (..NAMED PORT OF DESTINATION. "CIF")

"Cost, Insurance and Freight" means that the seller has the same obligation as under CFR but with the addition that he has to procure marine insurance against the buyer's risk of loss of damage to the goods during the carriage. The seller contracts for insurance and pays the insurance premium.

The buyer should note that under the CIF term the seller is only required to obtain insurance on minimum coverage.

The CIF term requires the seller to clear the goods for export.

This term can only be used for sea and inland waterway transport. When the ship's rail serves no practical purposes such as in the case of roll-on/roll-off or container traffic, use of the CIP term is more appropriate.

CARRIAGE PAID TO (...NAMED PLACE OF DESTINATION. "CPT")

"Carriage paid to ... " means that the seller pays the freight for the carriage of the goods to the named destination. The risk of loss of or damage to the goods, as well as any additional costs due to events occurring after the time the goods have been delivered to the carrier, is transferred from the seller to the buyer when the goods have been delivered into the custody of the carrier.

"Carrier" means any person who, in a contract of carriage, undertakes to perform or to procure the performance of carriage by rail, road, sea, inland waterway or by a combination of such modes.

If subsequent carriers are used for the carriage to the agreed destination, the risk passes when the goods have been delivered to the first carrier.

The CPT term requires the seller to clear the goods for export.

This term may be used for any mode of transport including multimodal transport.

CARRIAGE AND INSURANCE PAID TO (..NAMED PLACE OF DESTINATION. "CIP")

"Carriage and insurance paid to ... " means that the seller has the same obligations as under CPT but with the addition that the seller has to procure cargo insurance against the buyer's risk of loss or damage to the goods during the carriage. The seller contracts for insurance and pays the insurance premium.

The buyer should note that under the CIP term the seller is only required to obtain insurance on minimum coverage. The CIP term requires the seller to clear the goods for export. This term may be used for any mode of transport including multimodal transport.

DELIVERED AT FRONTIER (...NAMED PLACE. "DAF")

"Delivered at Frontier" means that the seller fulfills his obligation to deliver when the goods have been made available, cleared for export, at the named point and place at the frontier, but before the customs border of the adjoining country. The term "Frontier" may be used for any frontier including that of the country of export. Therefore, it is of vital importance that the frontier in question be defined precisely by always naming the point and place in the term. This term is primarily intended to be used when goods are carried by rail or road, but it may be used for any mode of transport.

DELIVERED EX SHIP (...NAMED PORT OF DESTINATION. "DES")

"Delivered ex Ship" means that the seller fulfills his obligations to deliver when the goods have been made available to the buyer on board the ship without clearing for import at the named port of destination. The seller has to bear all the costs and risks involved in bringing the goods to the named port of destination.

This term can only be used for sea or inland waterway transport.

DELIVERED EX QUAY (DUTY PAID) (...NAMED PORT OF DESTINATION. "DEQ")

"Delivered ex Quay (duty paid)" means that the seller fulfills his obligation to deliver when he has made the goods available to the buyer on the quay (wharf at the named port of destination), cleared for importation. The seller has to bear all risks and costs including duties, taxes and other charges of delivering the goods thereto.

This term should not be used if the seller is unable directly or indirectly to obtain the import licence.

If the parties wish the buyer to clear the goods for importation and pay the duty the words "duty unpaid" should be used instead of "duty paid".

If the parties wish to exclude from the seller's obligations some of the costs payable upon importation of the goods (such as value added tax (VAT)), this should be made clear by adding words to this effect: "Delivered ex quay, VAT unpaid (… named port of destination)" This term can only be used for sea or inland waterway transport purposes.

DELIVERED DUTY UNPAID (NAMED PLACE OF DESTINATION "DDU")

"Delivered duty unpaid": means that the seller fulfills his obligation to deliver the goods at the named place in the country of importation. The seller has to bear the costs and risks involved in bringing the goods thereto (excluding duties, taxes and other official charges payable upon importation as well as the costs and risks of carrying out customs formalities). The buyer has to pay any additional costs and to bear any risks caused by his failure to clear the goods for import in time.

If the parties wish the seller to carry out customs formalities, bear the costs and risks resulting therefrom, this has to be made clear by adding words to this effect.

If the parties wish to include in the seller's obligation some of the costs payable upon importation of the goods (such as value added tax (VAT)), this should be made clear by adding words to this effect: "Delivered duty unpaid, VAT paid (… named place of destination)".

This term may be used irrespective of the mode of transport.

DELIVERED DUTY PAID (...NAMED PLACE OF DESTINATION. "DDP")

"Delivered duty paid" means the seller fulfills his obligation to deliver when the goods have been made available at the named palace in the country of importation. The seller has to bear the risks and costs, including duties, taxes and other charges of delivering the goods thereto, cleared for importation. Whilst the EXW term represents the minimum obligation for the seller, DDP represents the maximum obligation.

This term should not be used if the seller is unable directly or indirectly to obtain the import licence.

If the parties wish the buyer to clear the goods for importation and to pay the duty, the term DDU should be used.

If the parties wish to exclude from the seller's obligation some of the costs payable upon importation of the goods (such as value added tax (VAT)), this should be made clear by adding words to this effect: "Delivered duty paid, VAT unpaid (… named place of destination)".

This term may be used irrespective of the mode of transport.

COST SHARING BETWEEN SELLERS AND BUYERS – INCOTERMS

Seller's costs to provide goods:	Mode	Seller's obligations/costs	INCOTERM
At his own place			EXW – EX WOKS (------- named place)
At the named port of shipment (unloaded) Freight and other costs and risk to be borne by buyer	Ship Inland water-ways		FAS – FREE ALONDSIDE SHIP (… named port of shipment)
To first Carrier at the named place (unloaded). Freight and other costs and risks to be borne by buyer	Multi-modal		FCA – FREE CARRIER (------ named place)
Loaded on the named ship. Freight and other costs and risks to be borne by buyer	Ship		FOB – FREE ON BOARD (--- named port of shipment)
Unloaded at the port of destination. Freight is paid, but other costs and risks to be borne by buyer	Ship		CFR – COST AND FREIGHT (--- named port of destination)
At the named place of destination. Freight is paid, but other costs and risks to be borne by buyer	Multi-modal		CPT – CARRIAGE PAID TO (--- named place of destination)
At the named port of destination. Goods unloaded. Freight is paid but other costs and risks to be borne by buyer	Ship		DES – DELIVERED EX SHIP (-- named port of destination)
At the named port of destination. Freight and insurance paid. Goods unloaded but other costs to be borne by buyer	Ship		CIF – COST INSURANCE AND FREIGHT (--- named port of destination)
At the named port of destination. Freight and insurance paid. Goods unloaded but other costs to be borne by buyer	Multi-modal		CIP – CARRIAGE AND INSURANCE PAID TO (--- named place of destination)
At the named place. Goods unloaded but other costs to be borne by buyer	Multi-modal		DAF – DELIVERED AT FRONTIER (--- named place)
Goods on the ship at the named port of destination. Unloading and other costs, risks to be borne by buyer	Ship		DEQ – DELIVERED EX QUAY (-- named port of destination)
At the named place of destination. Import duty to be paid by buyer	Multi-modal		DDU – DELIVERED DUTY UNPAID (-- named place of destination)
At the named place of destination including import duty paid	Multi-modal		DDP – DELIVERED DUTY PAID (-- named place of destination)

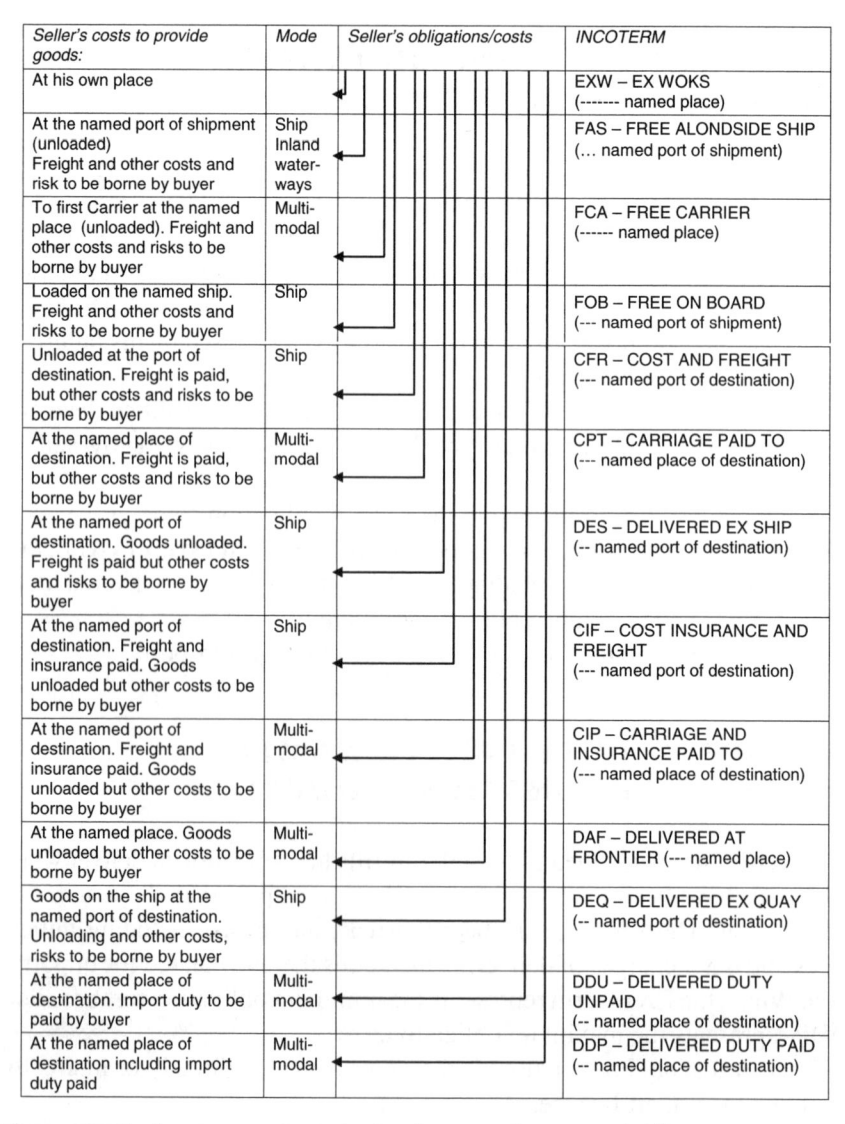

Figure 10.1 Incoterms – cost sharing between buyers and sellers

CHAPTER 11

Documents in Foreign Trade – Significance

GENESIS

A letter of credit is an undertaking between the issuing bank and the beneficiary to pay, accept bill(s) of exchange and make payment on maturity provided the beneficiary fulfills the requirement under a credit. The applicant requests the bank to issue a letter of credit to ensure that he receives the right quality and quantity of goods from the supplier. Banks do not deal in goods but only with documents. The issuing bank requires the beneficiary to present the documents evidencing the quality and quantity of the goods dispatched by him to meet the requirement of a letter of credit. Therefore, both the applicant and the issuing bank should be clear about the type of documents required and the significance of each document.

Extreme care must be taken in listing documents under a letter of credit transaction. The applicant must give precise instructions to the issuing bank. Some specific documents are a requirement when dealing with particular countries and import or export licences may be required etc. There are articles of the UCP 600, which refer to different type of documents. It is important that the documents required under a letter of credit mechanism must satisfy the requirements under UCP 600.

Banks require each document in original unless more copies are asked for under the credit. Under article 17(b)(c)(d) of UCP 600 banks accept as original(s), document(s) produced by reprographic, automated or computerised systems, and carbon copies, provided it is marked original and signed.

The applicant should specifically indicate the document(s) required and by whom these documents should be issued, and with required details or contents thereof. Otherwise banks will accept them as presented, provided they are in compliance with the terms and conditions of a letter of credit and are not issued by the beneficiary him or herself.

The details of most common documents are given hereunder.

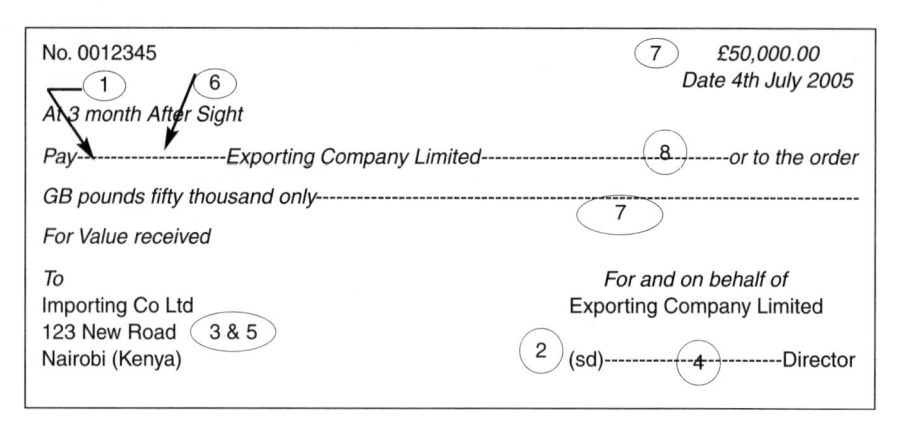

```
No. 0012345                                           7    £50,000.00
      1         6                                          Date 4th July 2005
At 3 month After Sight
Pay-------------------Exporting Company Limited-----------------8-------or to the order
GB pounds fifty thousand only----------------------------------------------------
                                                   7
For Value received

To                                              For and on behalf of
Importing Co Ltd                                Exporting Company Limited
123 New Road    3 & 5                        2
Nairobi (Kenya)                                   (sd)----------4---------Director
```

Figure 11.1 Specimen of bill of exchange

BILL OF EXCHANGE

The requirements of a bill of exchange are:

1. it must be written in ink or printed to prevent alteration

2. drawn by the seller/beneficiary

3. drawn on the drawee (IB in case of L/C)

4. must be signed by the drawer/beneficiary

5. requiring the person to whom it is addressed, drawee (on signature becomes the acceptor) to pay

6. on demand or at a fixed or determinable future time

7. a sum certain in money

8. to the payee, a specified person or to his order.

For ease of reference the phrases are numbered to correspond to the parts of the bill of exchange shown above. All of the information above must be shown on every bill of exchange.

A documentary letter of credit will stipulate when payment is to be made and the bill of exchange must be drawn accordingly. In the diagram the bill of exchange calls for payment three months after sight (this is known as a tenor bill). If a bill of exchange is drawn at sight i.e. without writing a period it is called a "sight" bill, which requires immediate payment by the drawee on presentation of the bill of exchange.

The bill of exchange must be worded to conform exactly to the terms of the credit and the sum specified must not exceed the amount of the credit. In addition the capacity of all signatories must be stated if the forms "for", "per" or "pro" are used.

Unless a documentary letter of credit stipulates that bills of exchange are required in duplicate, a single (sola) bill of exchange will be acceptable. Bill of exchange forms may be purchased from printers or stationers but bills of exchange may also be drawn on a company's notepaper or even a blank sheet of paper.

When a bill of exchange is being presented for payment it needs to be properly endorsed by the payee, if required.

INVOICE

A Commercial invoice must be issued by the beneficiary of a letter of credit addressed to the applicant/importer of the goods. An invoice gives details of the goods, which are the basis of the transaction between the exporter and the importer. It is usually completed on the exporter's own headed invoice form, and several copies are normally required for use by Customs and Excise authorities overseas (UCP 600 Article 18(a)).

The invoice must carry a description of the goods, stating prices and terms exactly as specified in the credit, as well as shipping marks. The following details are usually required and the inclusion of other information, for example export and/or import licence numbers, may also be necessary, if required under a letter of credit. Letter of credit usually requires three or more copies of the invoice.

1. Beneficiary's name and address (usually exporter/seller)

2. Accreditor's name and address (usually importer/buyer)

3. Place and date of issue

4. Shipment terms

5. Marks and numbers on packages

6. Number and type of packages

7. Description of the goods

8. Cost of freight and insurance (if specifically requested)

9. The quantity of goods

10. Total amount payable

11. Signature of the exporter, if required under L/C.

PRO-FORMA INVOICE

It is a price quotation by the seller/exporter to a potential buyer/importer. This document gives the details of goods and other terms and conditions of sale of the goods. The pro-forma invoice can serve various purposes for the buyer/importer i.e. to apply for import licence and can be used to tender for an export contract etc. If the buyer/importer accepts the quotation, he will place a firm order and it will be considered as a "sale contract". A commercial invoice will be sent later.

BILL OF LADING

DEFINITION: A Bill of Lading is a memorandum of the contract of carriage of goods signed by or on behalf of the master of a ship, certifying that goods have been received on board in good order for transportation and delivery as specified in the document.

It is a receipt given by the shipping company upon shipment of the goods and a document of title to the goods, enabling the consignee to transfer the title by endorsement and delivery. As such it will be required by the importer to clear the goods at the port of destination. It is a quasi-negotiable document because unlike a bill of exchange, the transferee takes it subject to equities. (The transferee will not have better title than the transferor).

In USA, Bill of Lading Act 1916 makes a Bill of Lading a fully negotiable instrument if issued in the USA.

A documentary letter of credit will specify what type of bill of lading is required. It will also indicate what additional information must be shown on the bill of lading.

A bill of lading normally embodies the following:

1. The name of the shipping company

2. The name of the shipper (usually the exporter)

3. The name and address of the importer (consignee) or ORDER

4. The name and address of the notify party (the person to be notified on arrival of the shipment, usually the importer)

5. The name of the carrying vessel

6. The names of the ports of shipment and discharge

7. The shipping marks and numbers identifying the goods

8. A brief description of the goods (possibly including weights and dimensions)

9. The number of packages

10. Whether freight is payable or has been paid

11. The number of originals in the set

12. The signature of the ship's master or his agent

13. The date on which the goods were received for shipment and/or loaded on the vessel (this must not be later than the shipment date indicated in the credit)

14. The signature of the exporter (or his agent) and his designation if applicable

Bills of lading are usually made out and signed in sets of two or three original copies known as negotiable copies, any one of which can give title to the goods. The number of copies in a set is shown on each copy. There may also be non-negotiable (unsigned) copies, which are not documents of title and are normally used for record purposes. The credit will indicate how the various copies of the bill of lading are to be distributed.

The reverse of the bill of lading bears the terms and conditions of the contract of carriage. The clauses on most bills of lading will be similar in effect if not in wording. A bill of lading should be "clean", i.e. contain no superimposed clause recording a defective condition of the goods or their packing.

The goods can be consigned to ORDER, which means the importer can authorise someone to collect the goods on his behalf. In this case, the exporter will endorse on the reverse of the bill of lading. If the importer (consignee) is named, the goods will only be released to him, unless the importer transfers his rights by endorsement. (The bill of lading must however provide for this).

TYPES OF BILLS OF LADING

"Shipped" or "Shipped on Board" bill of lading indicates that the goods have been received on board ship and will bear a clause to that effect.

A "Received for Shipment" bill of lading merely signifies that the ship owner has the goods in his custody, but they have not yet been placed on board the vessel. It can be marked "Shipped on Board" (or similar) by the shipping company once the goods have been received on the vessel. This is known as "on board" notation and should be dated and signed or initialled by the shipping company.

Through Bill of Lading: If ocean transport forms only part of the complete journey and overland transport has to be used as well, a "Through" bill of lading can be issued to cover all stages of the journey.

Clean Bill of Lading: A clean bill of lading is one which bears no superimposed clause or a notation that expressly indicates the defective condition of the goods or the packaging. The bill of lading indicates that the carrier has received the goods in apparent good order and condition.

Claused / Foul or Dirty / Unclean Bill of Lading: is a bill of lading, which contains a superimposed clause expressly declaring that the goods or packaging is defective. In this case the ship owners can refuse to accept liability to deliver the goods in good order and condition. This type of bill of lading is not acceptable to banks.

"Transhipment" bill of lading is issued if the goods have to be off-loaded and re-loaded on to a second ship because there is not a vessel available to complete the full journey to the port of destination. The transhipment port will be shown on the bill of lading.

Container Bill of Lading: Containers play an important role in the international business and "Container" bills of lading may be issued to cover goods from port to port or from inland point of departure to inland point of destination. It indicates that the goods are carried in a container as one cargo.

Stale Bill of Lading: If the original bill of lading reaches the consignee after the arrival of the vessel at the destination, is known as a "stale bill of lading". The consignee is not able to get the goods cleared from the port within the time allowed by the port authorities. In such cases the consignee has to obtain a bond, known as "Shipping Guarantee" from his bank to get delivery of the goods from the port authorities.

Charter Party Bill of Lading: A charter party bill of lading is by a charter party who has hired a ship/vessel or full or part of the space in the ship/vessel for his use. The charter party bills of lading are issued subject to the terms and conditions as agreed by the hirer and the ship owners. The charter party bills of lading are not acceptable to banks unless authorised under a letter of credit, because the ship owner may refuse to deliver the goods if the charter party does not pay hire charges.

House Bill of Lading: It is issued by Cargo Consolidators who collect cargo from various shippers and give it to the shipping company in their own name. By combining the shipment from various parties the consolidators are able to obtain bulk discount, which is better than the rates an individual shipper has to pay.

The shipping company issues one master bill of lading on the basis of cargo and the consolidator issues their own House bill of lading. The master bill of lading is sent to the cargo consolidator(s) and to their agents at the port of discharge to take the delivery of the entire cargo. The consignee holding the House bill of lading takes the delivery of the goods from the agent on presentation of the document.

Short Bill of Lading: It is also know as "Short Form of Bill of Lading". It is a bill of lading, which does not bear full details of the terms and conditions of carriage of goods that are printed on a full bill of lading.

AIR WAYBILL

An air waybill is a receipt for goods for despatch by air. It takes the place of the bill of lading but is not a document of title and the importer can take possession of the goods without it. Air waybills (or "air consignment notes" as they are also known) are issued in a minimum of three and frequently in sets of ten or more.

The credit may ask for certain specific information or instructions to be shown in the Air Waybill but the following details are those normally given.

- The names and addresses of the exporter, importer and the carrier (airline)

- The names of the airports of departure and destination together with details of any special route

- The date of the flight

- The declared value for customs purposes

- The number of packages with marks, weights, quantity and dimensions

- The freight charge per unit of weight/volume

- A description of the goods

- Whether freight charge has been prepaid or will be paid at destination

- The signature of the exporter (or his agent)

- The place and date of issue

- The signature of the issuing carrier (or his agent)

The air waybill should also bear the carrier's stamp indicating the flight number and departure date on which the goods were sent.

CERTIFICATE OF ORIGIN

This is a signed declaration stating the country of origin of the goods. This certificate may be required for various purposes i.e. by the customs and excise authority of certain countries for the purpose of assessing import duty. In some cases this certificate may be incorporated into the commercial invoice. Generally it has to be authenticated by a Chamber of Commerce of the exporter's country or as required by the letter of credit. A certificate of origin is a signed statement providing evidence of the origin of the goods. It is issued in a mandatory form and manner in most countries, although prepared by the exporter or his agent. It is usually certified by an independent official organisation, for example a chamber of commerce and contains details of shipment to which it relates:

- Origin of the goods.

- Bears the signature and seal or stamp of the certifying body.

- If the credit calls for a "certificate of origin" without giving further details, banks will accept the document tendered even if issued by the beneficiary (seller), providing it is not inconsistent with the other documents.

CERTIFICATE OF INSPECTION

A certificate of inspection is issued by an approved inspecting organisation after inspection or examination of the goods. It is used to ensure that the goods to be shipped are of the required standard and quality. Terms such as "first class", "well known", "qualified", "independent" etc. should not be used to describe the issuer. If used, the banks will accept the relative documents as presented.

Banks will accept such documents as presented where the credit does not stipulate by whom such documents are to be issued and their wording or data content.

PACKING LIST

Packing list gives the details of the goods i.e. item and number in a package. It is often required by the customs authorities to facilitate spot checks or thorough investigation. It does not necessarily give details of the cost or price of the goods.

POST PARCEL/COURIER RECEIPT

A post parcel receipt is issued by the post office for goods sent by parcel post – it acts both as a receipt and as proof of despatch. It is not a document of title. Goods sent by post should be consigned to the party specified in the documentary credit.

A courier receipt is an acknowledgement issued by the courier company for goods received for despatch by courier. It acts both as a receipt and as proof of despatch. It is not a document of title. Goods sent by courier should be consigned to the party specified in the documentary credit.

FORWARDING AGENT'S RECEIPT

A forwarding agent arranges the transport of the goods and will issue a receipt stating that he has taken charge of the goods for delivery to the importer. The forwarder is often the agent of the importer and exporters should ensure that the details on the receipt are exactly as required by the credit before relinquishing control of the goods.

RAIL, ROAD CONSIGNMENT NOTES/TRUCK AND CARRIER RECEIPT

These are issued by the rail authorities or road haulage companies and are receipts for the goods accepted for consignment. They are not documents of title and the goods are released to the importer on application, providing the importer has proof of identification. They should show the name of the importer, the date of despatch, bear the stamp of the issuing authorities and be marked 'Freight Paid' where appropriate.

CONSULAR INVOICE

This type of document is sometimes required by certain countries of the world for customs purposes. It is a specially printed document that can be obtained from embassies or consulates. It is completed by the exporter and usually authenticated by the consulate of the importer's country.

VETERINARY CERTIFICATE/HEALTH CERTIFICATE

This may be called for when livestock/domestic animals/agricultural products are being exported. A veterinary certificate or a health certificate must be signed by the approved Health Authority of the exporter's country.

NON-NEGOTIABLE SEA WAYBILL (UCP ARTICLE 21)

The use of this document is increasing in European, Scandinavian, North American and certain Far Eastern Trade areas. Under this article, banks will, unless otherwise stipulated in the credit, accept a document, however named, which appears on its face to indicate that the document covers all the terms and conditions of carriage relating to the goods in question and fulfills the normal requirement of documents under a credit and negotiable sea waybill.

MULTIMODAL TRANSPORT DOCUMENT (UCP ARTICLE 19)

It should be clearly understood by the parties to the credit that this covers a traditional ocean bill of lading and is one that allows for the contract of carriage from the place of receipt of goods to the place of delivery by more than one mode of transport. The document however named must appear to:

- indicate the name of the carrier and be signed by:

- The carrier or a named agent for or on behalf of the carrier or

- The master or a named agent for or on behalf of the master

Any signature by the carrier, master or agent must be identified as that of the carrier, master or agent.

The information in the document must match in accordance with the letter of credit.

COMBINED TRANSPORT DOCUMENT

Nowadays, with the widespread use of containerised transport, goods are transported from a place of "taking in charge" of the cargo (container) to a place of "delivery" in the same container, but on different modes of transport i.e. by lorry to a sea port and the container will be loaded on a ship. It will be shipped to a port of destination, unloaded, transferred to another lorry, and then by road, to a place of delivery.

The goods (container), although, carried by two or more modes of transport, are shipped under a single contract of carriage of goods. A single bill of lading is issued and it is known as "Combined Transport Document" (CTD).

FIATA BILL OF LADING

FIATA – (International Federation of Freight Forwarders Association). Documents are issued under licence only to members of FIATA or affiliated organisations, for example. The Institute of Freight Forwarders Limited. The exporter receives forwarder's receipt in exchange for the goods. The FIATA bill of lading is a combined transport document, which is issued by a member of the Institute of Freight Forwarders in the United Kingdom. FIATA bill of lading is approved by the International Chamber of Commerce and is acceptable to banks. A FIATA Combined Transport Bill of Lading serves as evidence that a freight forwarder is acting as a principal, i.e accepting carrier responsibility for performance of the entire contract of carriage and responsibility for loss or damage.

OTHER DOCUMENTS

If a credit calls for an attestation or certification of weight in the case of transport other than by sea, banks will accept a weight stamp or declaration of weight which appears to have been superimposed on the transport document by the carrier or his agent unless the credit specifically stipulates that the attestation or certification of weight must be by means of a separate document.

Note

If a person signs a document (e.g. a bill of exchange) on behalf of a company or another party his signature must be preceded by one of the following forms: "for and behalf of", "pp" or "per pro". If the first of the three forms is used the designation or official position of the signatory must be shown against the signature. The forms "pp" or "per pro" do not require further justification.

CHAPTER 12

Negotiation of Documents

MEANINGS OF NEGOTIATION

1. There are several meanings of the word "negotiation". The general term is applied to arranging a contract or discussing the terms and conditions of a contract. The legal connotation of the word "negotiation" refers particularly in connection to cheques and bills of exchange when transferred from one person to another. Negotiation is a means of financing an outward collection or funding the payee of a cheque, bill of exchange or the beneficiary of documents under a letter of credit payable abroad.

2. We refer to the meaning of the beneficiary of documents under a letter of credit payable abroad. When a bank negotiates an outward collection it is buying its customer's bills and/or documents drawn on an overseas buyer. It is a convenient method of providing the exporter with working capital. The bank in buying the bill and/or documents will look to the overseas buyer as a source of repayment. In the event of non-payment or delayed payment, the negotiating bank exercises the right of recourse to its customer, the drawer. Therefore, if payment does not arrive within a reasonable time, the negotiating bank will debit its customer's account with the amount advanced plus interest. The cost of negotiation is similar to loan interest when provided by a bank.

3. When a bank negotiates, it pays its customer/the beneficiary straight away and sends the bill and/or documents to the issuing bank.

4. Under English law the negotiating bank may become a holder in due course of the bill of exchange when it negotiates, and as such is given a right of action against the drawer in the event of default by the drawee. Should instruction be given for the bill not to be protested, this right is lost; as a result negotiating banks rely for reimbursement, when a bill is unpaid, on the specific right of recourse signed by their customer. The currency of the bill/or documents, be it in GB Pound or US Dollars, makes no difference.

ROLE OF ADVISING AND CONFIRMING BANKS

The seller may sometimes present documents that do not meet the letter of credit requirements. In such a case, the bank may act in one of the following ways:

1. Return the documents to the beneficiary (seller) to have them amended for re-submission within the validity of the credit and within the period of time after date of issuance specified in the credit.

2. Send the documents for collection. or

3. Return the documents to the beneficiary for sending through his own bankers, if the confirming or advising bank is not the beneficiary's bank. or

4. If authorised by the beneficiary, cable or send message by SWIFT or write to the issuing bank for authority to pay, accept or negotiate. The bank must provide a full list of irregularities to the issuing bank. or

5. Call for an indemnity from the beneficiary or from a bank, as appropriate, i.e. to pay, accept or negotiate on their undertaking that any payment made will be refunded by the party giving the indemnity, together with interest and all charges, if the issuing bank refuses to provide reimbursement against documents that do not meet the credit requirements.

6. Based on practical experience, and with the agreement of the beneficiary, pay, accept or negotiate "under reserve", i.e. retain the right of recourse against the beneficiary if the issuing bank refuses to provide reimbursement against documents that do not meet the credit requirements.

ROLE OF ISSUING BANK

In case of discrepancies in documents the following options are available to the issuing bank:

- Check all documents carefully
- Make a list of all irregularities
- Contact the buyer/applicant and seek his instructions immediately
- If the buyer/applicant is not ready to accept the documents, inform the advising/negotiating bank immediately of non-payment or non-acceptance of the documents with details of irregularities within five banking days following the day of presentation/receipt of documents (UCP 600 Article 14 (b)).

NEGOTIATION OF DOCUMENTS UNDER RESERVE

FORM OF AN INDEMNITY FOR DISCREPANCIES

The Manager   Date: _____

Bank's name _____

Address _____

_____

Dear Sir,

Letter of Credit No. _____ issued by _____

In consideration of your paying us the sum of _____ (amount in words and figures)

_____

under the above-mentioned credit we hereby indemnify you from all consequences which may arise notwithstanding the following discrepancies in the documents.

1. _____
2. _____
3. _____
4. _____
5. _____
6. _____
7. _____
8. _____
9. _____
10. _____

_____   _____
Signed by the beneficiary   Signed by the beneficiary's bank or third party

LETTER OF CREDIT – PROCESSING COST (INDICATIVES)

The following is an example of the cost of processing a letter of credit. The scale of charges may vary from one bank to another.

Activity	Scale of charges	Amount
Issuing of letter	Sight or Usance L/C 0.4% for 3 months or part thereof. Minimum £50 or US$80. Usance charges 0.1% per month	
Postage/Telex or SWIFT charges	£20/US$35. Courier charges UK/Europe £10/US$20 Other countries	
Advising bank's commission	By Mail £15 Brief telex/SWIFT £30. Full telex/SWIFT £50	
Advise of due date etc. Postage/Courier	Telex £20/US$35	
Handling charges	£20/US$35 per month or part thereof if bill not accepted within 30 days of intimation	
Amendment fee	£40/US$65 per amendment. Plus 0.3% for 3 months or part thereof 0.5% up to 90 days, thereafter 0.1% per month or part thereof	
Payment charges	0.2% per payment Minimum £40/US$65	
Advising L/C	£40/US$65	
Pre-advising L/C	£40/US$65.	
Discrepancy fee	£40/US$65 Plus £10/US$20 Postage/ telephone	
Confirmation charges L/C	0.3% for 3 months Minimum £50/US$80, thereafter 0.1% per month or part thereof 1 per mille per month confirmation commission	
Payment commission	2% Minimum £40/US$65 per payment plus telex/cable charges £20/US$35	
Transfer of L/C	0.4% of amount min. £50/US$80	
Any other out of pocket expenses		
Total		

Figure 12.1 Letter of credit – inactive processing cost

CHAPTER 13

Factoring and Forfaiting

FACTORING: GENESIS

Factoring represents the sale of outstanding receivables related to export of goods by the exporter to overseas buyers. The seller of the receivables thus transfers the risk of default on contractual obligations arising from non-payment by the buyer to a third party. The seller of the receivables is paid discounted value of the receivables, arising either from a letter of credit, guarantee or bill. Factoring is possible with recourse or without recourse. The advantages enjoyed by an exporter due to such financing are immediate payment after export. The exporter can enjoy financial benefit, in the case of without recourse, at no risks arising from the deal after factoring.

FACTORING AND CASH FLOW

Factoring is the selling of invoices by a seller to a third party called a factor. Factors may be independent or subsidiaries of major banks and financial institutions. The factor processes invoices and allows the seller to withdraw money against the amount owed under the invoices. It is used by businesses to improve their cash flow and also to reduce administration and overhead costs. Another method used to finance the exporters is called invoice discounting. This way the factor allows the business to withdraw money against the invoices. The business maintains control over the administration of the sales ledger. Both of the procedures are used by businesses to improve their cash flow. It helps the business to boost cash flow or release money for expansion or other purposes. Factoring is commonly used by companies selling goods on a wholesale basis to businesses on a credit basis. It is not normally available to retailers or to cash traders.

After signing the agreement, the factor will agree to advance up to an agreed percentage of approved invoices or up to a certain credit limit. All sales are required to go through the factor.

FACTORING AND LEGAL IMPLICATIONS

Most factors require notice of a certain period to end the service, though some have notice periods of a long time of up to for example a year or so which could be expensive. The debtor should understand the terms and conditions of the contract before signing the agreement. Factoring is a complex, long-term agreement that could have a major effect on the business development. It is advisable to the debtor to seek an independent legal opinion from a solicitor on the legal and financial implications of factoring.

FACTORING MECHANISM

1. Seller raises an invoice on buyer, with instructions to pay the factor directly, and sends it to the customer.

2. Seller sends a copy of the invoice to the factor.

3. The factor pays an agreed percentage of the invoice amount to the seller.

4. The factor operates credit control procedures including maintaining ledger, correspondence and telephoning the buyer, if necessary. The factor sends a statement of account to the buyer on behalf of the seller.

5. The buyer makes payment of the full amount of the invoice to the factor as per agreed terms.

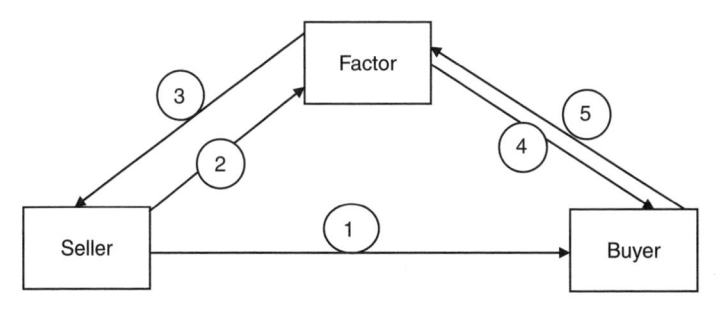

Figure 13.1 Factoring – mechanism

When an invoice is not paid on the due date the liability will depend on the type of agreement, for example whether it is with recourse or without recourse to the seller.

ADVANTAGES OF FACTORING

- The factor provides a quick boost to cash flow within a short time.

- It is a competitive business and competitively priced.

- It can be a cost-effective way of outsourcing sales ledger while freeing up owner's time to manage the business.

- It assists smoother cash flow and financial planning.

- Businesses may be given useful information about the credit standing of the customers (buyers) if they pay on time.

- The buyers can negotiate better terms with suppliers.

- Factors can provide an excellent strategic as well as financial resource when planning business growth.

- Businesses will be protected from bad debts if they choose without recourse factoring.

- Cash is released to the seller by the factor as soon as invoices are received by the factor.

DISADVANTAGES OF FACTORING

- It may be more expensive than a bank overdraft/loan.

- It may reduce the scope for borrowing from the bank because book debts will not be available as security.

- Factors may/would like to vet the customers (buyers) before a business sells goods.

- A business may find it difficult to end factoring at short notice as it will have to pay off any money the factor has advanced on invoices if the customers have not paid them yet.

- It may take a long time to settle in the case of a dispute.

INVOICE DISCOUNTING

Invoice discounting is an alternative way of drawing money against invoices. A business retains control over the administration of the sales ledger. It provides a cost-effective way for profitable businesses to improve their cash flow. It is only available to businesses that sell products or services on credit to other businesses.

The invoice discounter will first do a credit check on the business, its systems and also a credit check of its customers. It may then agree to advance a certain percentage of the total amount of outstanding sales ledger.

The business will pay a monthly fee to the invoice discounter and also interest on the net amount advanced. This is in addition to advances received or money repaid.

Each month, more money is advanced by the discounter or repaid by the business. This will depend on whether the total amount owing has gone up or down.

If the invoice discounter agrees to advance a certain percentage (say 80 per cent) of the total owing and the total of outstanding invoices is steadily changing, then so will the amount the business will receive. If the outstanding debt drops month on month, the business must repay a proportionate amount (say 80 per cent) of the fall in debt. If the debt rises month on month, the business will receive a similar amount of the increased amount.

ADVANTAGES TO EXPORTER

- The seller collects the debts and does the credit control.

- The customers do not usually know about the invoice discounting, although it is sometimes disclosed.

- Annual turnover must usually be at least £500,000, although increasingly, smaller businesses will be accepted. Generally, discounters will review the credit history and profit track record of the business. They will have stringent requirements regarding the quality of sales ledger systems and procedures.

- The invoice discounter will check regularly to see that business procedures are effective.

- A business can choose between recourse and without recourse facilities, determining who is responsible for recovering the amount of unpaid invoices.

EXPORT FACTORING

Some factoring companies offer a facility for the financing of international sales. They will typically work with a partner abroad who will be responsible for the collection of payment in the country to which the exports are made by the seller. The services of a local agent will prevent any problems that could arise because of differences in laws, customs and language.

In terms of credit limits and process, there is no material difference between local and international factoring and invoice discounting. Some factors will offer the exporter the choice of being paid in GB Pounds or in another currency. The exporter should carefully evaluate which is to his advantage. If the importer customer insists on being invoiced in their country's currency, investing in protection against currency fluctuations needs to be considered. Factors may approve a lower level of prepayment for export invoices than in local sales.

Export factoring – Sales criteria

- An annual turnover of at least £100,000, this may include domestic sales.

- Companies based in the European Union (EU) can still factor debts owed from other EU countries if sales within that country are relatively small.

- Outside the EU higher sales to a single country will be required. For the USA annual sales of £500,000 will typically be necessary.

Most companies, assuming that all factoring companies are the same, take the simplest route signing up with the subsidiary of their clearing bank without first establishing whether or not there are more suitable options available but unlike most other financial facilities, factoring and to a lesser extent invoice discounting, is the provision of finance geared to a service and that service element is not only highly important but equally highly variable from one factoring company to another. In general terms, factors owned by the big banks do not rank well in the service stakes with one even outsourcing its credit control function to India.

Selecting the right factoring company is important as some factors offer poor services and that is why the cheapest quote may work out much more expensive in practice, plus details of the hidden extra costs that some factors may add.

Amongst the factors we find major British banks, subsidiaries of major banks and financial institutions, independent financial institutions and factoring brokers.

FORFAITING: GENESIS

The word "forfait" is a French word meaning surrendering rights, which is of fundamental importance in forfaiting. Forfaiting is the purchase of a series of credit instruments such as bills of exchange, promissory notes, drafts drawn under usance (time), letters of credit or other freely negotiable instruments on a "non-recourse" basis (non-recourse means that there is no comeback on the exporter if the importer does not pay). The forfaiter deducts interest (in the form of a discount), at an agreed rate for the full credit period covered by the negotiable instruments. The debt instruments are drawn by the exporter (seller), accepted by the importer (buyer), and will bear an aval or unconditional guarantee normally issued by the importer's bank. In exchange for the payment, the forfaiter then takes over responsibility for claiming the debt from the importer. The forfaiter either holds the instruments until full maturity (as an investment), or sells them to another investor on a without recourse basis. The holder of the bills/notes then presents each receivable to the bank at which they are payable, as and when they fall due.

FIXED RATE EXPORT FINANCE

A proven method of providing fixed rate export finance for international trade transactions, in recent years, forfaiting has assumed an important role for exporters who wish to receive cash instead of deferred payments, especially from countries where protection against credit, economic and political risks has become more difficult. Typically the importer's obligations are evidenced by accepted bills of exchange or promissory notes which a bank avals or guarantees by way of a "per aval" endorsement on the instrument. The bills of exchange or promissory notes when endorsed as such are known as avalized bills/notes. Equally the receivable may take the form of term bills of exchange drawn under documentary letters of credit.

FORFAITING – CAPITAL GOODS SALE

Forfaiting is often applied where the exporter is selling capital goods, and having to offer export finance for a longer period such as up to five or more years. The forfaiter will then quote a price being a discount rate to be applied to the paper, calculated on the underlying cost of funds i.e. (LIBOR) plus a margin. It is usually possible to have a fixed price quoted for shipment taking place up to six months forward, and the exporter is thus able to lock into his profit from the outset.

FORFAITING – SECONDARY MARKETS

There is an active secondary market for avalized export finance papers in London. Forfaiting companies can offer a wide range of trade related services including various forms of buyers' credits, forfaiting and arranging bank-to-bank loans, loans to financial organisations as well as providing insurance for trade related business through confirming letters of credit and letters of guarantee. Significant export financing and insurance facilities support exports to the emerging markets. Export-credit financing and insurance facilities are provided in co-operation with the Export Credit Guarantee Department in the United Kingdom. There are similar agencies in other countries.

Forfaiting is used for international trade transactions. Normally, a forfaiting house would not expect to handle transactions worth less than $100,000. Forfaiting is at a fixed rate and is short- or medium-term (one to five years) finance, but forfaiters have become very flexible about the terms they will accept. Some forfaiting houses will accept paper with tenors up to ten years; and in other cases for shorter periods down to 180 days. The market for forfaiting generally ranges between one and ten years, depending upon various risks in respect of the country, the importer financed and the guarantor's financial standing.

Payments will normally be made semi-annually in arrears, but most forfaiters may accommodate payments which are made quarterly, semi-annually, annually, or on a bullet basis. These can include capital and interest repayment holidays.

Difference between factoring and forfaiting	
Factoring	Forfaiting
Factoring is suitable for financing the export of consumer goods	Forfaiting is used for financing capital goods
Credit terms between 90 to 180 days	Credit terms for medium- and long-term

RISKS IN EXPORT FINANCE

Political risk: Extraordinary state measures or political incidents like war, revolution, invasion or civil unrest can lead to losses for the exporter.

Currency risk: One of the most important risks in forfaiting is that of payment in a currency other than the exporter's local currency. Floating exchange rates can have the effect of changing the contract value by a considerable amount when converted into the exporter's own currency, and can lead to a loss for the eventual holder of claim.

Commercial risk: This risk concerns the inability or unwillingness of the obligator or guarantor to pay, and applies to all forms of credit as well as forfaiting. The danger is that commitment may not be honoured and necessitates in each case an evaluation of the creditworthiness of the guaranteeing bank. The commercial risk of default by state entities falls into the category of political risks.

Transfer of funds risk: This risk lies with the inability or unwillingness of states or other official bodies to effect payment in the currency agreed upon including the risk of moratorium.

ADVANTAGES TO THE EXPORTER

- Relieves the balance sheet of contingent liabilities
- Improves liquidity
- No interest rate risk
- No risk of inflation in the exchange rate
- No risk of changes in the status of the debtor
- No credit administration and collection problems and related risks and costs

DISADVANTAGES TO THE EXPORTER

- High cost of financing

REQUIREMENTS OF A FORFAITER

- Name of the buyer, his nationality
- Nature of the goods to be sold
- Date of delivery of goods
- Value and currency of the contract

- Date and duration of the contract

- Credit period and number and timing of payments (including any interest rate agreed with the buyer).

DOCUMENTS REQUIRED BY THE FORFAITER

- Evidence of debt to be used (bills of exchange, promissory notes or letters of credit), and the identity of the guarantor or name of the availing bank

- Date of delivery of the documents

- Import export licences, if required

- Exchange control permission to transfer funds, if required

- Copy of supply contract, or of its payment terms

- Copy of signed commercial invoice

- Copies of all shipping documents

- Letter of assignment and notification to the guarantor

- Letter of guarantee, or aval.

The letter of guarantee must be irrevocable and assignable. The forfaiter would like to have all this information, indications or quotations immediately.

Where a letter of credit to cover the debt under a supplier's credit is used, it may be a deferred payment letter of credit that specifies one or a series of more usance (time) bills of exchange, which the bank will accept (guarantee) upon presentation of the usual documents required by the letter of credit. The letter of credit must be subject to the Uniform Customs and Practice for Documentary Credits of the International Chamber of Commerce, Paris (Revision 2007 ICC Publication No. 600 (UCP)).

Charges would depend on the level of interest rates relevant to the currency of the underlying contract at the time of the forfaiter's commitment, and on the forfaiter's assessment of the credit risks and other risks related to the importing country and to the avalizing (or guaranteeing) bank

- Interest cost is made up of: a charge for the money received by the seller

FACTORING AND FORFAITING

- Forfaiter's refinancing costs

- Charge for covering the political, commercial, and transfer risks attached to the avalizor/guarantor.

- Commitment fee

FORFAITING PROCEDURES IN PRACTICE

The exporter approaches a forfaiter who confirms that he is willing to quote on a prospective deal, covering the export in "x" number of months' time bearing the aval of ABC Bank PLC.

If the transaction is worth $10M, the forfaiter will calculate the amount of the bills/notes, so that after discounting the exporter will receive $10M, and will quote a discount rate of 'y' per cent. The forfaiter will also charge for some days grace, if applicable, and a fee for committing him or herself to the deal, worth 'Z' per cent per annum computed only on the actual number of days from the date of commitment and discounting. The forfaiter will stipulate an expiry date for his commitment (that is, when the paper should be in his hands).

This period will allow the exporter to ship his goods and get his bills of exchange avalized and to present them for discounting. The exporter gets immediate cash on presentation of relevant documents, and the importer is then liable for the cost of the contract and receives credit for number of years at 'y' per cent interest.

Many exporters prefer to work with forfait brokers because they deal with a large number of Forfait Houses. They can assure the exporter of competitive rates on a timely and cost effective basis. Such brokers typically charge a nominal (1%) fee to arrange the commitment. This is a one time fee on the principal amount and frequently is added to the selling price by the exporter. The broker frequently consults with the exporter to structure the transaction to fit the forfait market.

MECHANISM OF A FORFAITING TRANSACTION

1. Commercial contract between importer and exporter

2. Delivery of goods by the exporter to the importer

3. Delivery of bill of exchange from importer to the avalizing bank

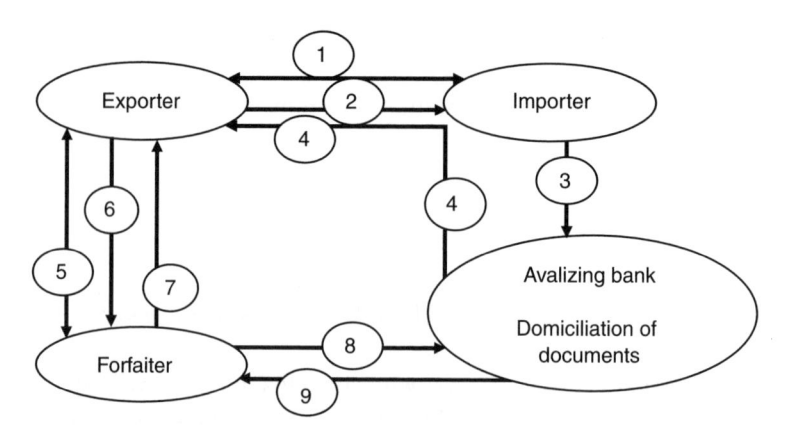

Figure 13.2 Forfaiting transaction – mechanism

4. Delivery of avalized bill of exchange by avalizing bank to the exporter

5. Forfaiting contract between exporter and the forfaiter

6. Delivery of bill of exchange by exporter to the forfaiter

7. Cash payment by forfaiter to the exporter

8. Presentation of the avalized bill of exchange to the avalizing bank on maturity

9. Payment made by the avalizing bank to the forfaiter.

CHAPTER 14

Electronic Documents (eUCP)

Background to eUCP (Uniform Custom and Practice) 600: The emergence of electronic commerce in the international trade system has completely transformed the way the business community does business with its overseas counterparts. This has created the need for a new set of rules and procedures governing global trade operations including entering into sale contracts, trade payment and handling of goods and documents. This has given rise to a new agency being introduced into the international trade mechanism, that of a reliable and trusted third party to do the important work of authentication and safe keeping of messages and their integrity, storage and retrieval, give instructions to various service providers and trigger release of goods and payment.

Development of Electronic Model: An acceptable electronic commerce model was evolved with the initiative of Bolero and other organisations. It will take care of electronic presentation of trade documents and with the passage of time the paper-based presentation of documents would vanish under a documentary credits system.

Banks have to be aware of the requirement of the rules, which can take care of presentations whether paper-based, electronic or both paper-based and electronic. The ICC started giving thought as to whether a revision of the then UCP 500 or some other mechanism could take care of the evolving system. A Task Force was constituted by the ICC Banking Commission at its meeting on 24th May, 2000 on the future of the Commission on Banking Technique and Practice with a main focus on electronic trade. The Task Force identified that there was a need to develop a bridge between the UCP and the processing of the electronic equivalent of a paperless documentary credit system. It is important to note that UCP has been extremely successful over many years of its history in providing self-regulation for the letter of credit trading system. It is time, however, to update the rules to accommodate the changes in developing technology.

Setting up of Working Group: A Working Group was set up, comprising experts from the UCP, electronic trade, legal and related industries such as transport, who after a very hard work of over a year and a half prepared a set of rules as a supplement to UCP. These rules are not a revision of UCP 600. The UCP 600 will continue to be the rules for paper-based documentary letters of credit. The eUCP is a supplement to the UCP 600 to provide necessary guidance for presentation of the electronic equivalents of paper documents under documentary letters of credits. Development of eUCP: The eUCP provides definitions to allow current UCP terminology to accommodate electronic presentation and the necessary rules to allow the UCP and the eUCP to work together. It has been written to allow for presentation completely electronically or for a mixture of paper documents and electronic presentation. Although the practice is evolving, providing exclusively for electronic presentation is not entirely realistic at this stage, nor will it promote the transition to total electronic presentation. It should be noted that the eUCP does not address any issues relating to the issuance or advice of letters of credits electronically. The current practice of issuing, advising and amendment of letters of credit is done electronically, through the Society for Worldwide Inter-bank Telecommunication (SWIFT) system. Many Articles of the UCP are not impacted by the electronic presentation of the equivalent of paper documents and do not require any changes to accommodate it. UCP 600 and eUCP together, are good enough to allow for developing practice in this area of trade. The eUCP is specific to UCP 600.

It is important to note that the eUCP has been drafted to be independent of specific technologies and developing electronic commerce systems. They do not address or define the specific technologies or systems necessary to facilitate electronic presentation. The technologies are evolving and the eUCP leave the parties free to agree on the technology or the format for example, e-mail or one of the various document processing programs to be used in the transmission of electronic messages. It is the responsibility of the parties concerned to decide it.

Synopsis of eUCP Articles: All the Articles of eUCP are consistent with the UCP except as they relate specifically to electronic presentations. Where necessary, changes have been made in the eUCP to address the differences between presentations in paper and electronic form. With a view to avoiding confusion between the Articles of the UCP and eUCP, the eUCP Articles have an "e" preceding each Article number.

Just as is the case with UCP 600, it will be necessary to specifically incorporate the eUCP if the parties wish them to apply for credits allowing for the presentation of electronic documents (or a mixture of paper and electronic presentation). Since the eUCP supplement incorporates the UCP 600 in any credit subject to it, it is not necessary to incorporate both in the same credit.

Among the key issues of electronic presentation addressed by eUCP include:

- The format in which electronic records are to be presented;

- The consequences if a bank is open but its system is unable to receive an electronic record;

- How notice of refusal of an electronic record is to be handled;

- How original documents are to be defined in the electronic world;

- What happens when an electronic record is corrupted by a virus or other defect.

UCP 500 has now been revised and the new publication is known as "2007 Revision ICC publication No. 600 (UCP)". It will be effective from July 2007

Supplement to the Uniform Customs and Practice for Documentary Credits (2007 Revision ICC Publication No. 600 (UCP)) for Electronic Presentation

Article e1   Outlines the scope of the eUCP including its applicability and incorporation in a credit. Just as UCP, eUCP will apply only if it is specifically incorporated in the credit calling for presentation of electronic records alone or in combination with paper documents; that it shall apply as a supplement to the UCP; and that unless a specific version is indicated, the version effective on the date the credit is issued, or amended will apply.

Article e2   Defines the relationship of the eUCP to the UCP. As per this Article, a credit subject to the eUCP shall also be subject to the UCP without express incorporation of the UCP; that eUCP shall prevail if they would produce a result different from that of the UCP; and if eUCP allows the beneficiary to choose presentation and he chooses paper presentation or eUCP permits paper presentation only, the UCP alone shall apply.

Article e3   Gives definition of terms that appear on its face (to apply to the examination of data content), document (to include an electronic record), place for presentation (to mean an electronic address), sign and the like (to include an electronic signature), superimposed notation or stamped (means data content whose supplementary character is apparent in an electronic record) in relation to electronic presentation. This Article further defines electronic record (to mean data created, generated, sent, communicated, received or stored by electronic means that is capable of being authenticated as to the apparent identity of a sender and the apparent source of the data contained in it, and that it has remained complete and unaltered, and is capable of being examined for compliance with the terms and conditions of the eUCP credit.), electronic signature (to mean a data process attached to or logically associated with an electronic record and executed or adopted by a person in order to identify that person and to indicate that person's authentication of the electronic record), format (the data organization in which the electronic record is expressed or to which it refers), paper document (a document in a traditional paper form) and received (the time when an electronic record enters the information capable of being accepted by that system. An acknowledgement of receipt does not imply acceptance or refusal of the electronic record) again in its application to UCP.

Article e4   Enjoins the eUCP credit to specify the formats in which electronic records are to be presented. If not specified, any format will do.

Article e5   Deals with the presentation. According to this Article, "an eUCP must state a place for presentation for the electronic records, if to be presented and also state a place for presentation of the paper documents, if both to be presented." It adds that electronic records may be presented separately from paper documents. If electronic record/s is part of the presentation, it is the responsibility of the beneficiary to provide a notice to the bank concerned as to when the presentation is complete. This notice may be an electronic record or paper document. If the necessary notice is not received, the presentation will deemed not to have been made.

Each paper document presentation under eUCP credit must identify the credit under which it is presented, failure to do so will render presentation as not received. If the system of the bank to which presentation is to be made is unable to receive the electronic record on the expiry date, etc. despite being open, it will be deemed to be closed and the date for presentation will set extended.

Article e6   Is another important Article, which deals with the examination of documents (or records in the case of electronic presentation). According to this Article, if an electronic record contains a hyperlink to an external system or a presentation indicates that it may be examined by reference to an external system, then the relevant hyperlink or external system will be the electronic record to be examined. It will be a discrepancy if the indicated system fails to provide access to the required electronic record at the time of examination. The forwarding of electronic records by the nominated bank will signify its having checked the apparent authenticity of the electronic record. It will, however, not be a basis for refusal if the bank concerned is unable to examine an electronic record in format required by the eUCP credit, or in the form presented if no format is stipulated.

Article e7   It covers the Notice of Refusal. The time period, according to this Article, commences on the banking day after receiving the notice of completeness. If this time period gets extended, the time for the examination of documents commences on the first following banking day on which the bank is able to receive the notice of completeness. It is added that the bank shall return any paper documents not previously returned to the presenter, if the concerned bank does not receive instructions from the party to which notice of refusal is given within 30 calendar days from the date of the notice. It may dispose of the electronic records in any manner deemed appropriate without any responsibility.

Article e8   Stipulates that any requirement for presentation of one or more originals or copies of an electronic record is satisfied by the presentation of one electronic record.

Article e9   The date on which an electronic record appears to have been sent by the issuer is deemed to be the date of issuance of that record, as per Article e9. If no other date is apparent, the date of receipt will be deemed to be the date it was sent

Article e10 Except for transport document, there is no other Article in eUCP covering documents. Article e10 states that if an electronic record does not indicate a date of shipment or despatch, the date of issuance of the electronic record will be the date. If, however, the electronic record bears a notation evidencing the date of shipment, that notation date will be the date of shipment or despatch. A notation showing additional data content need not be separately signed or otherwise authenticated.

Article e11 It deals with the corruption of an electronic record after presentation. As per this Article, the bank receiving an electronic record, which appears to have been corrupted may inform the presenter and may request for its re-presentation. If the bank concerned does not request re-presentation, the time for examination is suspended and resumes when the presenter makes re-presentation and that if the nominated bank is not the confirming bank it must provide the issuing bank and any confirming bank with notice of the request for re-presentation and also of the suspension. If the said electronic record is not re-presented within thirty (30) calendar days, the bank may treat the electronic record as not presented; and any deadlines are not extended.

Article e12   It is a disclaimer of liability clause for presentation of electronic records. It puts no liability on the bank, by checking the apparent authenticity of an electronic record, for the identity of the sender, source of the information, or its complete and unaltered character other than that which is apparent in the electronic record received by the use of commercially acceptable data process for the receipt, authentication and identification of electronic records.

Source: ICC

CHAPTER 15

Scrutiny of Documents – Procedures

Documentary Credits: Documentary credits are classic instruments for financing purchasing of foreign goods and foreign equipment. They may provide assistance to the issuing bank to grant financial facility to the importer. They may also provide assistance to the advising/confirming bank to grant financial facility to the exporter.

Scrutiny of Documents: A documentary letter of credit is a legal contract between the issuing bank and the beneficiary. The issuing bank undertake to honour its commitment to pay, accept bill of exchange and pay on maturity provided the beneficiary presents the documents in accordance with the terms and conditions mentioned in the credit.

It must be remembered that banks deal with documents and not in goods. Therefore, it is very important to ensure the quality and quantity of the goods be satisfied by presenting appropriate documents in this respect. The beneficiary is the party to supply the goods under a letter of credit and provide the appropriate documents to the issuing bank. If the documents presented do not satisfy the terms and conditions of the credit, the issuing bank cannot honour its commitment.

As a letter of credit is issued at the request and on behalf of the buyer/importer in favour of the beneficiary, the issuing bank is a middleman to facilitate completion of sale and purchase of the goods. There is a separate contract between the applicant and the issuing bank that he (the applicant) will honour his commitment provided the issuing bank also fulfills the requirements mentioned in the application for a letter of credit, which stipulates the documents.

Therefore the buyers and sellers have certain responsibilities in respect of documents required under a letter of credit.

BUYER'S RESPONSIBILITIES

The buyer must give clear and precise instructions to the issuing bank, without excessive detail. The issuing bank cannot guess what the buyer wants and cannot check complicated and technical specifications. The documents called for under the credit should be with the agreement of sale contract. The buyer should not ask for the documents that the seller cannot or may not be able to provide, or set out conditions that the seller cannot meet.

SELLER'S RESPONSIBILITIES

When a letter of credit is received by the seller/beneficiary he should immediately study the terms and conditions of the credit and ensure that these are in accordance with the sale contract between him and the buyer. If there is a need to make changes to the terms of the credit he must make such a request in writing without delay. Banks are not concerned with such contracts between them.

At the time of presentation of the documents the seller should present the required documents exactly with the same terms and conditions as called for by a letter of credit. The documents should be presented as soon as possible within the validity period specified in the credit.

The seller must remember that if the documents do not meet the terms and conditions of a letter of credit, the issuing bank will have no obligation to honour its commitment but will refuse to accept the documents.

RESPONSIBILITIES OF OTHER PARTIES (BANKS)

Advising/Confirming bank: It is very important for all other parties involved in a letter of credit to understand what documents are required and the terms and conditions that need to be fulfilled. There are three main parties involved in a letter of credit i.e. the applicant, the issuing bank and the seller. For the purpose of convenience in the process a fourth party is known as the advising bank/confirming and/or negotiating bank.

The advising/confirming bank: When documents are presented by the seller the advising and/or confirming bank need to check all the documents to ensure these are correct and satisfy the terms and conditions of the letter of credit. If they do not satisfy them, then the procedure mentioned under the section on "Negotiation of Documents" should be followed.

THE ISSUING BANK

When documents are received from the seller/advising/confirming bank the issuing bank must check all the documents to ensure these are correct and satisfy the terms and conditions of a letter of credit. If they do not satisfy them it must immediately inform the party seller/advising/confirming bank from where it received them that the documents do not meet the terms and conditions of a credit and it refuses to accept them.

It should also contact and inform the applicant of the irregularities and seek his mandate if he is willing to accept those documents.

Scrutiny of Documents: In order to ascertain the conformity of documents with the terms of a letter of credit it is necessary to carry out the following checks on various documents relating to letter of credit.

Letter of credit

- It is irrevocable.

- The signature on the letter of credit must be verified.

- All amendments must be attached to a letter of credit.

- Documents are submitted within the validity of a letter of credit.

- All the required documents are received.

- All documents should be presented/submitted by the original beneficiary unless it is a transferable letter of credit. In that event, documents would be accepted from a second beneficiary in accordance with the transferred letter of credit.

- If the documents evidence partial shipment it should not be accepted unless it is permitted by a letter of credit.

- If a forward foreign exchange contract is required it should be booked.

Bill of exchange

- It must be drawn in accordance with the terms of a letter of credit.

- It must be correctly dated.

- It must be signed by the drawer/beneficiary specified in a letter of credit.

- It must be drawn on the issuing bank.

- The currency of the drawing must be the same as of the letter of credit.

- The amount in words and figures must agree.

- Its value must be exactly the same as on the invoices – unless otherwise permitted by a letter of credit.

- It must be drawn at sight or usance as required and in accordance with the terms of a letter of credit.

- It must be drawn for a usance period from or after sight or from or after the "On Board" bill of lading date as per a letter of credit terms.

- Letter of credit reference number and date must appear on the bill of exchange as per letter of credit terms.

- Alteration to the instrument, if any, must be signed by the authorised signature.

- There must not be any irrelevant clauses mentioned.

- Stamp duty of the proper value must be affixed (wherever stamp duty is applicable). It is not applicable in the UK.

Commercial invoice

- It must be addressed to the buyer – unless a letter of credit stipulates otherwise. In that case it has to be addressed to the party stipulated.

- The value must not be in excess of that available under a letter of credit.

- The description of the goods on the commercial invoice must correspond exactly as given in a letter of credit.

- It must show import licence number, pro-forma invoice or other numbers, if required by a letter of credit.

- It must not evidence shipment of additional goods such as advertising samples, which are not required by a letter of credit.

- The price basis must not differ from any pro-forma invoice attached to a letter of credit or terms stated on a letter of credit.

- The calculations must agree with those in other documents and there must be no computational errors.

- There must be no extra charges or commission shown which are not permitted under a letter of credit.

- Invoice must show the beneficiary's name as per a letter of credit terms.

- The invoices must be certified, signed, legalised, if required under a letter of credit.

- Shipping marks, weight, number of packages/cases must agree with those shown on the bill of lading and other documents.

- Packing details must agree with other documents and must also be as required by a letter of credit.

- The correct number of copies of invoices must be submitted.

- If a letter of credit requires a combined certificate of value and origin, the certificate of origin section must be complete and signed.

- If a letter of credit requires that the transport documents evidence the amount of the freight paid, or that in some form the insurance premium is specified, the invoices must show such amounts exactly.

- The quantity of goods shown must be consistent with any part shipment clause in a letter of credit.

Insurance document

- It must evidence coverage of risks exactly as stipulated in a letter of credit.

- It must be issued/signed by an insurance company or underwriter or an agent on behalf of an insurance company or underwriter.

- It should not be a broker's certificate or cover note – unless it is specifically authorised in the letter of credit.

- It must not be dated later than the date of shipment, despatch or taking in charge. If it is, it must include "warehouse to warehouse" clause or "lost or not lost" clause.

- It must be issued in the currency of a letter of credit or as otherwise stipulated.

- It must be issued in a transferable form or endorsed to the order of a specified party if so required by a letter of credit.

- There must not be any unauthenticated alterations.

- It must show marks, numbers, weights, quantities and a description of the goods in accordance with the bill of lading and other documents.

- It must indicate the method of carriage of the goods, the port of loading, despatch, or taking in charge, name of the carrying vessel and port of discharge or place of delivery etc.

- It must state a named place where claims are payable (usually at the place of issuing bank) (if this is required by a letter of credit).

- When the transport document shows trans-shipment of goods, the insurance document must cover the trans-shipment.

- If the goods are being shipped in containers or if a letter of credit's terms permit shipment on deck, the insurance document must cover "Loaded on Deck" shipments.

- The document must be presented in original. Copies are accepted only if allowed in a letter of credit.

Bill of lading

- It must be issued and signed by a named carrier or on behalf of the named carrier by his agent.

- It must indicate that the goods have been "loaded" or "shipped on board" a named vessel.

- The bill of lading must not be issued by a freight forwarder, unless it indicates that the freight forwarder is acting as the actual carrier or as an agent for a named carrier.

- The documents presented must comprise a full set of originals and, if required, a set number of non-negotiable copies.

- If a letter of credit's terms require that the goods be consigned to the "order" of a nominated party it must not be otherwise consigned or endorsed by the seller.

SCRUTINY OF DOCUMENTS

- The date shown as being the "On-Board" date when goods were placed on the vessel must not be later than the latest date of shipment.

- If a "Received for Shipment" bill of lading is presented it is acceptable if it bears an "On-Board" notation and date, duly initialled by the carrier or his agent, if required by a letter of credit.

- The bill of lading must not indicate any detrimental clauses as to the defective conditions of goods and/or packing.

- The shipping marks or numbers must agree with those shown on other documents.

- There must not be any alterations, which have not been authenticated by the carrier or his agent.

- It must not show that any other goods have been shipped in addition to those required.

- It must not show that the vessels' name and/or the port of loading and/or port of discharge are "intended".

- It must not show that the goods have been loaded "On Deck" unless specifically authorised.

- It must not omit any required notify parties.

- It must be marked "Freight Paid" if the shipping terms are C & F or CIF.

- It must show the amount of the freight charge, if so required by a letter of credit.

- It must not bear a clause covering part container loaded stating that the goods will be released only when all original copies of bill of lading are presented by the holders.

- The bill of lading must have been presented within the period allowed under a credit or otherwise within 21 days from its date.

- If it is a charter party/short form bill of lading it must be allowed as per letter of credit terms.

- The vessel must not be on the banned list.

Air waybill and air consignment note

(Unless the letter of credit specifies otherwise)

- The air waybill must be issued and signed by a named carrier or signed on behalf of a named carrier by his agent.

- If it is a "House air waybill" it must be signed for and on behalf of a named carrier.

- The correct copy, which has been signed by the carrier or on behalf of a named carrier or by his agent, must be submitted.

- The "Freight Collected" and "Freight Prepaid" columns must be completed.

- The goods must be consigned as required under the letter of credit.

- The required notify parties must be shown.

- The despatch of goods must be made from and to the specified places.

- The despatch date must not be later than the latest shipment date.

- Trans-shipment must be effected, only if the letter of credit allows.

Parcel post/courier receipts

- They must show despatch of goods from a post office/courier in the nominated place.

- The date stamp must indicate that dispatch was made within the specified period.

- If the amount of postage paid is required to be shown, it must be stated on the receipt.

- The consignee as per a letter of credit's terms must be shown on the receipt.

Other transport documents

- It must show, on its face, that it has been issued by a named carrier and signed by the carrier or on his behalf by this agent.

- If it is issued in more than one original, a full set must be presented.

- There must be non-negotiable copies, if required by a letter of credit's terms.

- It must state that the goods have been despatched loaded, shipped on board or taken in charge as required by the letter of credit

- If shipment is by sea, that it must not be subject to a charter party.

- There must be no detrimental clause indicating defective goods or packing.

- The marks and numbers and description of goods must not differ from the other documents presented.

- Alterations, if any, in transport documents must be signed by the carrier or by the agent of the named carrier.

- It must not show shipment of goods in addition to those required by a letter of credit's terms.

- It must evidence notify party(ies) if required by a letter of credit.

- It must not show "loaded on deck" if shipment is by sea, unless specified in a letter of credit.

- It must be marked "Freight Paid" if shipment dispatch terms are C&F, CIF, DCP or CIP.

- If required by a letter of credit the document must show the freight charges.

- In case of combined transport document, the cross-border certificate should be attached, wherever required.

Certificate of origin

- The details must conform to other documents presented.

- It must indicate as the consignee, the applicant for a letter of credit.

- It must be issued by a Chamber of Commerce or other specified organisation.

- Any alterations must be authenticated.

- Marks, number, weight, etc must agree with those shown on other documents.

Packing list

- It must show the contents of each individual package.

- It must show marks, case numbers, weights etc. these should not differ from the other documents.

Weight list/note

- It must show both net and gross weights.

- It must quote a weight, which does not differ from that stated on other documents.

- It must not show details, which differ from other documents.

- It must state individual weights of the package.

- It must show weights, which add up to the stated total.

- It can be specifically identified with the other documents.

Other documents

In addition to the documents mentioned above, which are by far the most common, there are several other documents that are called for from time to time. Certain countries, particularly those in the Middle East, require certified invoices or certificates of origin confirming that the goods have been produced in a particular country. UK produced goods may have certificates of origin issued by local Chambers of Commerce who are authorised by the Department of Trade and Industry to make such declarations. These include:

- Inspection Certificates

- Health Certificates e.g. Fumigation, Sanitary, Veterinary

- Customs Invoices

- Pro-forma Invoices

- Legalised Invoices

- Consular Invoices

- The documents required must be stated in a letter of credit and the name of the organisation to issue such documents and the information should match with the requirement.

- Documents can be specifically identified with the other documents under the letter of credit.

- Documents describe the goods generally in accordance with a letter of credit description.

CHAPTER 16

Common Irregularities in Documents

COMPLIANCE OF TERMS

It is essential that documents called for in a documentary letter of credit comply correctly and are in accordance with the terms of the credit. However, mistakes do occur and these cause extra work for the exporter and the bank(s) involved. This extra work causes delay in receiving payment from the importer/bank, and may involve extra cost for the exporter. The irregularities/discrepancies can be avoided by paying due attention.

Documentary credit

- Does not comply strictly with the terms of sale contract.
- Has expired.
- Late presentation of documents.
- Difficult documents asked for under L/C.

Bill of exchange

- Drawn incorrectly or for a sum different from the amount of a credit.
- Capacity of signatories not stated, if required.
- Drawn in different currency.
- Tenor of the bill does not match with L/C.

- Bill of exchange not endorsed or incorrectly endorsed.
- Bill does not bear the notation "Drawn under L/C No. – Issued by – Bank".

Invoice

- Amount exceeds that of a letter of credit.
- Amount differs from that of the bill of exchange.
- Prices of goods different from those indicated in a letter of credit.
- Description of goods differs from that in a letter of credit.
- Price and shipment terms ("FOB", "CIF", "C&F", etc) not mentioned/incorrect.
- Extra charges included are not specified in a letter of credit.
- Is not certified, legalised or signed as required by a letter of credit.
- Does not contain declaration required under a letter of credit.
- Importer's name differs from that mentioned in a letter of credit.
- Is not issued by the exporter.
- Order or L/C. Number not stated, when required under letter of credit.

Bill of lading

- Not presented in full set when requested.
- Alterations not authenticated by an official of the shipping company or its agent.
- It is not "clean", i.e. carries remarks that the condition and packing of the merchandise is defective.
- It is not marked "on board" when so required.
- "On board" notation not signed or initialled by the carrier or agent as required under L/C.

- "On board" notation not dated.

- Is not endorsed by the exporter when drawn to "order".

- Is not marked "freight paid" as stipulated in the credit (under "C&F", "CIF" contracts).

- Is made out "to order" when the credit stipulated "direct to consignee" (importer) (and vice versa).

- It is dated later than the latest shipment date specified in the L/C.

- Is not presented within the period specified in the letter of credit.

- Included details of merchandise other than that specified in a credit.

- Rate at which freight is calculated and the total amount not shown when credit requires these details.

The following are acceptable only if expressly permitted in a credit:

- Shipment "on deck" i.e. the goods are not stored in the hold.

- Shipment from a port or to a destination other than that stipulated.

- Presentation of types of bills of lading not specifically authorised in a credit, for example Charter Party bill of lading etc.

Marine Insurance

- Amount of cover is insufficient.

- Does not include risks mentioned in a credit.

- Is not issued in the currency of a credit.

- Is not endorsed by the insured and/or signed by the insurers.

- Certificate or policy bears a date later than the date of shipment/despatch, except where a warehouse to warehouse clause is indicated.

- Incorrect description of goods.

- Alterations are not authenticated.

- It is not in transferable form when required.

- Carrying vessel's name not recorded.

- Does not cover transhipment when bills of lading indicate it will take place.

Note

When a policy is called for under a credit, a certificate is not acceptable. However, a policy is acceptable when a certificate is called for. Broker's cover notes are not acceptable unless specifically permitted in a credit.

Remember

When these and any other documents are required by a credit they should:
Comply with the stipulated terms and conditions of a credit.

- Properly signed.

- Have all alterations duly authenticated.

CHAPTER 17

Guarantees and International Bonds

Guarantees and international bonds are two separate subjects. A guarantee is usually an undertaking given by a person/guarantor as security for a credit facility offered by a creditor/bank to a borrower. An international bond is an undertaking given by a bank or issuer at the request of its customer (contractor/supplier) in favour of a project owner or beneficiary/buyer in another country.

GUARANTEES AS SECURITY

Definition: A guarantee is defined in section 4 Statute of Frauds 1677 as a "written promise by one person to be responsible for the debt, default or miscarriage of another person incurred to a third party".

From this simple definition it is evident that for a guarantee to be legally enforceable certain conditions must be present.

(a) The guarantee must be in writing. Thus, any oral promise expressed to be by way of a guarantee is legally unenforceable. However, if the oral promise is by way of an indemnity, then such promises are legally enforceable.

 1. "A" gives guarantee to the creditor (C)

 2. "C" gives money to the borrower (B)

 3. The creditor claims repayment from the borrower (B)

 4. If repayment does not come from the borrower (B), the creditor claims from the guarantor (A).

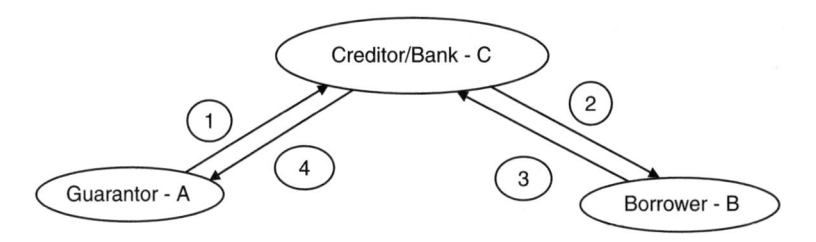

Figure 17.1 Guarantee as security – mechanism

(b) There are three parties to a contract of guarantee.

1. The person who gives the written promise – is known as the guarantor.
2. The person whose responsibilities are being secured is known as the debtor or more often is described as the principal debtor or the borrowing customer.
3. The third party – who is known as the creditor in actual fact is the bank.

(c) By another part of section 4, a guarantee is unenforceable unless signed by the guarantor(s) or his agent. Thus no one can be held liable on the guarantee unless they have actually signed the written document. This simple statement needs to be extended with regard to joint and several guarantees, i.e. promises by more than one person to sign the same guarantee. For, under English law, until all guarantors have signed the form of a guarantee, it is unenforceable even against those who have signed it.

(d) There is no provision within the definition for the signing to be witnessed. Thus, when a banker witnesses the signing of such forms, it is not out of legal compulsion. There are two reasons:

1. it avoids contentions that the form contains a forgery of a guarantor's signature.
2. it avoids claims that no one took the trouble to explain the contents of the document.

(e) A bank guarantee does not have to be in any set style. The only provision is that it must be in writing. However, banks today require guarantors to sign a very complex and lengthy document, which contains a lot of legal jargon. This is intended to give the bank the maximum possible protection against a whole range of contingencies, while at the same time it deprives the guarantors of many rights, some of which would be available through common law.

DISTINCTION BETWEEN GUARANTEES AND INDEMNITIES

By signing a bank guarantee, a guarantor promises to be collaterally answerable for the debt (default or miscarriage) which the principal debtor owes to the bank. So if the principal debtor who is primarily liable does not repay the bank debt, the guarantor, who is secondarily liable, will have to.

1. "A" gives guarantee to the creditor (C)

2. "C" gives money to the borrower (B)

3. The creditor claims repayment from the borrower (B)

4. If repayment does not come from the borrower (B), the creditor claims from the guarantor (A) who will have to pay to the creditor.

This should be compared with an indemnity, where there are only two parties to a contract of indemnity, and the person giving the indemnity (the indemnifier) assumes primary liability. Thus, the indemnifier undertakes to pay the debt to the bank (creditor) (rather than paying only if the principal debtor cannot or will not pay).

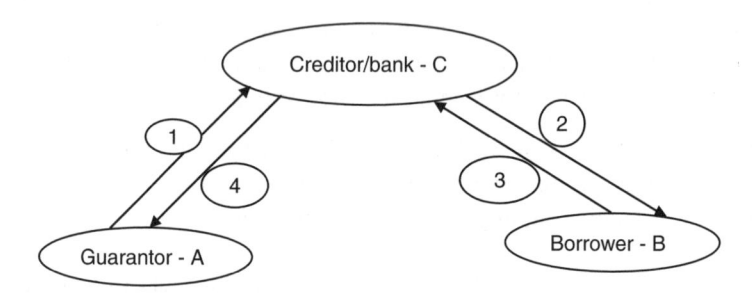

Figure 17.2 Distinction between guarantee and indemnity

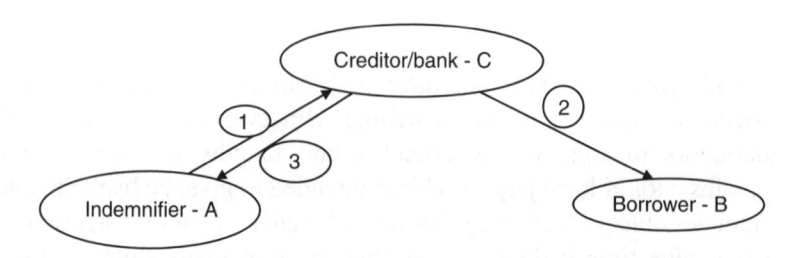

Figure 17.2a Distinction between guarantee and indemnity

1. "A" requests the creditor to lend money to "B" and indemnifies the creditor (C)

2. "C" gives money to the borrower (B)

3. The creditor claims repayment from the borrower (A)

This latter situation can be of considerable benefit to a banker particularly where the guarantee has been taken as security for a principal debtor who is not legally liable for a debt he has created – say because the principal debtor is a minor, or the guarantee is securing an advance which is ultra vires a company – even though in the latter case s.9 European Communities Act 1972 may be available as protection. In the past, when bankers have tried to enforce their security, they have been unsuccessful, and the classic legal case on the matter is Coutts & Co. V. Browne-Lecky (1947).

Banks overcome this general problem today by including a special clause known as an indemnity clause in their form of a guarantee. This clause converts the guarantee into an indemnity. Thus, if a bank had given an advance to a borrower that was secured by an indemnity, the bank could recover from the indemnifier even though recovery would not be possible from the debtor customer. The reason for this is that the indemnifier has assumed primary liability.

ADVANTAGES OF GUARANTEES AS SECURITY

The guarantees are easy to take, for it is not necessary to carry out an investigation of title or registration – even when given by a company. But remember if supported, then depending upon the nature of the supporting security, all the usual formalities regarding registration etc will be necessary for the latter.

The various clauses contained within a bank guarantee give the bank the maximum possible protection and powers.

With the exception of an unlimited guarantee, the guarantor's maximum liability is fixed to the amount quoted on the form.

With the exception of a specific guarantee all the principal debtor's liabilities are secured, both current and in the future.

Provided the guarantor remains financially sound (a point determined by status enquiry), the guarantee has a stable value.

Where supporting security has been taken, which itself is stable in value, then the security is a very strong one.

If the guarantor defaults on his promise, it is a simple matter to pursue recovery through the courts.

Because the guarantees are third-party securities, they can be ignored when claiming against the principal debtor for recovery. This is particularly useful if the principal debtor has had a receiving order presented against him as a proof can be submitted ignoring any payment made or promised from the guarantor.

Where the principal debtor has no assets to offer as security this is always given by a third party which may be the only alternative offered to the banker. If a guarantee is offered by someone of good financial standing then the bank will usually be happy to accept it.

Bankers often request directors of limited companies to give guarantees to secure the liabilities of their companies. This action will ensure that they have a greater incentive for the business to succeed particularly if they have been required to support the guarantee

DISADVANTAGES OF A GUARANTEE AS SECURITY FOR A CREDIT FACILITY

If the guarantee is not supported by tangible security having a stable value, then the worth of the guarantee is dependent on the financial stability of the guarantor. In situations where the guarantee has been given by director in favour of his company, then the downfall of the latter may lead to the downfall of the former for both are dependent on each other.

Although a guarantee contains many legal clauses, a guarantor may still be able to avoid liability on technical reasons. It is often considered that the giving of a guarantee is a formality – and that the liability is not a real one. This of course is not true. If the bank finds it necessary to call upon the guarantor for repayment, bad feeling often results, particularly where the guarantor is a customer of the bank. If the guarantor will not pay, then legal action may be necessary – which may be time consuming and expensive.

PROCEDURES FOR TAKING AS SECURITY

Establish the financial standing of the guarantor(s). If the guarantor is already a customer of the bank/branch, then the bank will be fully aware of his financial standing. However, if the guarantor is a customer of another branch or bank, then it will be necessary to carry out a status enquiry. If a joint and several guarantee is being taken, an enquiry for the full amount is made on all the guarantors, but the joint and several liabilities aspect of the guarantee must be mentioned.

Review the general considerations: It is essential that an intending guarantor must obtain independent legal advice. After this, the advising solicitor should add the attestation clause and act as a witness as regards the signing of the document.

Use the bank's standard guarantee form or a guarantee to be enforceable (as established earlier it must be a written document). Although the wording has not been provided for by statute, each bank has developed its own form, which affords it the best possible protection. Thus, a bank will not be prepared to accept any form of a guarantee which is not its own. Where a guarantor suggests alterations, additions or deletions, then reference will have to be made to the bank's legal advisor.

Place where the guarantee should be signed: A banker would prefer it if all guarantees given in favour of his customers were signed at his bank/branch in his presence. This is not always possible and so various alternatives must be considered.

(a) At one of the bank's branches (which is near to the guarantor's home or place of business).

(b) At a branch of a anoither bank. This procedure is used when the guarantor's bank does not have a branch in the locality of the guarantor(s) home or place of business.

(c) At a solicitor's office, if independent legal advice has been sought. Wherever it is signed, then, it is essential for the signature to be witnessed. The witness normally prints his name, address and occupation and, then adds his signature as confirmation. If the guarantor's signature is not known then the guarantee form must be sent to his bankers so that they can confirm its authenticity.

A bank must never send a guarantee form direct to a guarantor however unique the circumstances of the request might be. Although there is no legal justification for declining such a request, a guarantor should be told that it is not possible to meet this request. The guarantor should, however, be told that the guarantee can be made available for his signature at a convenient branch or bank. There are three main reasons for acting this way:

(i) It minimises the risk of a forged signature being placed on the form and the consequences of such a problem.

(ii) It minimises the risk of a guarantor claiming *nonest factum*. But as we have seen, pleas under this heading are very unlikely to succeed today

because the banks ask the solicitors to confirm the identity of the person signing the document.
(iii) It reduces the likelihood of a successful claim that there was no opportunity for the guarantor either to ask questions or to have the nature of the guarantee liability explained.

Joint and several guarantees: The bank must ensure that when there is more than one guarantor, all must sign, otherwise, the security is unenforceable. Furthermore, if the terms have been agreed, one guarantor cannot vary anything unless all other guarantors agree. A banker would be expected to specify the names of the principal debtor(s) and guarantor(s) correctly.

After the guarantee form has been completed and signed, each of the guarantor(s) should be provided with a copy. A receipt should be obtained from each guarantor. A diary card should be completed as a reminder to carry out an annual status enquiry on each guarantor. Where a subsequent enquiry shows deterioration in the guarantor's financial standing the matter should be discussed with both the principal debtor and the guarantor.

A diary card should also be completed as a reminder to advise the guarantor of his liability at reasonable intervals and obtain an acknowledgement from him. This is for convenience purposes and is not a procedure required by law nor does it have any relevance to the six or twelve years status barred time unit.

Precautions

Where the guarantee is being taken as additional security, then the other procedures have to be considered. If the guarantor had already given the bank a guarantee in favour of the same principal debtor, then a separate memorandum is usually taken or a clause added to indicate that the security is in addition to, and not in replacement of, the earlier one.

If the arrangement was to cancel one guarantee as soon as a new one was completed then a memorandum or clause similar to the one mentioned above would not be needed. Clearly no competent banker would cancel the old guarantee until the new one had been taken, even though a customer may try to indicate that this was the agreement between him and the banker.

If another security, irrespective of whether it is direct or indirect, is held, then it is not necessary to tell the guarantor of its existence or the earlier mortgagors that further security is lodged. For contracts of guarantee are not contracts *uberrirae fidei*.

INTERNATIONAL BONDS/BANK GUARANTEES

Introduction

Over recent years, the demand from overseas buyers for bonds to support contractual obligations entered into by UK exporters has increased substantially.

As a result of the increase in demand, coupled with an overall increase in the average size of contracts and recent litigation, the subject of foreign bonds and guarantees has gained greater attention in international trading.

Many exporters will be aware that Bid Bonds and Performance Guarantees are one of the basic ingredients of doing business overseas and that liability under the bond/guarantee will remain during the life of the bank contract and beyond.

A bank guarantee/bond is usually no more than a written undertaking to a foreign beneficiary that the bank will pay him a sum of money against the production of a document or documents, or when demanded upon the occurrence of a specified failure.

A bond or guarantee is often an indication of the financial standing of a supplier or contractor and his ability to fulfill a contract.

The bank puts its name and its reputation behind the promise to pay and will protect that reputation by paying a claim if, and only if, the claim meets the requirements set out in the guarantee.

PARTIES

There are mostly three parties involved in the provision of a guarantee/bond.

The Seller – is to perform the work covered by the bond (also known as the supplier or contractor, principal or exporter).

The Buyer – to whom the bond is issued (also known as the customer, client, employer or beneficiary).

The Guarantor – bank, surety or insurance company who issues the guarantee/bond on provision of a written Counter Indemnity from the seller.

BANK'S ROLE

It is often forgotten that important duties are owed by a bank issuing a guarantee to both the beneficiary and to its customer and that their interests must accordingly be balanced. The bank's role is restricted to that of ensuring that a claim is paid only if it complies with the literal terms of the guarantee issued, and it therefore does not wish to be put in a position of having to adjudicate the relative merits of the parties to the underlying contract.

When issuing guarantees, banks should not be concerned with the terms of the contract. The only reference to the contract which should appear in the guarantee is a reference sufficient to identify and connect the guarantee with the underlying transaction and such would normally appear in either the heading or in a preamble.

A guarantee/bond should be a stand-alone document, payable either on simple demand or against documents called for in the guarantee.

The neutral position of a bank between buyer and seller only holds after the guarantee has been issued. Beforehand the seller is the bank's customer and is entitled to as much advice and assistance as the bank is able to provide. All too often banks do not receive the opportunity of providing that help, for the first information they receive of an impending contract is frequently an urgent request to arrange the delivery of a tender bond in some distant corner of the world, in time for the opening of tenders at 9'clock the following morning.

FORMAT OF BANK GUARANTEES/BONDS

Over the years banks have accumulated a considerable volume of data on guarantee requirements, acceptable formats, local costs and so on, and are happy to share that data with customers whose own experience may well be more limited.

Advantages

Some countries nominally require all guarantees from abroad to be issued through a local bank. A determined exporter and a willing buyer can arrange for a direct guarantee to be given.

The advantages of a direct guarantee to the exporter are substantial:

(a) It is cheaper because it cuts out the correspondent bank's charges.

(b) It can be made subject to English law.

(c) Most important is the fact that the local bank is in charge of the operation of the guarantee and not the foreign bank.

If a claim materialises, local banks are in a better position to assess the validity of the claim than is the case when the guarantee is a correspondent bank's guarantee and if the correspondent has paid, a local bank must respond without question to this demand.

CATEGORIES OF BANK GUARANTEES/BONDS

Guarantees fall into two broad categories – on demand and conditional.

(i) An on demand guarantee/bond, once given, can be called at the sole discretion of the buyer as the nature of the document is such that claims must be met without being contested.

The unconditional nature of these guarantees/bonds makes it difficult – if not impossible – for the exporter to interfere with the bank's obligation to pay.

(ii) Conditional guarantees/bonds i.e. those specifying documentary evidence, give maximum protection to the exporter if claims made under the bond are required to be substantiated through the production of specified documents, for example certificate of an award by an independent arbitrator.

A contentious matter for many exporters is the question of expiry dates and in some countries the provisions of local law and practice permit claims to be submitted beyond the nominal expiry date of the guarantee – this prevails in Algeria for example.

Provisions such as these, which are generally applicable to guarantees issued by local banks, may well apply to guarantees issued by the bank direct to an overseas buyer. It is also important that both the exporter and his bank reach agreement on the wording format of a guarantee and if there is a strong possibility that guarantees are going to play an important role in gaining an overseas contract, an early approach to the bank would create the opportunity to provide helpful information on bonding in the country concerned. In particular, it would enable the bank to establish whether its direct guarantee is likely to be acceptable and – if necessary – to provide standard guarantee text. These may not always be acceptable to the buyer, but at least they can provide the exporter with a useful basis from which to begin negotiations.

TYPES OF BANK GUARANTEES/ INTERNATIONAL BONDS

During the last century overseas buyers of capital goods and large projects have increasingly demanded that suppliers and contractors provide them with a guarantee or bond covering them against non-performance. A bank issuing such bonds is liable to reimburse in full for the amount of the bond to the bondholder.

The main types of guarantees or bonds which banks are requested to issue on behalf of contractors or suppliers for large overseas projects are:

Bid bonds or tender bonds

Exporters who tender for foreign contracts often find that the conditions of tender require a bank guarantee to be established for a percentage. Usually one to five per cent of the value of the contract, to assure the buyer that the accompanying bid is a serious offer. This is known as a bid/tender Bond.

It is demanded by the buyer to protect the buyer if the seller refuses to accept or enter into a contract after the bid has been awarded to him. In the event that the seller refuses or fails to open a performance bond as required by the buyer, the buyer can call the bid bond and recover the losses suffered by him in re-inviting the tender.

This is issued in support of a customer's tender sometimes in lieu of a cash deposit. It is to confirm the genuineness of the tender so that, in the event of the failure of the contractor to enter into any contract granted in accordance with the terms of the tender, a sum (usually about five per cent, but sometimes as low as one or as high as ten per cent, of the total contract price) may be claimed by the company or organisation in whose favour it has been issued. Callings under such a bond are normally payable on demand. Such a guarantee usually takes the form of a request to a bank abroad to issue the bond against the British (or home) bank's indemnity. Like all types of guarantees given by banks, a counter indemnity is taken from the customer.

Mechanics of bid bond

1. Invitation for Bid. The project owner/promoter sends a tender to bid on a project to a contractor. The tender requires a bid bond and permits the bid bond to be in the form of a standby letter of credit.

2. The contractor applies to his bank for the issuance of a bid bond.

3. The contractor's bank (issuing bank) issues a bid bond and forwards it to the contractor.

4. The contractor forwards his bid together with the bid bond to the project owner

5. The project owner accepts the contractor's bid and sends a contract to the contractor.

GUARANTEES AND INTERNATIONAL BONDS

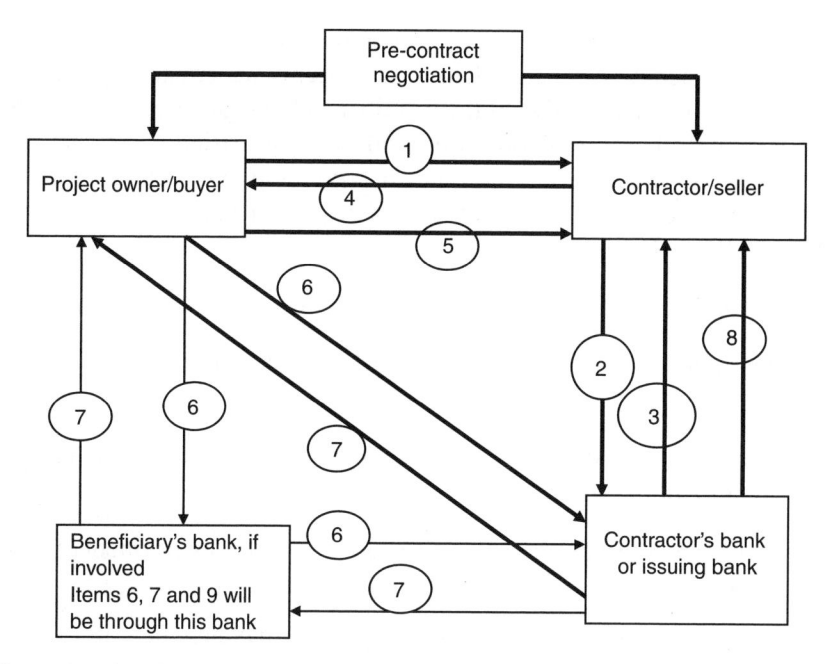

Figure 17.3 Bid bond – mechanism

6. If the contractor fails to sign the contract or fails to obtain and forward to the project owner a performance bond, the project owner will demand payment under a bid bond.

7. When the contractor has signed the contract and obtained a performance bond, or whatever else the contract may require, the project owner will return the bid bond to the contractor to be cancelled.

8. The issuing bank informs the contractor of his action. The matter is closed from the bank's point of view. However, in the case of a dispute between the two parties, it has to be resolved through a legal court in accordance with the conditions of the document.

Specimen of Bid Bond/Guarantees

From XYZ Bank PLC

To Name and address of beneficiary

Messrs ABC & Co. Limited (supplier) submitted on their bid for the supply of ---------- under your bid invitation No -------- dated ---------- According to your tender conditions a bid bond has to be provided.

At the request of Messrs .... (supplier), we, XYZ Bank of Address .... Postcode ...., hereby irrevocably undertake to pay to you on first demand, irrespective of the validity and the legal effects of such bid and waiving all rights of objection and defence arising therefrom, any amount up to .... (currency/maximum amount) (full amount in words) upon receipt of your duly signed request for payment stating that Messrs ABC & Co. Limited:

- have withdrawn their offer before its expiry date without your consent or
- have failed to sign the contract awarded to them in the terms of their offer or
- have failed to open the performance bond foreseen in the tender upon signature of the contract.

The total amount of this guarantee will be reduced by any payment effected hereunder.

For the purpose of identification, your request for payment in writing has to be presented through the intermediary of a first rate bank confirming that the signatures thereon are legally binding upon you.

Your claim is also acceptable if transmitted to us in full by encoded telex/SWIFT through a first rate bank confirming that your original claim has been sent to us by registered mail and that the signatures thereon are legally binding upon you.

Your claim will be considered as having been made once we are in possession of your written request for payment or the encoded telex/SWIFT to this effect.

Our guarantee is valid until .... (date in words) and expires in full and automatically if your claim has not been made on or before that date, regardless of such date being a banking day or not.

This guarantee is governed by English Laws of the United Kingdom and the place of jurisdiction is London.

Authorised Signature

Authorised Signature

Date: ....

Performance bond

If the exporter is subsequently awarded a contract, he is usually required to arrange a performance bond for perhaps five per cent or ten per cent of the value of the contract, which remains in force until the contract is completed. It guarantees satisfactory performance of the seller's obligations under the contract.

It is usual for the tender bond to be released shortly after the issue of the performance bond.

The issue of these bonds provides buyers with an indication of the financial standing of the tendering party. It is also intended to act as a safeguard should the contract not be carried out in a satisfactory manner.

This is given in support of a customer's obligation to fulfill a contractual commitment. When issued by a bank it usually provides for payment to the beneficiary of about ten per cent of the contract value in the event of the undertaking not being fulfilled. It may be payable on demand, but payment is often related to the production of evidence showing non-fulfilment.

A performance bond is usually issued after the tender guarantee is cancelled, although the tender guarantee may be extended to become a performance bond.

Specimen of a Performance Bond/Guarantee

Date: ------------------

From: XYZ Bank PLC

You have concluded on ----------- a contract No -------- with Messrs --------- ABC & Co. ----------- for the delivery of ----------- at a total price of --------. As security for the due performance of the delivery, a guarantee by a bank shall be furnished.

At the request of Messrs ------- ABC & Co. Limited, we, XYZ Bank PLC, of ------------------ Postcode -------, hereby irrevocably undertake to pay to you on first demand, irrespective of the validity and the legal effects of the above-mentioned contract and waiving all rights of objection and defence arising from said contract, any amount up to ----------- (currency and maximum amount in words) upon receipt of your signed request for payment stating that Messrs ------- ABC & Co. Limited ------ have failed to deliver the ordered merchandise or have not delivered such merchandise as specified in the above mentioned contract and that as a consequence you have suffered a loss equalling the amount requested under this performance bond.

The total amount of this guarantee will be reduced by any payment effected hereunder.

For the purpose of identification, your request for payment in writing has to be presented through the intermediary of a first rate bank confirming that the signatures thereon are legally binding upon you.

Your claim is also acceptable if transmitted to us in full by encoded telex/SWIFT through a first rate bank confirming that your original claim has been sent to us by registered mail and that the signatures thereon are legally binding upon you.

Your claim will be considered as having been made once we are in possession of your written request for payment or the encoded telex/SWIFT to this effect.

Our guarantee is valid until _____ (date in words) and expires in full and automatically if your claim has not been made on or before that date, regardless of such date being a banking day or not.

This guarantee is governed by English Laws of the United Kingdom and place of jurisdiction is London (UK)

---------------------------   ---------------------------
Authorised Signature   Authorised Signature

Advance or progress payment bonds

This guarantee is usually 10 to 20 per cent of the contract value and is provided by the seller for the money given to him by the "buyer" in advance to finance initial stages of the contract.

Specimen of Advance Payment Guarantee/Bond

From: XYZ BANK PLC   Date: _____

Dear Sir/Madam,

You have concluded on a contract No._____ with Messrs _____ ABC Co. _____ for the delivery of _____ at a total price of _____. As security for the payment of the merchandise, a guarantee by a bank shall be furnished.

At the request of Messrs _____ ABC & CO _____ we, XYZ Bank PLC, of _____ Postcode _____, hereby irrevocably undertake to pay to you on your first demand, irrespective of the validity and the legal effects of the above-mentioned contract and waiving all rights of objection and defence arising from said contract, any amount up to _____ (currency/maximum amount in words) upon receipt of your written request for payment and your written confirmation that:

(a) you have delivered the merchandise to Messrs ABC & Co in conformity with the contract and that

(b) you have not received payment on the due date for the sum claimed under this guarantee.

The total amount of this guarantee will be reduced by any payment effected hereunder.

For the purpose of identification, your request for payment in writing has to be presented through the intermediary of a first rate bank confirming that the signatures thereon are legally binding upon you.

Your claim is also acceptable if transmitted to us in full by encoded telex/SWIFT through a first rate bank confirming that your original claim has been sent to us by registered mail and that the signatures thereon are legally binding upon you.

Your claim will be considered as having been made once we are in possession of your written request for payment or the encoded telex/SWIFT to this effect.

Our guarantee is valid until -------------- (date in words) and expires in full and automatically if your claim has not been made on or before that date, regardless of such date being a banking day or not.

This guarantee is governed by English Law and place of jurisdiction is London (UK)

---------------------------   ---------------------------
Authorised Signature   Authorised Signature

RETENTION OR MAINTENANCE BONDS

By providing such a bond a seller can obtain 100 per cent of payment, instead of a portion being withheld by the buyer to cover possible future maintenance obligations.

BANKING FACILITY

The above-mentioned guarantees can be conditional or unconditional, open ended, or providing an expiry date or method by which they can expire or be cancelled.

OTHER TYPES OF BONDS

Bonds or guarantees may also be required to cover completion of a project, purchase of equipment, transportation of crude oil or bulk commodities and retention monies etc.

Where the provision of bonds and guarantees is a feature of a contract, the exporters/importers are advised to seek the advice of the local branch of their bank.

PRECAUTIONS

Sellers and issuing banks should resist issuing unconditional guarantees. Banks should advise their customers of the consequences and dangers of providing such guarantees.

However, in view of big projects and supply contracts, exporters, often for fear of losing a contract, submit too easily to erroneous bonding conditions without first trying to negotiate more satisfactory terms.

This is a variation on a performance bond, whereby guarantees the refund, in the event of certain terms and conditions not being completed (e.g. if goods are not shipped or a contract complied with), of amounts paid by the purchaser in advance to the contractor; it is therefore issued in favour of the buyer. It can provide for an increase as further amounts are paid to the contractor, or for a reduction as various portions of the contract arc fulfilled.

Most contracts provide for a period during which the contractor or supplier is responsible for the maintenance and effectiveness of the completed project. The bond guarantees financial support to the buyer for the warranty period. It is often issued to obtain the release of funds on completion of the contract, which under the terms and conditions of the contract would not otherwise be paid over until the warranty period had expired.

Note: all these bonds are normally payable on the demand of the claimant. Banks are not able to act as arbitrators in deciding whether or not the contractor has fulfilled his obligations. Any claims made will be paid in full and it is then for the parties to refer the matter to an arbitrator or take the matter up in court.

INTERNATIONAL BONDS/GUARANTEES – PRECAUTIONS

- The name and address of the guarantor (bank) should be clearly written.

- Names and addresses of the other parties involved should also be stated.

- The tender to which a tender guarantee relates and the contract to which any other guarantee relates should be clearly identified in the guarantee. The reference number (if any) and date should also be mentioned. This is important as the guarantee may not be valid for any other, or an amended tender or contract.

- The guarantee should indicate the maximum liability of the guarantor. Care should be taken if the contract price is variable, or expressed in amounts involving different currencies, or by using a percentage figure if an amount and currency of the guarantee. The amount or the percentage figure of a guarantee should be realistic and avoid over-protection, since the cost of such over-protection may be reflected in the contract price.

- In the case of an Advance Payment Bond, it may well be appropriate to specify in the guarantee pro rate reduction in the guarantee amount as part re-payments are made by the principal. Performance bonds may also be treated in a similar way, i.e. by specific provision for pro rate reduction in the guarantee amount to match partial performance.

TIME FOR PAYMENT

- When a claim has been presented, duly supported by the appropriate documentation, payment is to be effected by the bank without any delay other than that necessary for the bank to check the documentation and satisfy itself that requirements stipulated in the guarantee have been met. No particular time for paying a claim under a tender guarantee can be defined.

- In the case of a performance or repayment bond the procedure for checking the documentation, for example where an arbitral award may have to be translated, may take some time. It is advisable to specify in the guarantee a maximum period for the checking of documents.

ARBITRATION CLAUSE

- All guarantees may provide for an arbitration clause in the case of disputes. If the parties prefer to delete the provision on arbitration, disputes will then be settled by the courts at the guarantor's (main) place of business or, at the option of the beneficiary, at the competent court covering jurisdiction where the guarantee was issued

Documentation

- It is obviously desirable that these details should as far as possible be clearly defined in the guarantee. Considerations to be taken into account may, however, differ according to the type of guarantee and the problem.

Expiry date

- The expiry date is a matter of primary importance for all parties concerned. If, after the expiry date, the bank has not received any claim, its liability to the beneficiary comes to an end. It is, therefore, advisable for such date and the place to receive claim, to be specified in the bond itself.

Return of guarantee document

- When a guarantee has ceased to be valid in accordance with its terms and conditions it should be returned to the bank without delay.

ISSUING BANK GUARANTEES – ACTION STEPS

All customers who wish the bank to issue a guarantee on their behalf are required to make a request in writing to the bank giving all the details to be given in the Letter of Guarantee to be issued. On receipt of the request the following steps are to be followed:

1. Establish the time limit within which the guarantee has to be issued and presented to the beneficiary.

2. Check the mandate and the signature(s).

3. Check the contents/clauses in the letter as to whether they are acceptable.

4. Refer to legal department for any clarification, if required.

5. Check the balance of the account.

6. Check for existing facilities granted by the bank.

7. If the customer (applicant) is a company, follow points 8–10.

8. Check memorandum and articles of association.

9. Obtain necessary resolution of the Board of Directors.

10. Check quorum requirements for validity of the resolution.

GUARANTEES AND INTERNATIONAL BONDS

11. Obtain (necessary) counter indemnity, where required.

12. Prepare credit report and/or facility application to seek approval required of the competent authority.

13. Check details of the security to be offered by the customer.

14. Prepare credit line security to credit control department.

15. Submit draft to manager for approval and signature.

16. Prepare draft for the guarantee to be issued and submit to a credit control department for perusal and return.

17. Show/discuss the draft with the customer.

18. Obtain customer's signature on the draft.

19. Mark lien on the balance, if required.

20. Recover percentage of the facility as margin.
    - (a) DEBIT   Customer's account.
    - (b) CREDIT   Margin on guarantees' account.

21. Record the details on Liabilities Register.

22. (a) DEBIT   Customer Liabilities – Guarantees.
    (b) CREDIT   Bankers Liabilities – Guarantees.

23. Obtain authorised signatures on the Letter of Guarantee.

24. Obtain authorised signatures on the respective vouchers.

25. Recover commission and charges in respect of the guarantee issued (at appropriate rate according to the bank's schedule of charges for each 3 month period).

26. Post guarantee form to the principal.

27. Record a separate file and attach negotiation sheet.

28. Record expiry date on the negotiation sheet.

29. Diarise the expiry date.

30. Post vouchers on the terminal on the same day under the respective value date.

31. Amend all the records, if extension is requested.

32. Diarise to recover commission or charges periodically.

33. In the event of no reply being received from the customer, the facility will be withdrawn on the expiry date and entries on Liabilities Register will be reversed.

34. Advise the principal of withdrawal of bank facility.

35. Advise the customer accordingly.

INTERNATIONAL BONDS AND BANK GUARANTEES – SPECIMENS (amend wording as required)

Performance Bond

To:

XYZ Bank PLC   From: ABC Bank PLC

Address

At the request of ---------------------------- of -------------------------------
(hereinafter referred to as suppliers) we, ------------------- Bank PLC, hereby issue our letter of guarantee in your favour up to an amount of GB Pounds ---------------- (GB Pounds: -- only).

This guarantee is issued in consideration of suppliers, supplying --------------
to----------------on behalf of Messrs. ---
------------------- of ---------- under letter of credit no. --------- dated ---------,
opened by XYZ Bank of -------------------------- branch, -------------------- in favour of ----------------------------

This letter of guarantee is irrevocable on our part and we, hereby undertake to pay upon your first simple demand in writing that Messrs. ----------------
have advised to you that defective parts of ------------------------- equipment

and accessories supplied to _____ were not fitted and replaced by _____ and that they failed to do so within_____months and 15 days from the date of acceptance of merchandise as detailed in credit no._____ issued by _____, date of which to be advised to us by yourselves.

For and on behalf of:
ABC BANK PLC.

Signatures _____   _____

Advance Payment Guarantee/Bond Specimen
(amend wording as required)

From: XYZ Bank PLC   Date: _____

You have concluded on a contract no._____ with Messrs ABC & Co _____ for the delivery of at a total price of _____. According to the contract you will make an advance payment of_____ (_____ % of the total price) to Messrs _____ ABC & Co _____. As security for the claim for the refund of the advance payment, in the event that the merchandise is not delivered or not delivered in conformity with the terms of the contract, a guarantee by a bank shall be furnished.

At the request of Messrs _____ ABC & Co. _____ we, XYZ Bank PLC _____ hereby irrevocably undertake to refund to you on your first demand, irrespective of the validity and the legal effects of the above-mentioned contract and waiving all rights of objection and defence arising from said contract, any amount up to _____ (currency/maximum amount) (in words) upon receipt of your duly signed request for payment stating that Messrs _____ ABC & Co _____ have failed to deliver the ordered merchandise or have not delivered such merchandise as specified in the above mentioned contract.

The total amount of this guarantee will be reduced by any payment effected hereunder.

For the purpose of identification, your request for payment in writing has to be presented through the intermediary of a first rate bank confirming that the signatures thereon are legally binding upon you.

Your claim is also acceptable if transmitted to us in full by encoded telex/SWIFT through a first rate bank confirming that your original claim has been sent to us by registered mail and that the signatures thereon are legally binding upon you.

Your claim will be considered as having been made once we are in possession of your written request for payment or the encoded telex/SWIFT to this effect.

Our guarantee is valid until ---------- (date in words) and expires in full and automatically if your claim has not been made on or before that date, regardless of such date being a banking day or not.

This guarantee is governed by English Laws of the United Kingdom and place of jurisdiction is London (UK).

Authorised signature

Authorised signature

Banking Facility Guarantee Specimen
(amend wording as required)

To:

Bank ------------------------   Dated: ---------------------

Address

Test---------------- GB Pounds 0,000,000/=

RE: Our guarantee No: L/G--------------------------

We ------------------------ XYZ Bank PLC of------------------------ Postcode-----------, Hereby issue our letter of guarantee No L/G------------- in your favour for a maximum amount, not exceeding GB Pounds 0,000,000/= (GB Pounds: XXXXXXXXXXX only) inclusive of any interest and charges in consideration of your allowing banking facility to Mr/Messrs--------------------------

Any claims under this guarantee will be met on your first demand provided they are:-

1) Made in writing, by letter, or authenticated telex, cable stating that Mr/Messrs--------------------has failed to meet his/their obligations towards you in respect of the banking facilities extended to him/them by yourselves and

2) Lodged so as to reach us during the validity of the guarantee.

This letter of guarantee is valid for a period of six months i.e. up to ---------------------------- and any claims must be made so as to reach us before close of business on this date after which this guarantee will be considered null and void and our liability hereunder will cease to exist.

Signature---------------------------   Signature---------------------------

**Advance Payment Guarantee Specimen
(amend wording as required)**

To:

Bank's Name   Dated: 27-07-200X

Address

Jeddah
Saudi Arabia.

Test-------------------------- on S. Riyals 4,000.00

RE: Our letter of guarantee No: L/G -----------------------------

You are requested to issue your own letter of guarantee in the standard form acceptable to Saudi government and government agencies.

1. Favour---------------------------Ministry of Agriculture of Government of Saudi Arabia

2. Principal--------------------------M/S Together & Co. Limited – Istanbul, Turkey, on behalf of T & Z Ltd. Jeddah, Saudi Arabia

3. Amount------------------------S.R. 4,000,000.00 (Saudi Riyals: Four millions only)

4. Type of bond--------------------------advance payment, being 10% of the contract amount of S.R. 40,000,000.00 (Saudi Riyals: forty million only) for the project contract No. XXXXXX dated 1st January 200X

5. Starting from------------------.and validity --------------- months from the
   ----

6. Date of expiry date of--------------------- receipt of advance payment of S.R. 4,000,000/= (Saudi Riyals: four million only) by you for our account

7. This guarantee will only become operative subject to the strict compliance of the following terms and conditions: -

   a) Upon receipt of 100% advance payment of S.R. 4,000,000/= (Saudi Riyals: four million only) into and to the order of the XYZ Bank PLC Saudi Riyal A/C No. XYZ 12345678 held with you, receipt and crediting of which to be confirmed to us by your tested telex or swift advice.

   b) An irrevocable undertaking from the beneficiary to you, stating in writing that any payments by them to M/S Together & Co. Limited, Jeddah, Saudi Arabia, under the contract No. XXXXXX dated 1st January 200X for a total amount of S.R. 40,000,000/= (Saudi Riyals: forty million only) shall be paid to you only.

   c) That on receipt of proceeds, referred to in clause (b), above you will credit the entire proceeds of S.R. 40,000,000/= (Saudi Riyals: forty million only) into and to the order of XYZ Bank PLC account No. XYZ 12345678 held with you for account: M/S Together & Co. Limited, Istanbul, Turkey.

In consideration of your issuing the above-mentioned letter of guarantee, we, XYZ Bank PLC, of 300 commercial street, London E1 3AD, hereby absolutely irrevocably and unconditionally guarantee, under our counter guarantee No. 000000 to pay to you on your first demand by letter, telex or cable any amount upto Saudi Riyals 4,000,000/= (Saudi Riyals: four million only) as and when required to be paid by you to the above-mentioned beneficiary plus your charges and expenses as determined by you and to indemnify you against any loss or damage whatsoever resulting from issuing your guarantee, notwithstanding any objection and deficance by a third party arising from said obligation.

The validity of this guarantee extended to-----------------(allow ten days after validity of our guarantee to allow for processing) by which date all demand under this guarantee should be received by us. Any payment made hereunder shall be made free and clear of and without deduction for any present of future witholding or

Other taxes, duties, imports etc, of whatsoever nature and any whomsoever imposed. We hereby confirm that foreign exchange control and all other necessary approvals for the issuance of this counter guarantee have been obtained and are in full force and effect.

Our counter guarantee is subject to the laws and regulations of the Kingdom of Saudi Arabia.

Signature---------------------------   Signature-----------------------------

Customer's Request to Replace Earlier Guarantee Specimen (amend wording as required)

From: M/S ------------------------ Of -------------------------

To: XYZ Bank PLC   Date ---------------------

    Address

    Abu Dhabi

Test--------------------------On GB Pounds--------------------

Ref our guarantee number L/G-------------------------------------

At the request of -------------------- bank, -----------------branch London and on behalf of their clients M/S ------------------ we -------------------- bank PLC, of -----------------------------------, hereby request you to kindly issue a guarantee for USD ------------- (GB Pounds: ---------------------------------- only) in favour of M/S--------------------------Co. of -------------------------

as per following text: -

Quote

Messrs. M/S ---------------------------.

Address ------------------------------

At the request of M/S ------------------------of -------------------------------
-----------, we ---------------- bank PLC of -------------------------- guarantee to you for a sum of GB P------------ (GB Pounds: -------------------------------
------------ only).

This guarantee is in respect of replacement and fitting of defective parts of --- being supplied in accordance with our LC No. Lon ----------------- dated -------------

This guarantee will remain valid for a period of -------- months from the date of acceptance of merchandise to --------------------------and in case M/S -------------------------- or their nominee fail to replace the defective parts of the --------------------------, the beneficiary of the guarantee is authorised to claim the amount of the guarantee alongwith the letter from -------------------------- stating that despite their notification to M/S --------------------------of --------------------------, or their nominee the defective parts of the -------------------------- were not replaced.

Any claim made under this letter of guarantee must be presented at our office within the validity period, after which no claims will be entertained hereunder and our liability will cease to exist. Before any claim is made notification must be given to us --------------------------
M/S---------------------------

Unquote

1. Please treat this telex as an operative instrument and send us two copies of the guarantee issued by you for our record.

2. Please claim your charges in GB Pounds.

3. On the expiry of the above guarantee our liability thereunder will cease to exist.

In consideration of your issuing this guarantee we undertake to hold you harmless against any claim which may arise by reasons of your so doing provided that the amount does not exceed GB Pounds --------------- (United States Dollars-------------------------only). Please quote our reference No.------------in all communication relating to this guarantee.

Authorised Signature   Authorised Signature

------------------------------------   -------------------------------------

CHAPTER 18

SWIFT and Letters of Credit*

INTRODUCTION

SWIFT is an industry-owned co-operative supplying secure, standardised messaging services and interface software to nearly 8,100 financial institutions in 207 countries and territories. SWIFT members include banks, broker-dealers and investment managers. The broader SWIFT community also encompasses corporates as well as market infrastructures in payments, securities, treasury and trade.

Table 18.1 SWIFT statistics. SWIFTNet FIN traffic (in number of messages) January 2007 YTD (Posted 28 February 2007)

- Latest peak day: 13,663,975 messages on 20 December 2006

Total number of messages (year to date)	260,035,748
Message growth (total traffic year to date)	19.74%
Average daily traffic (year to date)	12,265,837
Message growth (average daily)	15.79%
Latest peak day: 20 December 2006	13,663,975
SWIFTNet FIN availability	
SWIFTNet FIN systems	99.993%
SWIFTNet FIN customer base	
Live countries	207
Live members	2,289
Live sub-members	3,124
Live participants	2,690
Total live users	

* The text reproduced here is valid at the time of reproduction. As amendments may from time to time be made to the text, readers are referred to the website www.swift.com for the latest version and for more information on this subject.

Source: SWIFT – www.swift.com

SWIFT Standard IPR Policy

End-User Licence Agreement
September 2005

1. *Definitions*

"**SWIFT**" is an acronym for Society for Worldwide Inter-bank Financial Telecommunication.

"**SWIFTStandards**" means any message-based standard or component thereof, developed by or for SWIFT, including the related business model, messages, message flows and documentation, whether in draft or final form.

"**IP Rights**" means all copyright, proprietary know-how, patent rights (including patent applications) or other intellectual or industrial property rights.

2. *Licence*

SWIFT hereby grants you a world-wide, royalty-free, non-exclusive licence to use or promote SWIFTStandards (i) for information transmission purposes in or outside the context of SWIFT messaging services and/or (ii) to develop software, products or services which support transmission of information in accordance with SWIFT Standards.

3. *Limitations*

You may not directly or indirectly sell SWIFTStandards. You may not modify SWIFTStandards while maintaining "SWIFTStandards" as a reference for the modified standard. This License Agreement does not grant you a license to use any of SWIFT's trademarks, except the trademark "SWIFTStandards" for the use as defined in Section 2.

4. *Sub-licensing*

You may grant sub-licenses on a royalty free basis only and provided that any such sub-license remains within the scope of your rights under this License Agreement.

5. *Ownership of SWIFTStandards*

All IP Rights, worldwide ownership of and rights, title and interest in and to SWIFTStandards, and all copies and portions thereof, are and shall remain exclusively in SWIFT and its licensors.

6. Termination

This license will terminate immediately without notice if you fail to comply with any material provision of this License Agreement.

7. Disclosure of IP Rights

During the thirty (30) days period immediately following the date that SWIFTStandards are provided to you, you may disclose that the publication of, use of or compliance with SWIFTStandards as presented, in whole or in part, would infringe any of your IP Rights. Upon timely disclosure and considering the non-commercial nature of SWIFTStandards, you agree to license any such IP Right to SWIFT (including the right to grant sublicenses) on royalty-free or otherwise reasonable and non-discriminatory terms and solely for the purpose of developing, implementing, promoting and using SWIFTStandards.

8. Non-Enforcement of IP Rights

Any non-disclosure of your IP Rights pursuant to Section 7 of this License Agreement, shall be considered as a final and irrevocable waiver to assert or enforce any such IP Right that you may own or control, against SWIFT or any other third party that may use SWIFTStandards, if the allegedly infringing activity is caused solely by the use of SWIFTStandards in accordance with this License Agreement.

9. Disclaimer

SWIFTStandards are provided "as is". SWIFT makes no express or implied representations, including but not limited to, warranties of merchantability or fitness for any particular purpose nor any warranty that the use of SWIFTStandards will not infringe any third party IP Rights.

10. Limitation of liability

Since SWIFTStandards result from industry consultation and are adopted by consensus amongst relevant industry participants, SWIFT will not be liable for any direct, indirect, special or consequential damages arising out of any use of SWIFTStandards even if SWIFT is expressly advised of the possibility of such damages.

11. Choice of Law – Arbitration

This License Agreement shall be governed by Belgian law.

Any dispute concerning this License Agreement, that cannot be amicably resolved, shall be finally settled under the Rules of Conciliation and Arbitration of the International Chamber of Commerce (ICC) by three arbitrators appointed in accordance with these rules. The arbitration proceedings shall take place in Brussels, Belgium and shall be conducted in the English language.

SWIFT UCP 600 Usage Guidelines
Exceptional update to achieve alignment
Published on 12 January 2007

During its 24–25 October 2006 meeting, the ICC Commission on Banking Technique and Practice approved new UCP 600 rules for documentary credits. These rules will take effect on 1 July 2007. With the purpose to remain aligned with the new UCP 600 from this date onward, the 'SWIFT UCP 600 Guidelines' provide guidance to banks on how to use today's category 7 standards in compliance with UCP 600.

Traditionally, SWIFT groups all its MT standards changes in one annual standards release, usually in October or November. In 2007, this will be on 27 October. In other words, the 1 July 2007 effective date of the UCP 600 does not coincide with the implementation date of SWIFT's Standards Release 2007.

This means that the only way to let the ICC and SWIFT 'live' dates coincide and to publish how the UCP 600 affects category 7 standards was by issuing 'SWIFT UCP 600 Guidelines' that financial institutions can start using as soon as the UCP 600 rules go 'live'. All guidelines are based on the use of narrative text in existing fields. This should ensure a seamless transition to the new rules.

The November 2006 SWIFT release caters for the UCP 600 using today's existing category 7 messages. A new mandatory field 40E Applicable Rules contains codes to indicate adherence to specific rules. Other changes as described below will be implemented in October 2007.

James Wills, Head of Trade Services Standards Development at SWIFT notes, "The difference in dates for UCP 600 (1 July 2007) and the annual SWIFT Standards Release (November 2006 and October 2007) has provided something of a challenge. However, SWIFT has worked with the industry to develop this approach to managing the issue, so that the community will be able to work successfully with the dates and guidelines."

The SWIFT UCP 600 Guidelines will be reflected in the official Standards Release 2007 documentation (Standards Release Guide and User Handbook) of 27 October 2007.

Changes that financial institutions can use from 1 July 2007

1. Date and place for presentation of documents under a credit

(a) Field 31D "Date and Place of Expiry" of the MT 700, 705, 710, 720 and 740. The definition of this field should be interpreted as follows: "This field specifies the latest date for presentation under the documentary credit and the place where documents may be presented." This guideline does not change the usage of this field.

(b) Field 41a "Available With ... By ... " of the MT 700, 705, 710 and 720. The definition of this field should be interpreted as follows: "This field identifies the bank with which the documentary credit is available (the place for presentation) and an indication of how the credit is available." This guideline does not change the usage of this field.

2. Expiry dates in reimbursement authorizations (or amendments thereof)

(a) Field 31D "Date and Place of Expiry" of the MT 740. The following usage rule should be added: "This field should not be used to specify the latest date for presentation of a reimbursement claim or an expiry date for the reimbursement authorization."

(b) Field 72 "Sender to Receiver Information" of the MT 740 The following usage rule should be added: "Any latest date for a reimbursement claim or an expiry date for the reimbursement authorization should be indicated in this field and not in field 31D."

(c) Field 31E "New Date of Expiry" of the MT 747 The following usage rule should be added: "This field should not be used to specify a new latest date for presentation of a reimbursement claim or a new expiry date for the reimbursement authorization."

(d) Field 72 "Sender to Receiver Information" of the MT 747 The following usage rule should be added: "Any new latest date for a reimbursement claim or a new expiry date for the reimbursement authorization should be indicated in this field and not in field 31E."

3. Details about the disposal of documents in a notice of refusal

Any details regarding the disposal of documents for which the two existing code words "HOLD" and "RETURN" in field 77B "Disposal of Documents" of the MT 734 Notice of Refusal cannot be used, must reflect the content of article 16.c of UCP 600 as follows:

(a) The code word "NOTIFY", to signify that "The issuing bank is holding the documents until it receives a waiver from the applicant and agrees to accept it, or receives further instructions from the presenter prior to agreeing to accept a waiver."

(b) The code word "PREVINST", to signify that "The bank is acting in accordance with instructions previously received from the presenter."

Because the contents (including code words) of field 77B "Disposal of Documents" of the MT 734 are not centrally validated (i.e. checked) by SWIFTNet, users may start using the above codes as of 1 July 2007 (live date of UCP 600). Alternatively, field 77B may contain a narrative text, reflecting the content of article 16.c of UCP 600.

Please refer to the usage guidelines section of field 77B of the MT 734 for further details. (Source: SWIFT)

Society for worldwide inter-bank financial telecommunications

SWIFT provides a means of communication among the financial institutions who are members of SWIFT.

The financial institutions can:

- Send and receive messages to themselves

- Send and receive messages within a "Close Group".

The policy of SWIFT is:

- To overview the SWIFT system

- Service Description

- The SWIFT system description

- Responsibility and liability

SWIFT administration:

- Issue and activation of login tables
- Authenticator keys
- Pricing structure
- Security procedures

SWIFT operations:

- Functional overview of the network
- System description: addressing, access, applications, message referencing
- Test and training
- System messages and reports
- User response to network faults

SWIFT address/ header:

- Name of the bank – (4 characters i.e. BARB for Bank of Baroda)
- Name of the country – (2 Characters i.e. GB for Great Britain)
- Location of the main server of the member bank – (2 characters i.e. 2 L for 2nd location in London)
- Branch address – (3 characters XXX)

Messages types (MT)

MT 0XX Series   Messages sent by SWIFT regarding:

- Network architecture
- System architecture

- Communication concepts

- Protocols

- Message and address standards

- General text and field rules

MT 103 Series	Customer fund transfers from one customer to another in another bank.
MT 200 Series	Financial institutions fund transfers (MT 202) from one bank to another bank (Institutional funds)
MT 300 Series	Treasury/Foreign exchange transactions, confirmations etc. (unauthenticated messages)
MT 400 Series	Collections / Cash Advices Foreign bills for collection, foreign bills purchased, acknowledgements / payment advices
MT 500 Series	Securities Dealing
MT 600 Series	Precious Metal Dealing
MT 700 Series	Documentary Credits / Guarantees
MT 800 Series	Travellers Cheques
MT 900 Series	Cash Management (Unauthenticated messages)

When the two Zeros (00) (unit and tens) are replaced in any of the above series of MT then messages indicate as:

99 – Free Format (i.e. MT 199) relating to customer fund transfer

92 – Request for cancellation (i.e. MT 192) relating to customer fund transfer cancellation request

95 – Query (i.e. MT 195) It is a query relating to customer fund transfer.

96 – Answer or Reply (i.e. MT 196) It is a reply relating to customer fund transfer.

Field groups format specifications

Tag	Field Name	Content/Options
19	Sum of Amount	17 number
20	Transaction Reference Number	16x
21	Transaction Reference	16x
23	Further Identification/Bank Operation Code	16x
26E	Number of Amendment	2n
26T	Transaction Type Code	3a
27	Sequence of Total	1n/1n
30	Value Date	6n
31C	Date of Issue	6n
31D	Date and Place of Expiry	6n29x
31E	New Date of Expiry	6n
32a	Principal Amount Paid/Accepted/Negotiated	A, B, K
32A	Value Date, Currency Code, Amount	6n3a15number
32B	Currency Code, Amount	3a15number
33a	Total Amount Claimed/Net Amount	A, B, C or K.
33B	Additional Amount	3a15number
34a	Total Amount Claimed	A or B
34B	Total Amount to be Paid	3a15number
36	Exchange Rate	12number
39A	Percentage Credit Amount Tolerance	2n/2n
39B	Maximum Credit Amount	13x
39C	Additional Amount Covered	4*35x
40A	Form of Documentary Credit	24x
40B	Form of Documentary Credit	2*24x
41-	Available with ---- by----	A or D
42a	Drawee	A or D
42C	Draft at	3*35x
42M	Mixed Payment Detail	4*35x
40B	Form of Documentary Credit	2*24x
41a	Available With ----By ----	A or D
42a	Drawee	A or D
42C	Draft at -----	3*35X
42M	Mixed Payment Details	4*35x
42P	Deferred Payment Details	4*35x
43P	Partial Shipments	1*35x
43T	Trans-shipment	1*35x

Continued

Tag	Field Name	Content/Options
44A	Loading on Board/Despatch/Taking in Charge	1*35x
B	For Transportation to ---	1*x
C	Latest Date of Shipment	N
D	Shipping Period	*x
A/B	Description of Goods and/or Services	50*x
A/B	Additional Conditions	50*x
48	Period of Presentations	A or D
49	Confirmation Instruction	x
50	Applicant	4*X
H	Applicant and Account Information	/x,4*x
A	Applicant bank	A or D
A	Ordering Institution	A, B, D
A	Sender's Correspondent	A, B, D or J
A	Receiver's correspondent	A, B, or D
A	Intermediary	A, B, D OR J
A	"Advise through" Bank	A, B, D, or J
A	Beneficiary's institution	A, D, or J
59	Beneficiary	(/x),4*x
70	Details of Payments	1*x
A	Details of Charges	4*x
B	Charges	6*x
F	Sender's Charges / Amount	3a15number
71G	Receiver's Charges / Amount	-a15number
72	Sender to Receiver Information	6*x
73	Charges to be Deducted	6*x
75	Queries	6*x
76	Answers	6*x
77A	Discrepancies / Narrative	20*x
77B	Disposal of Documents	3*x
77C	Details of Guarantee / Amendment Details	50*x
77D	Details of Dishonoured Items	6*x
78	Instructions to the Bank Paying/Accepting Negotiating	12*x
79	Narrative	35*50c

SWIFT CODE WORDS

SWIFT uses different types of code words in all categories of messages. The appropriate code words should be used in the narrative where required.

The following is a list of code words that are used for trade finance and payment messages.

Code word	Definition/Meaning	Message Type
/ICU	Instructions following are for the account with institution	100, 200, 201, 202, 203, 204, 205, 754
/ALCHARF/	All charges have been refused by drawee	400, 412
/BENCON/	Receiver is requested to advise the beneficiary's acceptance or non-acceptance of the terms and conditions contained in the amendment	707, 760, 767
/BENONLY/	Payment is to be made to the beneficiary customer only	103
/BNB/	Information following is for the beneficiary	202, 203, 204, 205, 400,
/CABLE/	Please advise account with institution by cable	100, 202
/CABLEBEN/	Please advise the beneficiary/ claimant by cable	100, 202
/CABLEIBK/	Please advise the intermediary by cable	100, 202
/CHECK/or/ CHEQUE/	Payment by cheque	100
/FORWARD/	Collection(s) is/are being forwarded to our branch. Please address any further communication to them.	410
/HOLD/	Beneficiary customer/claimant will call; pay upon identification.	100
/HOLDING/	The accepted draft(s) is/are held with us in safe custody and at your disposal for presentation for payment at maturity	412
/INS/	The instructing institution which instructed the sender to execute the transaction	100, 202, 203, 205

Continued

Code word	Definition/Meaning	Message Type
/OGB/	Information following the name and the location of the originator's institution which service the originator of the transfer	202
/OUCHARF/	Our charges have been refused by the drawee(s)	400, 412
/PHON/	Please advise accounts with institution by phone	100, 200, 201, 202, 203, 205
/PHONEBEN/	Please advise/contact beneficiary/claimant by phone	100, 202, 203, 205, 400, 700, 705, 707, 710, 720, 754, 760, 767.
/PHONIBK/	Please advise the intermediary by phone	100, 200, 201, 202, 203, 205
/RCB/	Receiver's correspondent	100
/REC/	Institution following is the receiver	100, 200, 201, 202, 203, 204, 205, 400, 410, 412, 754.
/SENDING/	The accepted draft(s) is/are being returned to you by airmail	412
/TELE/	Please advise the account with institution by telex	100, 200, 201, 202, 203, 205,
/TELEBEN/	Please advise the beneficiary/claimant by telex	100, 200, 201, 202, 203, 205,
/TELEBK/	Please advise the intermediary by the most efficient means of communication	100, 200, 201, 202, 203, 205,
/UCHREF/	Your charges have been refused by drawee(s)	

SPECIMENS OF FORMATS FOR SWIFT MESSAGES USED BY BANKS

Issuing documentary letter of credit using SWIFT
MT 700

Title				
Guide to message Text Standards				
Subject				
Issue of a Documentary Credit				
BKIDGBLAXXX Issue of a Documentary Credit MT 700 Please note that the boxes are compulsory and must be completed				
Message Addressing Details	PRIORITY: SEND TO:	K = Normal U = Urgent D = Deferred		
	FROM: Telegraph Serial No.		DATE	y y m m d d
Message TEXT	To:_____ or SWIFT address CBID CODE			
	From:			
M/#	Field Tag No	Issue of Documentary Credit-		
M	27	SEQUENCE OF TOTAL:		
M	40	Form of DC:		
M	20	DC No.	*IRREVOCABLE / REVOCABLE/TRANSFERABLE	
#	23	PRE-ADVISE		
				y y m m d d

SWIFT AND LETTERS OF CREDIT

#	31	Date of issue	D	d	m	M	y	Y									
M	31	Expiry date & Place															
#	51a	Applicant Bank (Max. 4 lines)															
M	50	Applicant. (Name & address)															
M	59	Beneficiary. (a/c no. if known)															
M	32B	Currency Code, Amt															
#	39a	%age of DC amt. tolerance															
#	39B	Max. DC Amt. Specification. Max. 4 lines															
#	39c	Additional amt covered															
M	41a	Available with/By	By Payment / Acceptance / Negotiation													
#	42c	Drafts At/ Drawn on	D	R	A	F	T		A	T							
#	42a	Drawee	D	R	A	W	N		O	N							
#	42m	Mixed Payment detail															
#	42P	Deferred payment details															
#	43P	Partial Shipments:	*ALLOWED / FORBIDDEN													
#	43T	Trans-shipment:	*PERMITTED / PROHIBITED													
#	44A	Loading on board/ Despatch/ Taking in charge at/from															

#	44b	For transport to												
#	44c	Latest date of shipment												
#	44D	Shipment period												
#	45A	Description of goods/services												
#	46	Documents required												
#	47A	Additional conditions												
#	71B	Charges												
#	48	Period of presentation												
M	49	Confirmation instructions												
#	53a	Reimbursing Bank												
#	78a	Instructions to paying/ accepting/ negotiating bank												
#	57a	Advise through Bank												
#	72	Sender to Receiver information												

# = Optional	M = Mandatory		* = Delete whichever not required		
Authorised Signature		Prepared by:	Taped by:	Checked by:	Sent by:

Issuing documentary letter of credit using SWIFT
MT (Page 701)

Title		Volume	Section	Page
Guide to message Text Standards		2	3	5
Subject				
Issue of a Documentary Credit				
BKIDGBLAXXX				
Issue of a Documentary Credit (701)				
Please note that the boxes are compulsory and must be completed				

Message Addressing Details	PRIORITY: SEND TO:	K = Normal	U = Urgent	D = Deferred
	FROM:			
	Telegraph Serial No.		DATE	y y m m d d
MESSAGE TEXT	To:_____ or SWIFT address CBID CODE From:			
M/#	Field Tag No.	Issue of a Documentary Credit		
M	27	Sequence of Total:		
M	20	DC No.		
#	45	GOODS: (maximum 20 lines)		
#	46	DOCUMENTS REQUIRED: (maximum 20 lines)		

#	47	ADDITIONAL CONDITIONS: (maximum 20 lines)					
		Col.:					
Authorised Signature				Prepared by:	Taped by:	Checked by:	Sent by:

Pre-advice of a documentary letter of credit

MT 705

Title	
Guide to message Text Standards	
Subject	
Pre-advice of a Documentary Credit	
BKIDGBLAXXX Pre-advice of a Documentary Credit MT 705 Please note that the boxes are compulsory and must be completed	

Message Addressing Details	PRIORITY: SEND TO:	K = Normal U = Urgent D = Deferred
	FROM:	
	Telegraph Serial No.	Date
		y y m m d d

Message Text	To:____ or SWIFT address CBID CODE	

M/#	Field Tag No	Pre-advice of a Documentary Credit	
M	40a	Form of Documentary Credit	Irrevocable / Revocable / Transferable
M	20	Documentary Credit No.	
M	31	Expiry Date & Place	
			y y m m d d
M	50	Applicant (name and address)	

M	59	Beneficiary: (a/c no. if known should be quoted on first line)	
#	32B	Currency Code, Amount	
M	39A	%age Credit Amount Tolerance	
#	39B	Maximum Credit Amount. Specification	
#	39C	Additional amount covered	
#	41a	Available with / By	
			Payment / Acceptance / Negotiation
#	44a	Loading on board/Taking in charge at/from/Shipment Details:	
#	44B	For transportation to	
#	44C	Latest date of shipment	
#	44D	Shipment period	
#	45A	Description of Goods and / or services:	
#	57A	Advise through bank	
#	79	Narrative	
#	72	Sender to receive information	

Advice of a third bank's documentary letter of credit

MT 711

Title				
Guide to message Text Standards				
Subject				
Advice of a Third Bank's Documentary Credit				
Bank Name				
Pre-advice of a Documentary Credit				
Please note that the boxes are compulsory and must be completed				
Message Addressing Details	PRIORITY: SEND TO:	K = Normal U = Urgent D = Deferred		
	FROM:			
	Telegraph Serial No.		Date	
				y y m m d d
Message TEXT	Continuation of DC No.			
#	27	Sequence of total Number of a message Total No. of Messages		
#	20	Sender's Reference number		
#	21	Documentary Credit No.		
#	45B	Description of goods and/or services		

#	46B	Documents Required													
#	47B	Additional Conditions													

Authorised Signature		Prepared by:	Taped by:	Checked by:	Sent by:

Documentary credit amendment

Page 1 (707A)

Title		Volume	Section	Page
Guide to message Text Standards		2	5	2
Subject				
Documentary Credit Amendment				
H K B G				
Pre-advice of a Documentary Credit Page 1 (707A)				
Please note that the boxes are compulsory and must be completed				
Message Addressing Details	PRIORITY: SEND TO:	K = Normal U = Urgent D = Deferred		
	FROM:			
	Telegraph Serial No.		DATE	y y m m d d
Message Text	To:_____ or SWIFT address CBID CODE			
	From:			
M/#	Field Tag No.	DOCUMENTARY CREDIT AMENDMENT		
M	20	OUR REF:		
M	21	YOUR REF:		
#	23	ISSUING BK'S REF:		
#	52	ISSUING BANK		
#	31	DATE OF ISSUE	y y m m d d	

INTERNATIONAL TRADE FINANCE

#	30	Date of Amendment:	y y m m d d	
#	59	Beneficiary: (a/c no., if known should be quoted on 1st line)		
#	31	New Expiry Date:	y y m m d d	
#	32	Increase of DC Amt:		
#	33	Decrease of DC Amt:		
#	34	New DC Amt:		
#	39	Amt. Specification:		
#	44	SHIPMENT DETAILS		

M = Mandatory   # = Optional   (Continued on page 2)

Documentary credit amendment

Page 2 (707B)

Title		Volume	Section	Page
Guide to message Text Standards		2	5	3
Subject				
Documentary Credit Amendment				
H K B G				
Pre-advice of a Documentary Credit Page 2 (707B)				
Please note that the boxes are compulsory and must be completed				

Message Addressing Details	PRIORITY: SEND TO:	K = Normal U = Urgent D = Deferred	
	FROM:		
	Telegraph Serial No.		Date y y m m d d

Message Text	Continuation of DC No.		
#	79	Other Documents:	
#	72	Bank to Bank information	

Authorised Signature		Prepared by:	Taped by:	Checked by:	Sent by:

Transfer of a documentary credit
MT 720

Title				
Guide to message Text Standards			
Subject			
Transfer of a Documentary Credit			
Name of Bank			
Transfer of a Documentary Credit			
Please note that the boxes are compulsory and must be completed			
Message Addressing Details	PRIORITY: SEND TO:	K = Normal U = Urgent D = Deferred		
	FROM:			
	Telegraph Serial No.		Date	
			y y m m d d	
Message Text	To:_____ or SWIFT address CBID CODE From:			
M/#	Field Tag No.	Transfer of a Documentary Credit		
M	27	Sequence of total:		
M	40B	FORM OF DC	IRREVOCABLE/REVOCABLE TRANSFERABLE	
			ADDING / WITHOUT OUR CONFIRMATION	
M	20	Transferring Bank's Reference:		
M	21	Documentary Credit No:		

#	23	PRE-ADVICE: Ready	P	R	E	A	D	V				y	y	m	m	d	d
M	31C	DATE OF ISSUE	y	y	m	m	d	d									
M	31D	DATE & PLACE: OF EXPIRY	y	y	m	m	d	d									
M	52A	Issuing Bank of the original documentary Credit															
M	50	First Beneficiary															
M	59	Second Beneficiary															
M	32B	Currency Code, Amount															
#	39A	%age Credit Amount Tolerance															
#	39B	Maximum Credit Amount															
#	39C	Additional Amounts covered															
M	41a	Available with/By:															
			BY PAYMENT/ACCEPTANCE/NEGOTIATION														
#	42C	Drafts at															
#	42a	Drawee															
#	42M	Mixed Payment Details															
#	42P	Deferred Payment Details															

#	43P	Partial Shipment																		
#	43T	Trans-shipment																		
#	44A	Loading on Board/Despatch/Taking in Charge at/from ----																		
#	44B	For Transportation to --																		
#	44C	Latest date of Shipment																		
#	44D	Shipment period																		
#	45A	Description of goods and/or services																		
#	46A	Documents required																		
#	47	Additional conditions																		
#	71B	Charges																		
#	48	Period for Presentation																		
M	49	Confirmation Instructions																		
#	78	Instructions to the paying/ Accepting/ Negotiating Bank																		
#	57a	Advise through Bank.																		
#	72	Sender to receive information																		
Authorised Signature				Prepared by:			Taped by:			Checked by:			Sent by:							

SWIFT format of a letter of credit

To swift

40A	Form of documentary credit	Irrevocable
20:	Documentary credit no:	XXXXXXX
31C	Date of issue	YY-MM-DD
31D:	Date & place of expiry	YY-MM-DD, London
51A:	Applicant bank	Bank ID
50:	Applicant	Full name and address including post code
59:	Beneficiary	Full name and address including post code
32B:	Currency code and amount	USD XXX,XXX.XX
41A:	Available with ..... by	Advising bank by negotiation
42C:	Draft at	Sight
42A:	Drawee	Bank ID Name of bank, London
43P:	Part-shipment	Allowed in full container load only
43T:	Trans-shipment	Allowed
44A:	Onboard/disp/taking charge at/f:	Name of port & country
44B:	For transportation to	Name of port & country
44C:	Latest date of shipment	Year-MM-DD
45A:	Description of goods and/or services	

Full details and specifications as per beneficiary's proforma invoice no:XXXXXXXX dated XXXX-XX-XX.

46A:	Documents required	
47A:	Additional conditions	
71B:	Charges	All charges outside UK are for beneficiary's account
48:	Period for presentation	No. of days as appropriate
49:	Confirmation instruction	Without
51D:	Advice through	Full name and address of the bank

78:     Instruction to paying/accepting/negotiating bank

         We hereby engage with drawers and/or bonafide holders that the drafts drawn under and in strict compliance of this letter of credit will be honoured and paid on due date as per their instruction.

All documents should be sent in one lot and to us (name and address of the issuing bank)

79:     Except as otherwise expressly stated, this documentary credit is subject to UCPDC 91993 Revision ICC Broucher no. 500

CHAPTER 19

ICC DOCDEX RULES
ICC Rules for Documentary Instruments Dispute Resolution Expertise*

ARTICLE 1: DISPUTE RESOLUTION SERVICE

1.1 These rules concern a service called Documentary Instruments Dispute Resolution Expertise (DOCDEX) which is available in connection with any dispute related to:

- a documentary credit incorporating the ICC Uniform Customs and Practice for Documentary Credits (UCP), and the application of the UCP and/or of the ICC Uniform Rules for Bank-to-Bank Reimbursement under Documentary Credits (URR),

- a collection incorporating the ICC Uniform Rules for Collections (URC), and the application of the URC,

- a demand guarantee incorporating the ICC Uniform Rules for Demand Guarantees (URDG), and the application of the URDG. Its objective is to provide an independent, impartial and prompt expert

---

* The text reproduced here is valid at the time of reproduction. As amendments may from time to time be made to the text, readers are referred to the website www.iccdocdex.org for the latest version and for more information on this ICC dispute resolution service.
Source: International Chamber of Commerce, Paris www.iccdocdex.org

decision (DOCDEX Decision) on how the dispute should be resolved on the basis of the terms and conditions of the documentary credit, the collection instruction, or the demand guarantee and the applicable ICC Rules, be it the UCP, the URR, the URC or the URDG (ICC Rules).

Any reference to DOCDEX will be deemed to apply to the latest version of the DOCDEX Rules and the applicable version of the ICC Rules, unless otherwise stipulated in the documentary credit, the collection instruction or the demand guarantee.

1.2 DOCDEX is made available by the International Chamber of Commerce (ICC) through its International Centre for Expertise (Centre) under the auspices of the ICC Commission on Banking Technique and Practice (Banking Commission).

1.3 When a dispute is submitted to the Centre in accordance with these rules, the Centre shall appoint three experts from a list of experts maintained by the Banking Commission. These three experts (Appointed Experts) shall make a decision which, after consultation with the Technical Adviser of the Banking Commission, shall be issued by the Centre as a DOCDEX Decision in accordance with these rules. The DOCDEX Decision is not intended to conform with any legal requirements of an arbitration award.

1.4 Unless otherwise agreed, a DOCDEX Decision shall not be binding upon the parties.

1.5 In the DOCDEX procedure the communication with the Centre shall be conducted exclusively in writing, i.e. by communication received in a form that provides a complete record thereof, via teletransmission or other expeditious means.

ARTICLE 2: REQUEST

2.1 The Initiator shall apply for a DOCDEX Decision by submission of a request (Request). The Initiator may be one of the parties to the dispute applying individually, or more or all parties to the dispute submitting jointly a single Request. The Request, including all documents annexed thereto, shall be supplied to the Centre in Paris, France, in four copies.

2.2 A Request shall be concise and contain all necessary information clearly presented, in particular the following:

> 2.2.1 full name and address of the Initiator, clearly stating such Initiator's function(s) in connection with the documentary credit, the collection, or the demand guarantee, and

2.2.2 full name and address of any other party to the dispute (Respondent), clearly stating such Respondent's function(s) in connection with the documentary credit, the collection, or the demand guarantee, where the Request is not submitted jointly by all parties to the dispute, and

2.2.3 a statement of the Initiator formally requesting a DOCDEX Decision in accordance with the ICC DOCDEX Rules, ICC Publication No. 811, and

2.2.4 a summary of the dispute and of the Initiator's claims, clearly identifying all issues related to the documentary credit, the collection, or the demand guarantee and the applicable ICC Rules to be determined, and

2.2.5 copies of the documentary credit, the collection instruction, or the demand guarantee in dispute, all amendments thereto, and all documents deemed necessary to establish the relevant circumstances, and

2.2.6 a statement by the Initiator that a copy of such Request, including all documents annexed thereto, has been sent to each Respondent named in the Request.

2.3 The Request must be accompanied by the payment of the Standard Fee as per the Appendix hereto. No Request shall be processed unless accompanied by the requisite payment.

ARTICLE 3: ANSWER

3.1 The Respondent may submit an Answer to the Initiator's Request. The Respondent may be one or more of the parties to the dispute named in the Request as Respondent, each submitting an individual Answer or submitting jointly a single Answer.

The Answer must be received by the Centre within the period stipulated in the Centre's Acknowledgement of the Request (see Article 5). The Answer, including all documents annexed thereto, shall be supplied to the Centre in Paris, France, in four copies.

3.2 An Answer shall be concise and contain all necessary information clearly presented, in particular the following:

3.2.1 name and address of the Initiator, and

3.2.2 date of the relevant Request, and

3.2.3 a statement of the Respondent formally requesting a DOCDEX Decision in accordance with the ICC DOCDEX Rules, ICC Publication No. 811, and

3.2.4 a summary of the Respondent's claims, clearly referring to all issues related to the documentary credit, the collection, or the demand guarantee and the applicable ICC Rules to be determined, and

3.2.5 copies of all additional documents deemed necessary to establish the relevant circumstances, and

3.2.6 a statement of the Respondent that a copy of such Answer, including all documents annexed thereto, has been sent in writing to the Initiator and to the other Respondent named in the Request.

3.3 If the Respondent does not provide a statement pursuant to Article 3.2.3, then the final DOCDEX Decision will not be made available to him.

ARTICLE 4: SUPPLEMENTS

4.1 Request, Answers and Supplements shall be final as received.

4.2 The Centre may ask the Initiator and Respondent, by way of an Invitation, to submit specific supplementary information, including copies of documents, relevant to the DOCDEX Decision (Supplement).

4.3 Supplements must be received by the Centre in four copies within the period stipulated in the Invitation. The Supplement shall be concise and contain all necessary information clearly presented and include copies of relevant documents. It shall also contain:

4.3.1 date and reference as stated in the Invitation, and

4.3.2 name and address of the issuer of such Supplement, and

4.3.3 a statement of the issuer of such Supplement that a copy of the Supplement, including all documents annexed thereto, has been sent to the Initiator or Respondent.

4.4 Supplements shall only be submitted to the Centre upon and in accordance with an Invitation issued by the Centre.

ARTICLE 5: ACKNOWLEDGEMENTS AND REJECTIONS

5.1 The Centre shall confirm the receipt of Requests, Answers and Supplements to the Initiator and Respondent (Acknowledgement).

5.2 The Centre will stipulate a reasonable period of time within which each Answer or Supplement must be received by the Centre. The stipulated time should not exceed 30 days after the date of the Acknowledgement of the receipt of a Request or 14 days after the date of an Invitation to submit a Supplement.

5.3 Any Answer or Supplement received by the Centre after expiry of the period of time specified in the relevant Acknowledgement or Invitation, or any communication not solicited by the Centre, shall be disregarded.

5.4 By advice to the Initiator and Respondent, the Centre may reject at any time, before or after its Acknowledgement, any Request, Answer or Supplement, in whole or part,

> 5.4.1 where the Centre or Appointed Experts deem any issue to be determined to be unrelated to the applicable ICC Rules, or
>
> 5.4.2 which in other respects, in particular regarding form and/or substance, does not fulfil the requirements of these rules, or
>
> 5.4.3 in respect of which the Standard Fee has not been received by the Centre within 14 days after the date of the Request.

5.5 Periods of time specified in these rules or in any Acknowledgement or Invitation referring to days shall be deemed to refer to consecutive calendar days and shall start to run on the day following the date of issuance stated in the relevant Acknowledgement or Invitation. If the last day of the relevant period of time is, or any fixed day falls on, a non-business day in Paris, France, then the period of time shall expire at the end of the first following business day in Paris.

ARTICLE 6: APPOINTMENT OF EXPERTS

6.1 The Banking Commission will maintain internal lists of experts having profound experience and knowledge of the applicable ICC Rules.

6.2 Upon receipt of a Request, the Centre shall appoint three independent experts from the list. Each Appointed Expert shall declare his independence of the parties indicated in the Request. The Centre shall designate one of the three Appointed Experts to act as their Chair.

6.3 An Appointed Expert shall at all times keep strictly confidential all information and documents related to any DOCDEX case.

6.4 Where an Appointed Expert deems that he is unable to carry out his functions, he shall immediately give notice of termination to the Centre. Where the Centre deems that an Appointed Expert is unable to carry out his functions, it shall immediately give notice of termination to such Appointed Expert. In either case, such Appointed Expert shall immediately return to the Centre the Request, Answer(s) and Supplement(s) received, including all documents annexed thereto, and the Centre shall inform the other Appointed Experts of such termination.

6.5 The Centre shall, without delay, replace an Appointed Expert whose appointment is prematurely terminated pursuant to Article 6.4 of these rules and the Centre shall inform the other Appointed Experts accordingly.

ARTICLE 7: APPOINTED EXPERTS' PROCEDURE

7.1 The Centre shall submit to the Appointed Experts the Request, Answer(s) and Supplement(s) received in connection therewith.

7.2 The Appointed Experts shall render their decision impartially and exclusively on the basis of the Request, Answer(s) and Supplement(s) thereto, and the documentary credit and the UCP and/or URR, or the collection and the URC, or the demand guarantee and the URDG.

7.3 Where it is deemed necessary by the Appointed Experts, their Chair may ask the Centre to invite the Initiator and Respondent, pursuant to Article 4 of these rules, to provide additional information and/or copies of documents.

7.4 Within 30 days after they have received all information and documents deemed by them to be necessary and appropriate to the issues to be determined, and provided that the Additional Fee as mentioned in Article 10.1 is paid, the Appointed Experts shall draft a decision and their Chair shall submit the decision to the Centre.

7.5 Neither the Initiator nor the Respondent shall

- seek an oral hearing in front of the Appointed Experts,
- request ICC to reveal the name of any Appointed Expert,
- seek to have an Appointed Expert or officer of the Banking Commission called as witness, expert or in any similar function to an arbitral tribunal or a court of law hearing the dispute in connection with which such Appointed Expert or officer of the Banking Commission participated by rendering a DOCDEX Decision.

ARTICLE 8: DOCDEX DECISION

8.1 Upon receipt of the decision of the Appointed Experts, the Centre shall consult with the Technical Adviser of the Banking Commission or his nominated delegate, to ascertain that the DOCDEX Decision will be in line with the applicable ICC Rules and their interpretation by the Banking Commission. Amendments suggested by the Technical Adviser (or his delegate) shall be subject to the consent of the majority of the Appointed Experts.

8.2 Subject to Article 10.2 of these rules, the Centre will issue and make available the DOCDEX Decision without delay to

    8.2.1 the Initiator and

    8.2.2 the Respondent who has requested, pursuant to Article 3.2.3, a DOCDEX Decision in accordance with the ICC DOCDEX Rules, ICC Publication No. 811.

8.3 The DOCDEX Decision shall be issued by the Centre in the English language, unless the Appointed Experts decide otherwise, and shall contain, inter alia, the following:

    8.3.1 names of the Initiator and Respondent, and

    8.3.2 summary of the representations relevant to the issues determined, and

    8.3.3 determination of the issues and the decisions taken with succinctly stated reasons therefor, and

    8.3.4 date of issuance and signature for and on behalf of the Centre.

8.4 The DOCDEX Decision shall be deemed to be made at Paris, France, and on the date of its issuance by the Centre.

ARTICLE 9: DEPOSIT AND PUBLICATION OF THE DOCDEX DECISION

9.1 An original of each DOCDEX Decision shall be deposited with the Centre and shall be kept there for 10 years.

9.2 ICC may publish any DOCDEX Decision, provided always the identities of the parties to the dispute are not disclosed.

ARTICLE 10: COSTS OF DOCDEX

10.1 The costs of the DOCDEX service shall be the Standard Fee set out in the Appendix. The Standard Fee shall not be recoverable. In exceptional circumstances, an Additional Fee may be payable which shall be fixed by the Centre at its discretion, taking into account the complexity of the issue and subject to the ceiling set out in the Appendix under 'Additional Fee'. Such Additional Fee shall be invoiced to the Initiator within a reasonable time, at the latest within 45 days after the date of the Acknowledgement of the Request. The Centre will fix a time limit for the payment of the Additional Fee. The Centre may stay the procedure at any time, and instruct the Appointed Experts to suspend their work on the case, until the Additional Fee is paid by the Initiator. No Additional Fee will be charged where the amount of the letter of credit, the collection, or the demand guarantee in dispute does not exceed the minimum amount stated in the Appendix.

10.2 The DOCDEX Decision shall not be issued until the Centre has received the Additional Fee, if invoiced.

ARTICLE 11: GENERAL

11.1 In all matters not expressly provided for in these rules, the Centre, experts, Appointed Experts, officers, officials and employees of ICC shall adhere to strict confidentiality and shall act in the spirit of these rules.

11.2 Appointed Experts, officers, officials and employees of ICC assume no liability or responsibility for the consequences arising out of delay and/or loss in transit of any message(s), letter(s) or document(s), or for delay, mutilation or other error(s) arising in the transmission of any telecommunication, or for errors in translation and/or interpretation of technical terms.

11.3 Appointed Experts, officers, officials and employees of ICC assume no liability or responsibility for the discharge or purported discharge of their functions in connection with any DOCDEX Decision, unless the act or omission is shown not to have been in good faith.

APPENDIX TO THE ICC RULES FOR DOCUMENTARY

Instruments Dispute Resolution Expertise

1. *Standard Fee*

The Standard Fee, which includes administrative expenses and expert fees, is US$ 5000.

2. Additional Fee

Pursuant to Article 10.1 of these Rules the Centre may, if the amount of the letter of credit, of the collection, or of the demand guarantee exceeds US$ 500 000, charge an Additional Fee of up to 100% of the Standard Fee.

3. Payment

Any payment made towards such fees shall be made in United States dollars to the International Chamber of Commerce in Paris, clearly marked with the reference of DOCDEX

- by bank transfer to UBS SA

    35, Rue des Noirettes
    P.O. Box 2600
    CH-1211 Geneva 2 – Switzerland
    Account No.: 240-224534.61R
    Swift code: UBSWCHZH12A
    IBAN: CH06 0024 0240 2245 3461 R

    or

- by cheque payable to the International Chamber of Commerce, or
- by Visa card stating

    Expiry date _____
    Visa card number _____
    Name on card _____
    Signature _____
    Date _____

4. Transmission

Any such payment shall be accompanied by an advice in writing to: International Chamber of Commerce

International Centre for Expertise
38, Cours Albert 1er
F-75008 Paris France
Fax: +33 1 49 53 29 29
E-mail: docdex@iccwbo.org

stating the following data:

Name: --

Business title: --

Company: ---

Address: ---

Code/postal code: --

Date of Request: ---

5. General

This Appendix is subject to change without notice. Please enquire with the International Chamber of Commerce as to the applicable version of this Appendix.

ICC at a Glance

ICC is the world business organization, a representative body that speaks with authority on behalf of enterprises from all sectors in every part of the world. The fundamental mission of ICC is to promote trade and investment across frontiers and help business corporations meet the challenges and opportunities of globalization. Its conviction that trade is a powerful force for peace and prosperity dates from the organization's origins early in the last century. The small group of farsighted business leaders who founded ICC called themselves "the merchants of peace". Because its member companies and associations are themselves engaged in international business, ICC has unrivalled authority in making rules that govern the conduct of business across borders. Although these rules are voluntary, they are observed in countless thousands of transactions every day and have become part of the fabric of international trade.

ICC also provides essential services, foremost among them the ICC International Court of Arbitration, the world's leading arbitral institution. Another service is the World Chambers Federation, ICC's worldwide network of chambers of commerce, fostering interaction and exchange of chamber best practice. Within a year of the creation of the United Nations, ICC was granted consultative status at the highest level with the UN and its specialized agencies. Business leaders and experts drawn from the ICC membership establish the business stance on broad issues of trade and investment policy as well as on vital technical and sectoral subjects. These include financial services, information technologies, telecommunications, marketing ethics, the environment, transportation, competition law and intellectual property, among others.

ICC was founded in 1919. Today it groups thousands of member companies and associations from over 130 countries. National committees work with their members to address the concerns of business in their countries and convey to their governments the business views formulated by ICC.

For More information on ICC and ICC publications please visit:

www.iccwbo.org

www.iccbooks.com

ICC Publication No. 811

ISBN-10: 92-842-1325-8

ISBN-13: 978-92-842-1325-2

International Centre for Expertise

38, Cours Albert 1er, 75008 Paris, France

Telephone +33 1 49 53 30 53 Fax +33 1 49 53 29 29

www.iccdocdex.org E-mail docdex@iccwbo.org

International Chamber of Commerce

Source: International Chamber of Commerce, Paris

CHAPTER 20

Export Risks Insurance and ECGD

GENESIS

In the case of normal trade, a small seller/exporter may be able to protect him or herself against non-payment by his local buyers for whatever reason provided that it cannot be shown that the seller was responsible for the non-payment, i.e. by not fulfilling his side of the contract. Non-payment is not the only risk faced in the selling of goods and/or services overseas. These risks may be beyond the control of the overseas buyer. Therefore, exporters and service providers do not wish to take such risks in selling their goods and services overseas. To protect exporters from these types of risks cover can be provided by the ECGD.

BACKGROUND

The term "ECGD" stands for Export Credit Guarantee Department. It is a separate department of the British government. It was set up in 1919 to help British exporters to export goods to other countries. Like any other country the UK also needs foreign exchange but there are more risks in exporting overseas than selling in the local market. Manufacturers and services providers are not willing to take such risks in selling their products and services overseas. The ECGD encourages exporters to export more of their products and services by providing insurance against the commercial and political risks of not being paid by overseas buyers after goods were exported. A section of ECGD dealing with exporters trading on short terms of credit basis (i.e. up to two years) was sold to Atradius (formerly NCM Credit Insurance Limited) in 1991.

ECGD derives its powers from the 1991 Export and Investment Guarantees Act and reports to the Secretary of State for Trade and Industry who provides parliament with a report on its activities and trading operations on an annual basis.

OPERATION ON BREAK-EVEN BASIS

ECGD operate on a break-even basis, by charging exporters premiums at levels to match the risks of non-payment. The premium rates charged depend on various considerations and the individual assessment of the risks of each contract i.e. the nature of the project, its duration, and the type of risks to be covered, buyer or borrower and country risks. This means under their Active Portfolio Management (APM) ECGD assess risks systematically. The charge or premium fee may therefore vary from case to case. Some reserves are built up from the revenue earned from the premiums to pay for claims, if overseas buyers/borrowers default on payments.

ECGD'S SAFEGUARD FINANCE

The Export Credits Guarantee Department does not provide finance itself for exports, but it may become very much involved in indirect export finance. It also plays a vital role by safeguarding the finance that banks and other financial institutions make available to exporters. It would otherwise appear to be too risky a proposition to a bank if asked to make an advance without tangible security. ECGD offers various types of policies, often as a result of long discussions between the department, the government and the banks. The result is that the amount of export finance available is increasing. The security offered by ECGD enables exporters to offer better credit terms to buyers and to break into new markets.

The UK has for some time been playing a leading role in pushing forward initiatives to help the poorest developing countries, emerging from debt and poverty burdens, return to the international trading community. ECGD is also committed to supporting productive expenditure for countries as they emerge from their debt problems.

Guarantees

ECGD issue about £3.5 billion of guarantees a year to cover a variety of exports of capital goods such as, multi-million textile machinery, power stations, defence-related equipment and civil aircraft/Airbus. It also supports the supply of telecommunication technology and the construction of the new north runway at Hong Kong International Airport.

Loans to overseas borrowers

ECGD provides loans to overseas borrowers to facilitate the purchase of a wide range of capital goods from a number of British suppliers under an overall financing scheme. These types of lines of credit have been made available to foreign governments or government agencies under projects for which they are responsible. Examples of buyers credit guarantee are:

- Tanzania £204 million

- Guyana £90 million

- Zambia £83 million

- Bolivia £49 million

- Uganda £27 million

- Mozambique £90 million

If a buyer or importer's country defaults on payments which ECGD have guaranteed, it seeks to recover the amounts of the guarantees issued through negotiation with overseas buyers/borrowers. It has a specific financial objective to operate with a reasonable confidence of breaking even. This is achieved by charging their customers premiums at reasonable levels, which are sufficient to match their perception of market/buyer risk and to cover administration costs. Apart from providing support directly to large UK exporters, ECGD guarantees also indirectly benefit hundreds of smaller companies in the UK. When ECGD provides support to major companies, smaller manufacturers also get benefit by supplying various items to the main contractors.

Use of ECGD Guarantees: The ECGD guarantees can be used not only to cover the risks of non-payment but also as a means of obtaining finance from banks pending receipt of payment from the overseas buyers. Specific guarantees issued by ECGD can be assigned to banks to get exporters finance facilities from their banks.

Capital goods and projects involve a credit period of up to five years or more and also involve lengthy manufacturing periods prior to shipment. The most usual form of payment is by way of a series of bills of exchange or promissory notes payable at intervals.

ECGD's specific guarantee is designed to meet the specific needs of the contract, and premiums are paid to the department according to the nature, length of the project and manufacturing period.

Capital goods

The following are some examples of the types of contracts ECGD have supported. Light capital goods include buses, fire engines, airport runways, industrial pumps, anti-pollution equipment for projects, production lines, housing, digital broadcasting and mattress making equipment. Capital goods also include heavy engineering goods, plant, power stations, dams, turbines, oil and gas pipelines, aircraft, ships and heavy construction equipment.

ECGD cover for shipments of consumer goods and light engineering goods that are sold on a short-term credit basis. Such shipments are usually frequent and repetitive and therefore call for a comprehensive policy that enables the exporter to cover them on a continuous basis without reference to ECGD. For exports of capital goods and large capital projects, rather different treatment is called for. Individual negotiation with ECGD for such large-scale transactions is essential and specific guarantees have to be issued that take into account the particular requirements in each case.

SPECIFIC GUARANTEE

The Specific Guarantee is available from either the date of contract or the date of shipment, but the majority of policies are in the former category in view of the lengthy manufacturing periods involved. The risks covered are the same as under a Comprehensive Short-Term Guarantee except that there is no cover against the failure of private buyers to take up the goods. This cover is, however, provided in respect of government buyers. The maximum cover is 90 per cent and Specific Guarantees cover sales of up to five years' credit. If it can be proved/shown that a credit facility is being offered by foreign competitors for a longer period, ECGD may be able to give equivalent support to UK exporters.

Specific Guarantees need to be negotiated with ECGD at the same time as the contracts to which they apply and a premium is agreed at an early stage. The premiums may vary according to the risks involved. There are modified forms of Specific Guarantee that apply to exports of aircraft and to construction work contracts. These take into account the special factors involved, for example the need for certificates of airworthiness in the case of aircraft and the fact that constructional works contracts are concerned with both the supply of goods and the performance of services. Services include consultancy, manpower, installation, refits or conversion of machinery, licensing, leasing, training and "know-how" (i.e. technical information).

Overseas Investments include food manufacturing facilities, communications assembly lines, equipment leasing, waste treatment plants etc. and are investments made overseas by UK companies.

TYPES OF ECGD GUARANTEES

Comprehensive guarantees

A Comprehensive Guarantee issued by ECGD covers exports often with the same regular buyers, and involving goods which are being sold for cash or on a short-term to medium-term basis of up to five years. The exporter pays a premium at the rate of a certain percentage agreed between the exporter and ECGD (apart from an annual lump sum), which is a very modest fee considering the risks that are covered. These risks are as follows:

(a) Insolvency of the buyer;

(b) The buyer's failure to pay within six months of due date for goods which he has accepted;

(c) The buyer's failure to take up goods which have been despatched to him (where not caused or excused by the policy holder's actions, and where the ECGD decides that the institution or continuation of legal proceedings against the buyer would serve no useful purpose);

(d) A general moratorium on external debt decreed by the government of the buyer's country or of a third country through which payment must be made;

(e) Any other action by the government of the buyer's country which prevents performance of the contract in whole or in part;

(f) Political events, economic difficulties, legislative or administrative measures arising outside the UK which prevent or delay the transfer of payments or deposits made in respect of the contract;

(g) Legal discharge of a debt (not being legal discharge under the proper law of the contract) in a foreign currency, which results in a shortfall at the date of transfer;

(h) War and certain other events preventing performance of the contract provided that the event is not one normally insured with commercial insurers;

(i) Cancellation or non-renewal of a UK export licence or the prohibition or restriction on export of goods from the UK by law (this risk is covered only where the pre-credit risk section of the guarantee applies).

Important points:

1. To ensure that the exporter retains an interest in recovering unpaid debts and that he does not enter into sales contracts recklessly without consideration for the financial consequences.

2. ECGD does not normally provide 100 per cent cover. The normal percentage guaranteed is 90 per cent of the loss where the buyer is insolvent or fails to pay within six months.

3. There are other risks, apart from the buyer's failure to take up the goods, the proportion is 90 per cent if the cause arises before despatch overseas, and 95 per cent if it arises after despatch. Where the buyer fails to take up the goods, the exporter must bear the "first loss" of 20 per cent of the full price and ECGD bears 90 per cent of the balance.

4. The time taken to pay out on claims varies with the cause of loss. For insolvency of the buyer, the payment is made immediately on proof of insolvency.

5. Where there has been protracted default on goods accepted, payment of claims is made six months after the due date of payment, and where the importer has failed to take up the goods, the period is one month after resale. For other causes, payment is made four months after the due date of payment or the date of the event causing the loss.

6. After paying a claim the Department does not normally interfere in the contract of sale between the exporter and the foreign buyer and expects the exporter to protect its interests by pursuing the buyer for payment.

7. All transactions between ECGD and the exporter are confidential, so that the importer does not become aware that the goods are insured, as this might encourage him to default. Only in exceptional circumstances will the Department agree to its interest being disclosed to the buyer.

8. The Comprehensive Short-Term Guarantee normally covers the whole of the policyholder's export turnover for a minimum period of a year. In some cases ECGD will accept business on a range of markets selected by the policyholder.

Buyer Credit Guarantees

If a contract amounts to over a certain amount an exporter may be able to persuade a bank or other financial institution to make a loan direct to the buyer, backed by an ECGD Buyer Credit Guarantee. The overseas purchaser must pay 15 to 20 per cent or more according to the scale of ECGD of the contract price direct to the supplier out of his own resources and the rest is paid to the supplier out of the loan provided by the bank. ECGD give the bank a guarantee for the money that it lends to the foreign buyer and the British supplier is thus relieved of risk.

BUYER CREDIT (BC) FACILITY

Buyer Credits are individually tailored to finance high value capital goods and services exports. Because of the amount of work normally involved, a Buyer Credit loan normally has to support a contract of at least £5 million or its equivalent in other acceptable currencies. Loans are made by lending bank(s) in the United Kingdom to overseas buyers or other borrowers, usually their bank(s), to fund purchases from the UK. Once the contract and loan are effective the exporters will be paid from the loan as they fulfill the terms of the contract with the buyers, just as if these were cash contracts.

The supplier credit finance facility (SCF)

The Supplier Credit Finance facility allows the supplier to pass the payment risk to the bank. This can be used for light capital goods and related services. The SCF is designed to enable exporters to receive payment as though the contracts were on a cash basis while allowing the buyers to pay on credit terms. This facility can be used to finance contracts with values of GB Pounds 25,000 or more. If the overseas buyers are paying the exporter using promissory notes or bills of exchange, the exporters can obtain finance on cash terms by selling or getting these negotiable instruments discounted from the participating banks as they continue performing the contracts. The exporters may be paid out of the proceeds of the promissory notes or bills of exchange, which their banks may arrange with the overseas borrowers. ECGD normally provides a 100 per cent guarantee to the bank.

The main difference between the SCF and Buyer Credit from an exporter's point of view is that ECGD does not examine the loan documentation under this facility. The Lender may therefore be able to put straightforward loan documentation in place very quickly. To keep procedures streamlined, approved banks are issued with a Master Guarantee Agreement, which is an umbrella policy covering a range of transactions.

The Export Insurance Policy (EXIP)

The Export Insurance Policy protects the exporter against purchaser and political risks. It can be used by light capital goods exporters and related services, and freestanding support of services. In the event of non-payment by the overseas buyer attributable to an insured cause of loss, the EXIP normally provides for cover of 90 per cent of such losses on an approved transaction.

INSURANCE FOR CASH PAYMENTS

The EXIP protects an exporter against not receiving payments to which the exporter is contractually entitled under a contract as a result of specified commercial and political risks. It is suitable for the sale of capital goods, major services, and construction projects.

The EXIP would normally be used where the buyer is obliged to pay the exporter on or shortly after delivery. Cover for payment on credit terms may also be considered, but for credit terms of two years or more the exporter should consider arranging an ECGD supported finance package.

Export credit insurance package

It is insurance for cash contracts, which have long delivery periods and business involving medium/long-term credit.

Supplement export credit guarantees

Supplement Export Credit guarantees for risks not covered under an ECGD finance package. For example, during the manufacturing period, cover for consumer goods, raw materials and the like is provided by the private sector. The exporters of these goods should seek the advice of their brokers or the private sector credit insurers.

Export credit guarantees

Where a potential overseas buyer seeks payment terms of over two years, an ECGD backed loan may be a suitable solution. ECGD may offer a 100 per cent repayment guarantee to an eligible UK based bank, to assist the financing of exports of capital goods and/or services contracts to overseas buyers.

ECGD conforms to the OECD guidelines on length of credit and can support credit for finance packages of typically from 2 to 10 years. Longer credit terms may be available, within OECD guidelines, depending upon the nature of the goods/project being supplied.

ECGD may support funding in a wide range of currencies, from hard currencies such as GB Pound, US Dollars and the Euro, to some local currency denominated loans, which match revenues earned by buyers, thereby reducing the risk of the buyer defaulting when its country is experiencing shortages of foreign currency to repay principal and interest on loans.

OVERSEAS INVESTMENT INSURANCE

This policy protects UK companies against certain political risks involved in investing overseas. Overseas investment insurance is available even if no UK goods are exported as part of the investment and also for bank loans to overseas companies.

Bond Insurance Policy (BIP)

Bond risk cover can only be considered under a Bond Insurance Policy where one of their main facilities is being provided (i.e. EXIP, Supplier Credit Finance, or Buyer Credit) for the related export contract. It normally provides cover for 100 per cent of bonding liabilities against the risk of a bond being called unfairly or as a result of the contract being frustrated solely due to political or force majeure circumstances. Cover is available for Bonds given in favour of public or private buyers. The benefits of the cover can normally be assigned to banks or other financial institutions with ECGD's permission. This cover is issued as a separate policy, and a separate premium is charged by ECGD.

Tender To Contract (TTC) Forward Exchange Supplement (FES)

Exchange rate movements can pose a significant risk during the tendering process for major overseas projects. This policy allows the exporter or service provider to commit a firm foreign currency price.

FINANCING FACILITIES FOR EXPORTERS

Finance facilities enable exporters to offer credit to overseas buyers whilst receiving cash payments themselves. Working within OECD guidelines, ECGD can support contracts eligible for at least two years credit and cover finance up to a maximum of 85 per cent of the contract value.

ECGD reserves the right to take recourse against the exporter in certain cases where it is considered necessary.

General lines of credit (LOCs)

It is an agreement between a UK based bank and an overseas bank to finance a number of contracts between UK suppliers and various overseas buyers, minimum contract value varies but may be as low as US$25,000. These are set up in advance of any contract award and are a useful way of speedily financing an export deal.

Project Line of Credit finances a range of UK export contracts for a specific project or identified export programme from any number of UK suppliers.

Recourse indemnity policy (RIP)

It is an insurance product available to exporters to enable them with respect to buyer's credit financing, to transfer the risk and contingent liability associated with their recourse obligations to insurance underwriters, subject to underwriting considerations.

ECGD provides a 100 per cent guarantee to pay the bank if the overseas borrower fails to repay the loan. ECGD can also provide a lower percentage guarantee at a lower cost, but the exporter will need to determine the impact of such cover on the overall cost of finance before entering into any commitment.

In the event of a default under the loan agreement, access to further funds under the loan (known as "Simple Buyer Credit") can be withdrawn by ECGD and the lending bank. This means the exporter can face the risk of non-payment by the buyer where the contract has not yet been fully completed. One option is for the exporter to take out additional insurance i.e. Export Insurance Policy or ask for a loan to finance termination settlements or arbitration awards (known as a "Complex Buyer Credit").

ECGD normally reserves the right to recover from an exporter all or part of a claim paid to a lending bank if a loan default occurs when the exporter has failed to meet the terms of the contract.

Overseas investment insurance

As part of the UK government's drive to encourage investment in developing countries, ECGD provide political risk insurance for long-term equity and loan investments made overseas by UK companies. In addition, an increasing amount of business is providing cover for UK banks lending to overseas companies.

PROJECT FINANCING FACILITY

"Project Financing" is a technique to finance a major new project or large project expansion whereby the lenders place primary reliance on the revenues of the project for repayment. The project owners are usually responsible for ensuring that the project is built and operated successfully, taking responsibility for making up any shortfall in the project's earnings.

Other terms used to describe these arrangements include "limited recourse" and "Build Own Operate Transfer (BOOT)" schemes, although there are many variants on this theme. It is unlikely to be cost effective for a contract of less than £20 million or its equivalent to be financed in this way.

Project Financing Scheme is a variant on the Buyer Credit technique and aims to help UK exporters win business by operating in a flexible, responsive, and cost effective way to meet the needs of all the parties involved. Many bankers and sponsors have already found that the involvement of ECGD can bring forward additional funding to this type of project. ECGD will usually expect the project sponsors to provide a minimum equity participation of 25 per cent of the capital cost and the lenders to share risks with ECGD.

The exporter should bear in mind that all of the above facilities are based on guarantees to banks. Therefore the exporter should consider whether his interests are adequately protected. Even if the Buyer Credit is of a "Complex" nature, he may still want additional security by taking out one or more of the insurance policies mentioned above.

The insurance provides cover against expropriation, war, and restriction on remittances and, subject to individual consideration, other political risks. This insurance is available for up to 15 years and is renewable annually by the investor with the terms fixed for the life of the policy.

Supplemental extended terms guarantee

This is a self-contained guarantee with its own premium to cover such goods as commercial vehicles, machine tools, machinery, contractor's plant, and general engineering goods which necessitate granting credit terms to the buyer in excess of six months. This credit may be granted by the supplier himself, through a UK merchant or confirming house. This type of guarantee is also used where, although credit terms do not exceed six months, pre-credit risk cover is required and the delivery period exceeds twelve months. This supplemental guarantee is normally limited to a delivery period not exceeding two years and a credit period of five years. The premium or this guarantee is assessed separately for each individual contract or branches of business and depends upon the period that ECGD is at risk and the grading of the buyer's country, the guarantee can be varied to cover the pre-credit risk and invoicing in foreign currencies.

SUBSIDIARIES GUARANTEE

This is a special guarantee designed to cover the sale of goods to an overseas subsidiary and the sale of the goods by that subsidiary.

SUPPLEMENTARY STOCKS GUARANTEE

Sales from stock held overseas are normally covered under the standard Comprehensive Short-Term Guarantee, but in addition ECGD will issue a supplementary guarantee to cover the goods prior to sale against loss arising from certain events. These include war between the UK and the country when the stocks are held, the requisitioning or confiscation of the goods and measures preventing the re-export of the goods.

There is an agreed limit for the amount of stocks that can be held and a flat-rate premium per £100 is payable on this limit. This type of cover can be taken out in respect of stocks held at an overseas trade fair or sent abroad on trial and demonstration.

External trade guarantee

This guarantee covers the goods that are shipped direct from one country to another without first being imported into the UK, the goods may be covered by an External Trade Guarantee. This cover is rather similar to that provided by the Comprehensive Short-Term Guarantee and the risks covered are broadly the same except that they do not include failure of the buyer to take up the goods or the imposition of either import or export licensing or the cancellation or non-renewal of existing licences. The cover is limited to 90 per cent. Premiums are assessed and collected in the same manner as for a Comprehensive Short-Term Guarantee, but they are somewhat higher than it. Premium rates are available from the offices of ECGD.

Services policies

The income earned/derived from services provided to overseas clients is covered by two types of policies:

(a) The Comprehensive "Services Rendered" Guarantee or

(b) The Comprehensive "Services Due" Guarantee.

Under (a) services actually completed can be covered, whereas under (b) contracts for services to be carried out in the future can be covered. These two policies are in respect of services provided on the basis of a continuing pattern of business, but if this does not apply, for example where an engineer's services are provided in respect of a "one off" construction project, a Specific Services "Sums Due" Guarantee can be obtained.

COMPREHENSIVE BILL GUARANTEE

This guarantee is additional to the Comprehensive Short-Term Guarantee and covers exports of goods with a credit period of less than two years where the buyer accepts a bill of exchange or signs a promissory note.

The sole purpose of this guarantee is to provide the exporter's bank with 100 per cent security for advances made against such bills or promissory notes.

COMPREHENSIVE OPEN ACCOUNT GUARANTEE

This is similar to the Comprehensive Bill Guarantee in that it is intended to give gilt-edged security to the bank that makes a loan against exports on an open account or cash against documents basis.

In the same way that direct guarantees between the banks and ECGD are available in respect of short-term loans, it is possible for the exporter of capital goods to obtain finance more easily, or to arrange for his buyer to raise finance, by taking out additional special policies.

SPECIFIC BANK GUARANTEE

Where the terms of payment are two years or more (under an extended terms policy or specific policy) a Bank Guarantee giving 100 per cent protection to a bank making a loan to an exporter is available. The exporter takes out this additional guarantee and negotiates this at the same time as the main ECGD policy, i.e. when negotiating the contract with the buyer. Normally this type of contract involves payment by the buyer by bills of exchange or promissory notes maturing at six-monthly intervals and if payment for any of these is not received within three months after the due date of payment the bank receives payment in full from ECGD. The exporter pays a fixed and favourable rate of interest on this type of finance.

BUYER CREDIT GUARANTEES

If a contract amounts to GB Pounds 2 million or more, an exporter may be able to persuade a bank or other financial institution to make a loan direct to the buyer backed by an ECGD, i.e. a Buyer Credit Guarantee. The overseas purchaser must pay 15 per cent to 20 per cent of the contract price direct to the supplier out of his own resources and the rest is paid to the supplier out of the loan provided by the bank. ECGD gives the bank a 100 per cent guarantee for the money that it lends to the foreign buyer and the British supplier is thus relieved of risk. Recently the government has tried to ensure that most of the finance under Buyer Credit Guarantees is provided in foreign currencies. The rate of interest is the same as for Specific Bank Guarantees.

Under a similar Buyer Credit scheme ECGD provides loans to overseas borrowers to facilitate the purchase of a wide range of capital goods from a number of British suppliers under an overall financing scheme. The minimum limit of £1 million does not apply to these lines of credit and finance and contracts for as little as £5,000 or £10,000 have been provided. Some of these lines of credit have been made available to foreign governments or government agencies under projects for which they are responsible.

Lines of Credit support smaller exporters and these can enable an exporter to offer a finance package to the buyer while the exporter is paid "cash" soon after the goods are delivered. Line of Credits can be used for light capital goods, capital goods exports and related services.

MONEY LAUNDERING AND TERRORIST ACTIVITIES

ECGD provides support to the exporters of various export items and services. The exporters and investors must be exporting or investing from the United Kingdom. Some foreign goods and/or services as part of an export may be eligible. It is important to note that the OECD countries, including the United Kingdom, are committed to combating corruption and money laundering.

The laws in the UK have been strengthened in order to prevent money laundering and terrorism activities. The applicants are responsible for ensuring that their activities comply with all laws that are relevant to the transaction in respect of which they are applying for ECGD support.

Applicants' attention is also drawn in particular to the amendments to the applicable laws on corruption contained in the Anti-terrorism, Crime and Security Act 2001 and to the laws on money laundering contained in the Proceeds of Crime Act 2002. Certain acts committed abroad now constitute criminal offences in the UK. Applicants should also be aware that ECGD refers allegations of bribery, corruption and money laundering to the appropriate authorities.

Applicants are required to complete the appropriate application form for the type of facility required by an exporter or service provider. Before completing the application forms the applicant should read the terms and conditions for the Supplier Credit Finance facility carefully, as by signing the form he agrees and is bound by the terms and conditions.

All relevant questions must be answered fully and truthfully to the best of the applicant's knowledge and belief. If the space provided is insufficient, the applicant should continue answers on his business headed notepaper and attach it to the application form.

The applicant must disclose all material facts; failure to do so may nullify any Export Insurance Policy based on the proposal. It is the applicant's duty to disclose material facts and this continues from the date of signature of the proposal until the date cover under the Export Insurance Policy commences. A material fact is one likely to influence ECGD's acceptance or assessment of the proposal. If the applicant is in any doubt as to what is a material fact he should consult ECGD or his broker.

There are, also, a number of private insurance companies who can offer short-term insurance cover to exporters of consumer goods, other than capital goods. Help or advice can be obtained from commercial banks involved in trade finance or from the British Insurance Brokers' Association (BIBA). ECGD still provide exporters of British capital goods and services with finance and insurance packages to help them win valuable overseas orders. It can also insure British companies who invest abroad against the political risks of a non-return on their investments.

ECGD sources

CHAPTER 21

Marine Insurance

INTRODUCTION

Marine insurance began in the cities of Northern Italy, about the end of the twelfth century. Italian merchants came to the United Kingdom in the thirteenth and fourteenth centuries and brought with them their trading customs, including marine insurance. Initially merchants entered into marine insurance contracts as incidental to their general trading activities and later specialised in this business.

Do we need marine insurance? There are various risks of loss and damage to goods when transported from one place to another, depending upon mode of transport. The loss could be partial or total loss of goods and this could cause financial loss to the importers and/or other parties involved such as banks etc.

To protect the importers/parties involved, especially in international trade, insurance companies are prepared to offer protection against such risks, on payment of a premium to the insurers according to the protection required for loss or damage to the goods.

IMPORTANCE OF MARINE INSURANCE

Most ship owners and those responsible for cargo, resort to marine insurance for the protection of their ships, goods, freight and other interests against marine perils. Very heavy capital values are locked up in ships, the loss of which might easily prove financially crippling for the strongest shipping companies. Marine insurance, therefore, occupies an important position in international trade business. By affording protection against accidental losses, it enables those engaged in overseas trade to venture their capital more freely, without keeping large reserves of their own to meet disasters, and to expand the scope of their operations.

Business transactions, whether internal or international, necessarily involve movement of goods by sea, air, and/or land from one place to another. In the course of the journey the goods sustain various types of loss or damage including non-delivery. The marine insurance policy is the best means to protect the owner against possible loss or damage to cargo in transit. With a view to understanding the implications of a policy of marine insurance, in particular the person who can effect insurance, it is necessary to understand the terms and conditions of a contract of sale and also whether the person will stand to gain by the safe arrival of the cargo or sustain loss by damage to the cargo. When the seller executes an order as per directions of the buyer the contract of sale is performed and the property in the goods passes from the seller to the buyer. With the transfer of ownership the risk of loss also passes from the seller to the buyer and the terms of the contract of sale determine when the ownership of the goods passes on to the buyer.

DEFINITION

Marine insurance is a contract *uberimae fidei* representing an agreement whereby the insurer undertakes to indemnify the insured, in the manner and to the extent agreed, in terms of space-time and risk clauses subject to the principle of proximate clause, for insurable property lost or damaged by maritime perils, incidental to marine adventure. The contract can be assigned by endorsement and delivery to the other party.

CLASSIFICATION OF MARINE INSURANCE COVER

Marine insurance against loss of or damage to property by the perils of the sea, may be classified under these headings:

HULL: This refers to the insurance of the ship (i.e. hull and machinery), by the ship owners against maritime perils, which are briefly, perils of the sea, such as heavy weather, stranding or collision, fire and similar perils. Such insurance is normally arranged for a period of 12 months.

CARGO: This refers to goods and/or merchandise imported or exported to and from various ports of the world. Insurance interest exists on behalf of both buyer and seller. Cargo is normally insured against all maritime and transit risks, including war perils etc.

FREIGHT: Freight is the sum paid for transportation of goods to the ship owners. When goods are lost or damaged by marine perils, freight, or a proportion of it, will be lost. The person involved therefore, has an insurable interest. If the freight is prepaid, it is merged with the insurable value of the cargo. If it is payable at destination it is a ship owner's risk.

MARINE INSURANCE ASSOCIATIONS

- British Insurance Association
- Lloyd's Underwriters' Association
- The Institute of London Underwriters
- Liverpool Underwriters' Associations

TYPES OF INSURANCE INSTRUMENTS

BROKER'S NOTE: It is issued by an insurance broker/agent. Usually it is not acceptable to banks because its validity is for a short period only (say 28 or 30 days).

COVER NOTE: It is issued by an insurance company/broker or insurance agent. Generally it is not acceptable to banks unless issued under an "open policy".

INSURANCE CERTIFICATE: It is issued by an insurance company and is acceptable to banks.

MARINE INSURANCE POLICY: It is issued by an insurance company and is acceptable to banks.

Marine insurance policy

Marine insurance plays a very important role in overseas trade as it affords protection against accidental losses and enables the various trading interests to deploy their capital freely and thus help them to expand the scope of their activity. It is very important to insure the goods against the risks of loss or damage. It depends upon the sale contract as to who will take the insurance policy (the buyer or the seller of the goods). An insurance policy explains in detail the terms and conditions of the risks covered. An insurance policy covers cargo, hull freight or any other insurable interest allied to these, against marine perils or perils incidental to a marine adventure.

As per the Institute of London Underwriters Cargo Clauses policies can be classified into three types viz Clause (A) Clause (B) and Clause (C).

Institute cargo clauses (a) risk covered

This insurance policy covers all risks of loss of or damage to the subject matter insured except as provided in clauses 4, 5, 6 and 7 of the policy.

This insurance covers general average and salvage charges, adjusted or determined according to the contract of affreightment and/or the governing law and practice, incurred to avoid or in connection with the avoidance of loss from any cause except those excluded in Clauses 4, 5, 6 and 7 or elsewhere in this insurance.

This insurance is extended to indemnify the assured against such proportion of liability under the contract of affreightment "Both to Blame Collision" clause as is in respect of a loss recoverable hereunder. In the event of any claim by ship owners under the said clause the assured agree to notify the underwriters who shall have the right, at their own cost and expense, to defend the assured against such claim.

Institute cargo clauses (b) risks covered

This insurance covers, except as provided in clauses 4, 5, 6 and 7 in the policy, loss of or damage to the subject-matter insured reasonably attributable to, fire or explosion, vessel or craft being stranded, grounded sunk or capsized, overturning or derailment of land conveyance, collision or contact of vessel craft or conveyance with any external object other than water, discharge of cargo at a port of distress, earthquake, volcanic eruption or lightning, loss of or damage to the subject-matter insured caused by general average sacrifice, jettison or washing overboard, entry of sea lake or river water into vessel craft hold, conveyance container lift-van or place of storage. Total loss of any package lost overboard or dropped whilst loading on to, or loading from, vessel or craft.

Institute cargo clauses (c) risks covered

This insurance covers, except as provided in clauses 4, 5, 6 and 7 of the policy, loss of or damage to the subject-matter insured reasonably attributable to fire or explosion, vessel or craft being stranded, grounded, sunk or capsized, overturning or derailment of land conveyance, collision or contact of vessel craft or conveyance with any external object other than water, discharge of cargo at a port of distress, loss of or damage to the subject-matter insured caused by general average sacrifice, jettison clauses.

This insurance covers general average and salvage charges, adjusted or determined according to the contract of affreightment and/or the governing law and practice, incurred to avoid or in connection with the avoidance of loss from any cause except those excluded in clauses 4, 5, 6 and 7 or elsewhere in this insurance.

This insurance is extended to indemnify the assured against such proportion of liability under the contract of affreightment "Both to Blame Collision" clause as is in respect of a loss recoverable hereunder. In the event of any claim by ship owners under the said clause the assured agree to notify the underwriters who shall have the right, at their own cost and expense, to defend the assured against such claim.

CONTENTS OF A MARINE INSURANCE POLICY

A marine insurance policy may be issued at the time when the contract is concluded or afterwards. It should give the following information, which must be checked by a banker dealing with documentary credits.

1. Amount of Insurance
2. Currency of Policy Money
3. Name of the Insurance Company
4. Name of the Assured
5. Name of the Carrier
6. Merchandise Description
7. Ports of Loading and Discharge
8. Party to Whom Insurance is Payable
9. Place of Payment of Policy Money
10. Technical Information
11. Number of Copies, Original, Duplicates etc.
12. What Risks are Covered
13. Signature/countersignature

14. Facsimile Signature

15. Date of Issue

INSURANCE CERTIFICATE

The credit will indicate what insurance cover is required and will call for either an insurance policy or insurance certificate.

An insurance policy may only be issued by the insurer and is usually in standard form covering the customary risks for any voyage. The form of policy in general use today is Lloyd's SG (Ships and Goods) policy.

Regular exporters normally arrange an open contract to cover all exports during a specific period. This provides insurance cover at all times within the agreed terms and conditions of the contract and avoids having to obtain separate cover and a new policy for each shipment.

Insurance certificates are issued for each shipment by either the insurers and/or by the exporters.

The certificate must contain the same details as the policy with the slight difference that it will carry a shortened version of the provisions of the policy under which it is issued. An insurance certificate should be issued and signed by the insurance company or its agent.

Insurance documents normally show the following details:

- The name and signature of the insurer.

- The name of the assured.

- A description of the risks covered.

- The sum or sums insured expressed in the same currency as that of the credit.

- A description of the consignment.

- The place where claims are payable together with details of the agent to whom claims may be directed.

- The declaration of the assured together with his designation where applicable his endorsement on the reverse of the document is also required so that the right to claim may be transferred to another party (usually the importer).

■ The date of issue. This must be the same as or earlier than the date of the document evidencing despatch, except where warehouse-to-warehouse cover is indicated.

Insurance, particularly marine insurance, is a complicated subject and exporters should arrange cover for their shipments through a professional insurance broker.

Source: Marine Insurance Acts

Annexure (i)

SPECIMEN OF APPLICATION FOR L/C

(Banks do have their own style of format but the information required for issue of a L/C is usually similar)

Dear Sirs,

Please issue by Airmail/Brief or Full Cable/Swift your Irrevocable Documentary Letter of Credit available by negotiation/payment/acceptance as per details below

Name of Issuing Bank Branch	Application to Issue Irrevocable ----------------- Documentary Credit	L/C Number

Date of Application:	Date LC issued:	Date of Expiry (for negotiation in the country of beneficiary)

Applicant's full name and address	Beneficiary's full name and address
Advising Bank's name and address (Issuing Bank to write)	Amount in words and figures – State *FOB, FAS, CIF, C&F as applicable
	Partial Shipments: allowed/forbidden*
	Trans-shipment: permitted/ prohibited*

Shipment from _____ to _____ not later than _____
Documentary credit to be available by draft(s) at _____ drawn on us/yourselves for full invoice value of shipment purporting to be

Accompanied by the following signed documents marked (X)

- ☐ Commercial invoice in _____ copies certifying goods to be of _____ origin

- ☐ Full set of clean "shipped on board" marine bills of lading made out or endorsed to your order showing "Freight prepaid"/ _____ and marked notify us and you

- ☐ Air Waybill bearing your Credit number showing the goods consigned to _____ and showing 'Freight prepaid*/ Freight to pay _____ and marked notify you and us.

- ☐ Insurance policy/certificate in duplicate issued to beneficiary's order and bank endorsed covering goods for the invoice value plus 10% covering marine and war risks including Institute Cargo Clauses (All risks) and Institute Strike Riots and Civil Commotion. Claims payable in _____ Additional Risks:

- ☐ Insurance covered by _____. The details of the shipment under your credit must be advised by the beneficiary by air mail/telex immediately after shipment to us and _____ referring to cover note number _____ of _____

- ☐ Two copies of this advice should accompany the original set of documents.

- ☐ Certificate of origin issued by a Chamber of Commerce.

- ☐ Packing list in _____ copies.

- ☐
- ☐
- ☐
- ☐
- ☐
- ☐

Additional conditions:

1 short form of Bills of Lading not acceptable.

2. ----------------------------------

3. ----------------------------------

☐ Advising and Negotiating Bank charges are for ( ) our account ( ) Beneficiary's account

N.B. If any special documents (over and above those termed "shipping documents" are required such as health, inspection certificate etc. or certificate covering any special or unusual class of insurance, such documents should always be included in the application and specifically mentioned

Documents to be presented within ------------------- days after the date of issuance of the shipping documents but within the validity of the credit.

☐ We request you to arrange / not to arrange the forward exchange cover subject however to your rights under your terms and conditions.

We agree that the documentary credit issued by you is subject to Uniform Customs and Practice for Documentary Credits (2007 Revision, International Chamber of Commerce, Publication No. 600) except as otherwise stated herein.

The Documentary Letter of Credit shall be deemed to have been issued when an advice thereof has been despatched to the beneficiaries.

In consideration of your issuing the Documentary Credit in accordance with the details set out above we agree to be bound by the above terms and conditions and without prejudice to the generality of the same we specifically instruct you to pay or accept, as the case may be, for our account all drafts drawn pursuant thereto.

Applicant's Signature-------------------------   Date: --------------------

Account No. ------------------------------------

(Please note the applicant's signature(s) on the application must be in accordance with the customer's mandate for the operations of the account)

Basic Terms and Conditions for Issuing of Letters of Credit

The applicants agree to be bound by the following terms and conditions (in addition set out on the application form)

The applicant undertakes to:

1. pay at maturity in legal tender of the place of payment or in any currency in which the drafts are drawn at any offices of the bank or its agents all or any of the drafts together with interest that may be due there-under or the terms of the said letter of credit.

2. reimburse you with the amounts required to effect such payments together with interest at such rate as may be currently charging or as may be obtainable at the due date or the date of payment etc.

3. pay on demand commission, which shall be determined from time to time of the full amount of the credit.

4. to acquire sufficient foreign currency for delivery immediately thereafter or at such time as may be necessary or as may appear necessary to effect such.

5. to repay all indebtedness and the discharge of all liabilities absolute or contingent which may be now or hereafter, may be due or owing or become due or owing in respect of any transaction now or subsequently entered into.

6. to transfer all rights and interests that customer may acquire in goods and chattels relating to the credit and when such goods or chattels are at sea or in foreign ports.

7. that all goods be fully insured against all risks including war risks with insurers approved by the bank, that the insurance policies shall be assigned to the bank until all amounts due to in respect of the said credit or discharge of all liabilities.

8. acknowledge that all documents or goods pertaining to the said credit at any time held by the bank or its agents may be regarded as deposited with the bank or its agents as pledges in the absence of specific contrary arrangements and that as such you are entitled to sell or otherwise dispose of the said goods or documents in such way and on such terms as you think fit.

9. to assign to the bank his right in the said goods or chattels as unpaid sellers on the bank's first demand.

10. pledge or any other security at such time as the bank may think fit and in particular not withstanding that drafts relating to the said credit may not have matured.

11. to obtain relevant instructions from the applicant, or the bank or its agent may in its discretion (without having any obligation so to do) accept as tender in lieu of Bills of Lading any documents issued by a carrier (including a lighter age receipt), which acknowledges receipt of goods for transport.

12. be responsible for the risks arising for the bank's acts or any other person acting or purporting to act on bank's behalf together with all responsibility for the character, kind, quantity, delivery or existence of the merchandise purporting to be represented by any document and/or for any difference of character quality or quantity of merchandise shipped under this credit from that expressed in any invoice accompanying any of the said drafts and/or for the validity genuineness sufficiency from or correctness of any documents.

13. ensure that all necessary export and import authorisation is obtained in respect of the transaction to which the letter of credit relates.

14. to give the bank on demand any further security that may be required and further agree that all the other funds, credit instruments and securities including proceeds thereof, now or hereafter handed to the bank or left in its possession by the applicant or by any other person for his account or held by the bank for transit to or from the bank by mail or courier are hereby made security for this obligation.

15. continue in force notwithstanding any change in the constitution of the undersigned whether arising from the death or retirement of one or more partner or partners or the accession of one or more new partners, or otherwise howsoever.

16. to debit the account with all charges on account of this credit including amendments or extensions of this credit, as well as charges levied by the overseas correspondents or agents. We also authorise you to make payments of the premium to the insurance company concerned by debiting our account.

17. this letter of credit can be revoked or altered only with consent of all parties interested.

18. irrespective of the port to which shipment is effected the applicant shall retire the bills on demand of payment.

19. the documents accepted in connection with the credit may be those which are generally acceptable in accordance with the laws customs and usages at the place of negotiation.
20. this will also constitute an agreement between the undersigned and your correspondent whom you employ (as you are at liberty to do so) for the purpose and in connection with this letter of credit agreement.
21. it is a term of this letter of credit agreement that it is to be subject to and interpretation in accordance with English law and that it is to be subject to the exclusive jurisdiction of the English courts (save and except that you are not thereby to be prevented from commencing proceedings before any other court).
22. we agree that the address mentioned on the application is an effective address for service in respect of any proceedings commenced in the English courts as hereinbefore described.

I/WE request you to *arrange / *do not arrange the forward exchange cover subject however to your rights under the terms and conditions of your bank.

We agree that the documentary credit issued by you is subject to Uniform Customs and Practice for Documentary Credits (2007 Revision, International Chamber of Commerce, Publication No. 600) except as otherwise stated herein.

The Documentary Letter of Credit shall be deemed to have been issued when an advice thereof has been despatched to the beneficiaries.

In consideration of your issuing the Documentary Credit in accordance with the details set out above we agree to be bound by the above terms and conditions and without prejudice to the generality of the same we specifically instruct you to pay or accept, as the case may be, for our account all drafts drawn pursuant thereto.

Applicant's Signature_____   Date: _____

Account No. _____

(Please note the applicant's signature(s) on the application must be in accordance with the customer's mandate for the operations of the account)

Annexure (ii)

GENERAL GUIDANCE FOR COMPLETION OF L/C APPLICATION FORM

The application forms for letters of credit are usually designed by most banks using the same format as the bank's letter of credit. This facilitates the easy transfer of details from the application to the letter of credit itself.

When completing the application the following information should be given:

1.	L/C number	This is a serial number assigned by the issuing bank. Some banks may allocate a block of serial numbers to authorised branches of the bank.
2.	Date of application	The date should be written as follows: 22 December 2006 i.e. date in figures, month in words and year in figures.
3.	Date of expiry	Date of expiry is written in the same style as in paragraph (2) above.
4.	Mode of issue	Applicant should state the method of issue of letter of credit i.e. by airmail or telex, SWIFT etc.
5.	Applicant	Applicant should state full name and postal address including postcode. This information will be incorporated on the L/C by the bank in the letter of credit when issued.
6.	Beneficiary	Beneficiary's full name and postal address including post code should be mentioned.

7.	Advising bank	This is written by the issuing bank. In countries where there is a branch of the issuing bank, the letter of credit should be advised through that branch. In other places, the bank would advise through its correspondent banks.
8.	Amount	Amount of the credit should be written in figures and words e.g. US$50,000. CIF (US Dollars fifty thousand only). The currency should be mentioned in words together with the appropriate "incoterm".
9.	Partial shipment/ trans-shipment	The appropriate term/clause must be clearly stated. Trans-shipment should be allowed when multimodal transport is to be used.
10.	Port of shipment	The following should be clearly mentioned on the application form; 　i) Port of loading 　ii) Port of destination 　iii) Latest date of shipment. The date should be mentioned in the same style as in paragraph (2) above.
11.	Tenor of bill	The tenor of the draft (i.e. 30 days, 60 days etc.) should be written in the space provided on the form.
12.	Drawee	Under the Article No. 6(c) of the UCP 600 the bill of exchange is required to be drawn on the issuing bank. If the bill of exchange is to be drawn on the applicant or on any other party it will be considered as an additional document, the drawee's name should be written in the space provided.
13.	Description	The brief but precise description of the goods concerned should be given. If the space provided is too small to accommodate the description then it should be continued on a separate sheet to form part of the application. It may be convenient for the applicant to refer to the pro-forma invoice number and date etc than to a list of different items.

14.	Invoice	Number of copies required should be indicated.
15.	Country of origin	Required country of origin of the goods covered in the credit should be stated, if necessary.
16.	Shipment	Tick the appropriate box for shipment of goods or state the shipment By sea or By Air
17.	Terms of shipment	"Freight prepaid" or "Freight to pay" according to the incoterms.
18.	Name of the consignee:	Name of the consignee should be stated. Usually the IB insists that the goods are consigned to its order to protect its security position. Air waybills are non-negotiable receipts and not documents of title.
19.	Terms of air freight	If freight has not been prepaid the term "Freight prepaid" should be deleted and applicable term inserted i.e. "Freight payable at destination".
20.	Insurance cover	a) If the insurance is to be covered by the beneficiary e.g. under CIF term, it should be stated. b) If the insurance is to be covered by the applicant e.g. under FOB term, it should be stated. Prior arrangements in this respect should be made. c) The name and address of the insurance company/broker should be stated so that insurance can be arranged in time.
21.	Where claims payable:	Country/place where claims under insurance are payable should be clearly indicated.
22.	Cert. of origin	It should be stated, if required.
23.	Other documents	Details of other documents that may be required to cover the risks relating to goods, should be mentioned.
24.	Other conditions	Any other condition(s) to be fulfilled should be written clearly. Write condition No.1 – Short form bill of lading not acceptable.
25.	Advising and/or	Mention who should bear these charges i.e.

	negotiating banks charges	the applicant or the beneficiary.
26.	Period for presentation of doc.	The number of days allowed for presentation of documents after the issuance of transport document should be stated. If this period is not stated on the L/C then documents must be presented within 21 days after the issuance of the transport documents under Article No. 14(c) UCP 600. The presentation of documents must be within the expiry date of the L/C.
27.	Applicant's signature on application form	Applicant should sign the application form in accordance with the mandate held by the bank.

Annexure (iii)

NEGOTIATION OF DOCUMENTS UNDER RESERVE

Form of an Indemnity for Discrepancies
(Amend wording to suit requirements)

The Manager   Date _____

Bank's name _____

Address _____

_____

Dear Sir,

Re:_____

In consideration of your *negotiating/accepting/paying on presentation a Bill of Exchange (*delete as appropriate)
dated_____ for _____ amount in words _____

_____

Drawn under letter of credit no._____ dated _____ Issued by _____ notwithstanding that the documents tendered therewith fail to conform with the requirements of the said letter of credit by reasons of (State here specifically the irregularities in documents tendered together with the relative precise requirements of the letter of credit)

_____

_____

_____

We undertake to indemnify you from and against all losses or damage, which you may incur or sustain because of the above irregularities in the documents. Provided that any claim upon us hereunder shall be made before the expiration of six months from the date hereof.

Yours faithfully

Signature(s) _____

Annexure (iv)

Form of an Indemnity for Discrepancies
(Amend wording to suit requirements)

The Manager ------------------------------   Date: ------------------------

Bank's name ------------------------------

Address ----------------------------------

Dear Sir,

Letter of Credit No. -------------------- issued by --------------------------------

In consideration of your paying us the sum of ----------(amount in words and figures) --

Under the above-mentioned credit we hereby indemnify you from all consequences, which may arise notwithstanding the following discrepancies in the documents.

1. ---

2. ---

3. ---

4. ---

5. ---

6. ---

7. ---

8. _____

9. _____

10. _____

--------------------------------- ------------------------------------
Signed by the beneficiary   Signed by the beneficiary's
                                   bank or third party

Index

A/D 24
A/S 24
acceptance L/C 102
acceptance letter of credit 89, 104
acceptance of a bill of exchange 26
accommodation bill 37
accommodation bill of exchange 24
advance or progress payment bonds 178
advance payment 7
advances against shipping documents 6
advantages and disadvantages of letters of credit 45
advantages of factoring 134
advantages of guarantees as security 167
advantages to exporter 45
advantages to importer 45
advantages to the exporter 135
advising bank 54
advising or confirming bank 59
air waybill 123
anticipatory drawing red clause 61
applicant 62
arbitration clause 181
assignment of prime letter of credit 72
assurance of payment 45, 57
assured delivery of goods 45

background to eUCP 600 143
back-to-back L/C: salient features 67
back-to-back letter of credit 67
back-to-back transactions risks 68
balance of payment 14
bank draft 9
bankers' acceptances 90
banking facility 179
bank's accounting system 11
bank's role 171

beneficiary's responsibilities 42
bid bonds or tender bonds 174
bill of exchange 20, 23, 24
bill of lading 127
bills discounted 37, 38, 49
bills purchased 37
blank endorsement 27
buyer and the seller 43
buyer credit (BC) facility 239
buyer credit guarantees 238, 245, 246
buyer's responsibilities 41, 150

capital goods sale 137
capital transactions 15
carriage and insurance paid to 114
carriage paid to 113
cash flow 46, 135
cash margin 72
cash on delivery 7
categories of bank guarantees/bonds 173
certificate of inspection 124
certificate of origin 124
CHAPS 10
charter party bill of lading 122
cheque 9
CHIPS 10
circular or traveller letter of credit 53
classification of marine insurance cover 249
clauses on bills of exchange 24
clean bill of lading 122
clean bills of exchange 23
clean letter of credit 53
collection of bills 5, 32
collections 8
combined transport document 127
commercial risk 139

INDEX

common irregularities in documents   160
competitive terms   46
compliance with regulations   45
comprehensive bill guarantee   245
comprehensive open account guarantee   245
conditional endorsement   29
confidence in a currency   15
confirming bank   43
consular invoice   125
container bill of lading   122
contents of a sale contract   50
contracts and regulations   48
cost and freight   112
cost, insurance and freight   113
credit facility from the issuing bank   45
credit information   4
credit line   45
currency risk   138

D/P   24–32
deferred payment letter of credit   101
deferred payment letter of credit – mechanics   79
definition of a bill of exchange   20
definition of letter of credit   40
delivered at frontier   114
delivered duty paid   115
delivered duty unpaid   115
delivered ex quay   111
delivered ex ship   114
development of electronic model   143
difference between factoring and forfaiting   138
difficult terms & conditions of l/c   46
direct debit   10
disadvantages of factoring   134
disadvantages of guarantee as security for a credit facility   168
disadvantages to applicant/importer   45
disadvantages to the beneficiary   46
disadvantages to the exporter   139
discharge of bills of exchange   31
discrepancies in documents   46
distinction between guarantees and indemnities   166
documentary bill of exchange   24
documentary letter of credit   53
documents delayed   46
documents in foreign trade   117
documents required by the forfaiter   140

ECGD   233
economic and political reports   4
EFT   10
electronic documents (eUCP)   143
endorsement of bills of exchange   27

eUCP   143
ex works   111
exchange control   2
exchange control regulations   4, 45
exchange controls   5
exchange rates quotation   12
exchange risks   2
expensive   46
export credit guarantee department   233
export credit guarantees   240
export credit insurance package   240
export factoring   136
export factoring – sales criteria   136
export/import facilities   3
exporters' risks   2
external trade guarantee   244

factoring   132
factoring and cashflow   132
factoring and forfaiting   132
factoring and legal implications   133
Fed wire   10
FIATA bill of lading   127
finance for exports   6
financial load variations   98
financing facilities for exporters   241
fixed forward exchange rates   13
fixed rate export finance   137
foreign currencies   5
foreign currency transactions   11
foreign exchange market   12
foreign exchange spot transaction   15
forfait houses   141
forfaiter   141
forfaiting   141
forfaiting procedures in practice   141
format of bank guarantees/bonds   172
forward exchange contract   17
forward exchange rates   13, 15
forwarding agent's receipt   125
fraudulent documents   45
free alongside ship   112
free carrier   111
free on board   112

general acceptance   26
general lines of credit (LOCs)   241
geographical factors   2
goods delayed   46, 47
green clause   62
guarantees and international bonds   164
guarantees as security   164

house bill of lading   123
how exchange rates are determined   14

INDEX

how the forward exchange rate is
    calculated   14

importance and requisites of acceptance   25
importance of marine insurance   248
importers'risks   2
incoterms   109
insurance for cash payments   240
international bonds/bank guarantees   184
international bonds/guarantees – precautions   180
invoice   119
invoice discounting   135
irrevocable confirmed letter of credit   56
irrevocable letter of credit   54
issuing bank   54
issuing bank guarantees – action steps   182

language   2, 5
legal system   2
letter of credit – processing cost (indicatives)   130
letter of guarantee   140
letter of pledge or hypothecation   70
letters of credit   8, 52
letters of credit – types   52
liability of acceptor   25

mail transfer   9
manufacturing risks   2
marine insurance   162, 248
marine insurance associations   260
meanings of negotiation   92
mechanics of bid bond   174
mechanism of a forfaiting   141
methods of payment settlement   9, 87
methods of payment/settlement of account   9
methods of trade   7
money laundering and terrorist activities   246
multimodal transport document   126

negotiability of bills of exchange   30
negotiation   92, 95
negotiation is with recourse   6, 105
negotiation of a letter of credit   92
negotiation of bills of exchange   6
negotiation of documents   128
negotiation of documents under reserve   95
nominated bank   43
non-negotiable sea waybill   125
non-payment   2, 5, 25
noting of the bill   32

open account   8
option forward contract   18

option forward exchange rates   14
other documents   127
other types of bonds   179
overseas investment insurance   241, 242

packing list   125, 158
parties to a bill of exchange   22
parties to a letter of credit and their
    responsibilities   41
payment L/C   87
performance bonds   181
policy of SWIFT   197
political risk   2, 137, 139
post parcel/courier receipt   125
presentation for acceptance   26
presentation of a dishonoured bill   31
pre-shipment facility   45
pricing   68, 72
prime L/C   69, 70
prime letter of credit   71
procedures for taking as security   168
pro-forma invoice   120
project financing facility   242
protest   32, 128

qualified acceptance   26

rail, road consignment notes   125
ready negotiability   45
received for shipment bill of lading   122
recourse indemnity policy (RIP)   242
red clause   59
red clause letter of credit   59
red clause payment at maturity   61
reimbursing bank   43
requirements of a forfaiter   139
responsibilities of other parties   150
restrictive endorsement   29
retention or maintenance bonds   179
revocable letter of credit   53
revolving letter of credit   57
revolving letters of credit- mechanism   58
risk factors: 61, 68
risks in export finance   138
role of advising and confirming banks   129
role of issuing bank   129

safeguards   76
sale contract   50
scrutiny of documents   149
secondary markets   138
seller's responsibilities   150
services policies   244
'shipped' or 'shipped on board' bill of lading   122

INDEX

sight bill of exchange   23
sight negotiation letter of credit   104
silent confirmation   57
special endorsement   28
specific bank guarantee   245
specific guarantee   235
specimen of a performance bond/
    guarantee   177
specimen of advance payment guarantee/
    bond   178
specimen of bid bond/guarantees   175
spot exchange rates   13
stale bill of lading   122
standby letter of credit   81
stand-by letter of credit – mechanism   82
subsidiaries guarantee   242
supplement export credit guarantees   240
supplemental extended terms guarantee   243
supplementary stocks guarantee   244
SWIFT address/ header   198
SWIFT administration   198
SWIFT code words   201
SWIFT operations   198

technical details   73
telegraphic/swift transfer   10
tender to contract (TTC) forward exchange
    supplement (FES)   241
the acceptor   22, 25
the carrier   43
the drawer   22
the drawee   22

the endorsee   22, 28
the endorser   22
the export insurance policy (EXIP)   239
the holder   22
the holder in due course   22
the holer for value   22
the insurer   43
the issuing bank   43, 44, 45, 129
the payee   22
the supplier credit finance facility
    (SCF)   239
third country or transit letter of credit   77
through bill of lading   122
trade enquiries   4
transfer risk   141
transferable credit – limitations   63
transferable letter of credit   66
'transhipment' bill of lading   122
truck & carrier receipt   125
types of acceptances   26
types of bank guarantees/international
    bonds   173
types of bills of lading   122
types of ECGD guarantees   237
types of endorsements   27
types of insurance instruments   250
types of qualified acceptances   26

usance bill of exchange   23
usance negotiation   105

veterinary certificate/health certificate   126